Digital Dilemmas

Diana C. Parry • Corey W. Johnson
Simone Fullagar
Editors

Digital Dilemmas

Transforming Gender Identities and Power Relations in Everyday Life

palgrave
macmillan

Editors
Diana C. Parry
University of Waterloo
Waterloo, ON, Canada

Simone Fullagar
Department for Health
University of Bath
Bath, UK

Corey W. Johnson
Department of Recreation & Leisure Studies
University of Waterloo
Waterloo, ON, Canada

ISBN 978-3-319-95299-4 ISBN 978-3-319-95300-7 (eBook)
https://doi.org/10.1007/978-3-319-95300-7

Library of Congress Control Number: 2018959108

Cover illustration: FactoryTh

This Palgrave Macmillan imprint is published by the registered company Springer Nature Switzerland AG
The registered company address is: Gewerbestrasse 11, 6330 Cham, Switzerland

For all those in the world working for social justice one click/swipe at a time.

Acknowledgements

The terrain of this text was certainly an unpredictable, but delightful one. It started with a small amount of funding from the University of Waterloo International Partnership grant, the desire to connect three scholars in three countries, and keep pace with research on gender and leisure in the digital landscape. That inspiration has produced so much more: new colleagues, institutional affiliation changes, a conference, graduate student funding, new mentor-mentee relationships, keynote talks, and ultimately the text you hold in your hand. None of this comes without labour—labour of love. Consequently, there is the need for much gratitude. The book grew out of a conference that was funded by a Social Science and Humanities Research Council (SSHRC) connection grant, which brought together the authors with the likes of other presenters, including our keynotes Aimée Morrison and Brittney Cooper; we appreciate their inspiration. Special thanks to our chapter authors for committing to such unique, thoughtful, and timely contributions. Thanks to our partners Troy, Yancey, and Gill for their support and the real labour (childcare, baking cakes, and working registration tables), while we were burning the midnight oil. Most importantly, our huge gratitude to Luc Cousineau. He has been our event planner, author coraller, indexer, contributor (plus so much more), and could not have been more thoughtful, faithful, and diligent.

Contents

Notes on Contributors

Jen Apgar is an elementary teacher, working as a twenty-first-century technology coach for a school board in Ontario, Canada. A happily married lesbian mom with a daughter, Jen is an optimist and critical thinker who loves connecting with people with the hopes of making positive change.

Philippa Collin is a senior research fellow at the Institute for Culture and Society, Western Sydney University. She researches the role of the digital in the social, cultural, and political lives of young people, with a focus on the implications for the promotion of mental health, well-being, and citizenship. Her work is also concerned with method and how participatory and co-design approaches contribute to new forms of political participation, identity, and governance.

Luc S. Cousineau is a PhD candidate in the Department of Recreation & Leisure Studies at the University of Waterloo. Luc's research is focused on gender and power relations in work and leisure spaces, with a particular focus on anonymized online leisure and the effects of this leisure participation on masculinity. Using feminist theory, leisure theory, and new media/internet studies to ground his work, Luc's primary focus is men's involvement in men's rights activism—its roots, propagation, and transition from anonymous participation to identifiable personal ideology.

Annaleise Depper is a PhD candidate in the Physical Culture, Sport and Health research group at the University of Bath. Her research explores young people's experiences of embodied mobility and inequality in communities of disadvantage. Annaleise is particularly interested in using participatory, youth-led approaches to explore the affective, material, and discursive contexts of everyday lives.

Jessica Francombe-Webb is a lecturer at the University of Bath. Her research explores the contested politics of the (in)active body in relation to health practices, physical, and digital cultures and issues of power, gender, social class, and (dis)ability. Her work has been published in a variety of interdisciplinary journals.

Simone Fullagar is a professor and Chair of the Physical Culture, Sport and Health research group at the University of Bath. Simone is an interdisciplinary sociologist who has published widely using feminist post-structuralist and new materialist perspectives to critically explore active living policy, women's depression and recovery, and alternative physical cultures (from cycle tourism, parkrun to roller derby).

Alanna Harman is an assistant professor at Wilfrid Laurier University in the division of Kinesiology & Physical Education. Harman's research interests include the construction of gender in sport, psychological contracts, and organizational behaviour.

Corey W. Johnson is a professor in the Department of Recreation & Leisure Studies at the University of Waterloo. His theorizing and qualitative inquiry focuses its attention on the power relations between dominant and non-dominant populations in the cultural contexts of leisure.

Laura Kovac is an MA student in the Social Justice and Equity Studies programme at Brock University in Ontario, Canada. She is interested in adolescent females' participation in aesthetic sports and critically examines the ways in which a post-feminist girlhood culture shapes their experiences. Her research advocates for a diversity of gender expression.

Katie Lebel is an assistant professor at Ryerson University in the Ted Rogers School of Management. Lebel specializes in the area of sport marketing, with a particular focus on gender, digital image management strategies, and consumer engagement.

Ashley Love is a doctoral candidate at the University of Georgia in Critical Studies in Education. Her research encompasses the impact of digital discourses as public pedagogy and teacher education through the lens of study abroad experiences.

Aimée Morrison is Associate Professor of English at the University of Waterloo, specializing in new media studies, concentrating on social media as a mode of everyday life writing. She has recently published on virality in academic media, personal disclosure and new media, and conflict management in personal blogging.

Harrison Oakes is a PhD student and Vanier Scholar at the University of Waterloo. Trained in social psychological experimental methodology, he has recently begun diving into qualitative inquiry in an attempt to supplement not only his methodological tool belt, but also his understanding of psychological processes at the individual level. Outside of academia, Harrison is an avid coffee drinker, tropical plant enthusiast, and the world's biggest fan of his darling puppy, Zara.

Diana C. Parry is the Associate Vice-President, Human Rights, Equity and Inclusion at the University of Waterloo. As part of this portfolio, Diana leads the United Nations Women's HeForShe IMPACT 10 x 10 x 10 commitment on campus, including creating the strategy to ensure that the university obtains long-term, comprehensive, sustainable gender equity. A professor in Applied Health Sciences, Diana's research utilizes a feminist lens to explore the personal and political links between women's leisure and women's health, broadly defined. Diana's research privileges women's standpoints and aims to create social change and enact social justice by challenging the medical model of scholarship.

Ann Pegoraro is the Director of the Institute for Sport Marketing (ISM) and an associate professor in the School of Human Kinetics at Laurentian University.

Pegoraro focuses her research on the intersection of sport and social media from various lenses, including marketing, communication, and social issues.

Emma Rich is a reader in the Department for Health at the University of Bath. Her research examines sport, physical activity, and physical/health education from a critical/socio-cultural perspective. Her two main areas of expertise include critical perspectives of obesity, eating disorders, and weight-related issues and digital health technologies (e.g. mobile and digital health, big data, wearable technologies). Much of her research is focused on education and young people.

Iesha Small is a documentary photographer based in the South East of England. Her interest in mental health is shaped by personal and family experiences, and the building of Mindshackles was a way to move conversations about mental health issues into the open. In early 2013, Iesha decided to help tell the stories of ordinary people who have experienced depression at some point in their lives, or continue to do so, through photography and their own words.

Teresa Swist is Engaged Research Fellow at the Institute for Culture and Society, Western Sydney University. She researches the complexity and power relations of knowledge and cultural practices in the digital age, with a particular focus on creativity, co-design, technology, and well-being. Her work has been published in the *Journal of Youth Studies*, *New Media and Society*, *Communication and the Public*, and *Continuum: Journal of Media & Cultural Studies*.

Dawn E. Trussell is an associate professor at Brock University in Ontario, Canada. Her research focuses on leisure and sport culture in the lives of individuals, families, and communities. She seeks to understand diverse social contexts and issues of power and social inclusion, particularly related to family, children and youth, gender and sexual diversity, and rurality.

List of Figures

List of Tables

Digital Dilemmas: Transforming Gender Identities and Power Relations in Everyday Life

Diana C. Parry, Luc S. Cousineau, Corey W. Johnson, and Simone Fullagar

Every day, we are urged to turn more of the management of our lives over to technology and the corporations which develop it. From the measurement of our fitness, to the music we listen to, we trust the algorithms and programming in these technologies to help us know when we are hip, happy, and healthy. Beginning with Apple's Siri, the "digital assistant" has been gradually incorporated into the normative parameters of everyday life, and these digital helpers have now become desirable features of homes with products like the Amazon Echo and Google Home. But what

---

D. C. Parry (✉)
University of Waterloo, Waterloo, ON, Canada
e-mail: dcparry@uwaterloo.ca

L. S. Cousineau • C. W. Johnson
Department of Recreation & Leisure Studies, University of Waterloo, Waterloo, ON, Canada
e-mail: Luc.cousineau@uwaterloo.ca; corey.johnson@uwaterloo.ca

S. Fullagar
Department for Health, University of Bath, Bath, UK
e-mail: S.P.Fullagar@bath.ac.uk

D. C. Parry et al. (eds.), *Digital Dilemmas*,
https://doi.org/10.1007/978-3-319-95300-7_1

dilemmas are posed through the use of these technologies? Data are transmitted through (often poorly secured) internet connections, to major corporations to be processed, stored, acted upon, and sold through global networks that entangle gendered labour and leisure. In exchange for their convenience, personal information is extracted from the ebbs and flows of everyday activity. Perhaps this is why, as Kate O'Riordan (2006) demonstrated, these service technologies are imbued with historically feminine characteristics and voices, so that they feel less like HAL from *2001—A Space Odyssey* and more like Rosie from *The Jetsons*.

In this chapter, we will explore the nature of digital spaces and the connected and compounded effects that those spaces can have on shaping digital embodiments. Using various feminist theories, we discuss the discursive and ideological formation of gender imbricated in gender injustice, and outline how the intersection of gendered understandings with technological fluidity creates spaces where individuals can be simultaneously empowered and subjugated. In doing so, we will draw upon existing work that has explored elements of these dilemmas and bring those works together to examine the interrelationships of gendered leisure, advocacy, and civic engagement. We seek to advance new approaches to understanding, critiquing, and mobilizing action within the complex gendered relations that are entangled in leisure spaces and digital practices.

The proliferation of digital technologies, virtual spaces, and new forms of engagement raise key questions about the changing nature of relationships and identities within democratic societies. Scholars, policymakers, and activists have only begun to understand how everyday life is being transformed by technology in ways that inform and challenge social dynamics and norms, which govern our selves, our communities, and the spaces we inhabit. Nowhere are these issues more salient then when we explore the formation, regulation, and contestation of digital gender identities. The problems and paradoxes created through the intersection of gender ideology and the possibilities of digital environments create both spaces of positive explorations and embodiments, as well as sites of gender injustice. These opportunities and dilemmas, produced through leisure-related practices and digital public culture, are where attention is needed to produce cultural and critical inquiry. It is upon those dilemmas at the intersections of gender, oppression, opportunity, and digitality where we focus this book.

Our aim in compiling this book is to contribute to current debates in digital humanities and social science (digital sociology, science and technology studies, cultural studies, leisure studies, and pedagogy) through a focus on key dilemmas occurring at the intersection of public culture, policy, practice, and everyday gender relations. Specifically, we aim to generate new conversations across two broadly defined bodies of scholarship—gender studies/social justice and digital sociology/leisure studies. To date, there has been limited attention paid to questions of gender and power as they manifest in our digital leisure lives in relation to changing notions of freedom, choice, and social well-being. Gender issues have yet to be comprehensively addressed within the emerging focus on digital technologies, despite special issues of key journals, like *Leisure Studies* (2016), which focused on promoting the digital in leisure studies and building a "lively leisure studies that can make sense of the constantly changing worlds of lively devices and lively data" (Lupton 2016, p. 711), the *Leisure Sciences* (2018) special issue on popular leisure in a digital age, and texts such as Spracklen's (2015) *Digital Leisure, the Internet and Popular Culture*. We aim to begin the labour of ensuring that gender, and gender-related issues, are addressed in this literature. Exploring leisure-related digital practices that are virtual and visceral, the book is broadly oriented around three digital dilemmas:

- How do we theorize the influence of diverse virtual voices at the intersection of gender and (in)justice?
- How can innovative methodologies enable new insights into the social transformation of gender relations, digital cultures, and social justice?
- How is digital technology shaping relationships between diverse publics—citizens, communities, activists, policymakers—in terms of transforming gender injustice?

The exchange and flow of ideas between these different areas has yet to be fully explored (Johnson & Parry, 2016). There is a need to take stock of recent feminist research insights in both policy, activist, and academic arenas, and to identify the areas that still require greater research attention and policy debate. This edited collection seeks to share these insights among academics, policymakers, activists, and practitioners. This knowledge integration and synthesis is crucial to reshape the literature on gender and to inform future national and international debates. These debates include important ideas like technological access as a human right, public versus private data, how the data we generate is managed, disseminated, bought and sold, and net neutrality (the concept that all traffic on the internet should have equal value and that corporations should not limit, police, or enhance one type of traffic over another). Each of these, along with being technical issues, have deep social roots in who is valued and what is valuable about them. Issues of difference and inequality, user-generated content, and neoliberal economic policies do not create the same level of opportunity for everyone. They do not foster equitable distributions of power. The ubiquity of our technological connections subjugate us in ways that most individuals do not fully understand, while they also fuel forms of resistance, inventiveness, and feminist subversion.

Feminist Theories and Digital Contexts of Gender Injustice

Research on the digital contexts of gender injustice is rapidly evolving, and cutting edge conceptual work is taking place in both academic and non-academic arenas (government, think tanks, industry, etc.). Much of the critical work in this area has been undertaken by feminists and there is a growing global community of feminist scholars who are exploring questions of power, social justice, and change in leisure-related practices (Fullagar, Pavlidis, & Francombe-Webb, 2018; Harvey & Shepherd, 2017; Johnson & Parry, 2016; Lupton & Thomas, 2015; Morrison, 2014; Pavlidis & Fullagar, 2014; Rich, 2018). This scholarship has brought to the fore a strong focus on women and changing digital contexts through which girls are engaging with feminist practices. For example, Keller's (2016) book on American girls' feminist blogging, Dobson's (2015) Australian work on post-feminist digital cultures, Smith-Prei and Stehle's (2016) Canadian book on technologies of transnational popfeminist activism, as well as the UK work produced by Retallack, Ringrose, and Lawrence (2016) on girls' digital and creative engagement with feminism through school-based theatre. Building upon this work we add to this important body of research by foregrounding the question of intersectional power relations and bring into view ableism, racism, classism, and heterosexim as they play out through the mediated contexts of everyday life (Durham, Cooper, & Morris, 2013; Jones & Hughes-Decatur, 2012; Williams, 2015).

Cyberfeminism and Networked Leisure

Since the early writing about networked computer systems, virtual worlds, cyberspaces, and digital environments have been heralded as new landscapes, filled with possibility and promise about the role they might play in emancipation and empowerment. Early users and theorists saw the virtual worlds of networked computing as potential utopias (Turkle, 1996; Warf & Grimes, 1997), and this perspective was taken up by feminist authors and gender theorists in a significant way. They saw blank slates in the multi-user dungeons[1] (MUDs) and bulletin boards, which housed the text-based communications of these early digital-world systems and developed utopic theories about how they might bring about change.

The emancipatory potential of the new worlds of the net and web were expounded by cyberfeminist researchers and other authors (cf. Rheingold, 1993) who saw the internet as a technology that could facilitate gender and racial equality, through work on political economy and internetworked global feminism (Daniels, 2009). Authors like Norris (2001), Sassen (2002), and Eisenstein (1998) explored how, as the internet began to develop as a driving economic and social force in Western culture, individuals in developing societies, and particularly women, were less likely to have access to technologies and therefore

[1] Multi-user dungeons (MUDs) were text-based, online spaces where multiple users could create personal identities and interact with one another through a multi-user interface, normally moderated by the users themselves. Some MUDs had very long lifespans with users developing and interacting with the space for years.

less likely to reap the benefits of those technologies. Some 20 years after Eisenstein's work, as connectivity becomes more and more essential to life in a global community, the idea of internet access as a human right continues to proliferate; take, for example, the non-binding resolution at the United Nations in 2016 (United Nations, 2016) while individuals in developing countries, or even the poor and marginalized in Western countries, continue to struggle for simple connectivity, let along equitable access. In 2003, Radhika Gajjala cautioned that

> [i]f cyberfeminist agendas are to produce subversive countercultures or to succeed in changing existing technological environments so that they are empowering to women and men of lesser material and socio-cultural privilege the world over, it is important to examine how individuals and communities are situated within the complex global and local contexts mediated by unequal relations of power. (p. 54)

Gajjala's concern is about both the colonialist notions of Westernized technological adoption in other parts of the world, particularly South Asia, as well as the liberal feminist trappings of celebrating technology as liberating to *all* women. However, these critiques should not undercut the important effects that global or quasi-global interconnection have had on bypassing local, state, and mass media resistance to feminist causes globally (Everett, 2004; Sassen, 2002).

The intersections of gender and technologies have also been taken up by authors outside of feminism. Wajcman (2000, 2010) has written extensively on how gender interfaces with the technologies that we use every day, from our taken-for-granted assumptions about the technological acumen of men, to the co-mingling of technological development and gendered lives through domestication technologies like washing machines, and media like daytime television. There is current work exploring how our use of social media and its pervasive nature in our lives are affected by gender, not just in the ways that we interact with the technologies, but in the ways that those technologies code us knowingly and unknowingly (Bivens & Haimson, 2016; Bivens, 2017; Carstensen, 2014; Shepherd, 2013).

We are, through our engagement with social media and other interactive technologies, categorized, grouped, and reduced to discrete variables stored in databases. Some of these data points we provide willingly, like our name, or the high school we attended, but others are generated through complex algorithms which group us in ways we don't know about; they can even predict our behaviour. As we continually give up our (personal information) data in exchange for the use of these technologies, we must engage with the dilemmas of simultaneously being the user and the product, or face the repercussions of opting out. Work exploring both the surveillance and gendered implications of big data and technologies watching us as we use them is already underway, and their findings provide us with reason to question our technological choices (D'Ignazio, 2016; Noble, 2016; Whitson, 2014).

For early users and theorists of virtual communities and networked lives, the opportunities presented by the digital landscape were large in number and constantly evolving in nature, and the web has remained a space of perceived opportunity as it has developed. Although the utopic visions of a new digital social order may have faded, the web still represents opportunities for individual and social gain for users and consumers. Linking our offline and online lives, and allowing us to more easily coordinate social events or gain notoriety, we are consistently presented with the allure of being "internet famous" and becoming "real-life" rich, like Bethany Mota, a California teen whose shopping YouTube channel has over ten million subscribers and almost one billion views since 2009 (YouTube, 2018).

Particularly in our leisure, digitality has become an irrevocable part of how we communicate (Facetime, SMS messaging, Skype), coordinate (Eventbrite, Doodle, Facebook events), and mobilize meaning (phones, tablets, wearable tech). It provides the opportunity for large and small-scale real-time organization around social issues; movements like the Arab Spring, Black Lives Matter (BLM), or #idlenomore are good examples. These movements, along with being powerful calls for social justice, and individual and collective rights of citizens, are propagated by the intersections of technology and leisure for participants and supporters. Links between leisure, technology, and social movements have always been prescient, and the ability of digital technologies to link these elements together is rivalled in history only by the printing press (Goldin & Kutarna, 2016). Although the core and founding protestors in each of these movements spur initial interest, it is the proliferation of their messages through social networking sites like Twitter and Facebook (sites of dedicated leisure involvement for many people (Rose & Spencer, 2016)), which generate attention and public support. In the case of the Arab Spring, Twitter served as both a rallying cry and a means of coordination. Because of the decentralized nature of spreading messages on the platform, as well as the ability to use non-personal accounts managed by several people, protests' coordination on Twitter proved far more difficult to limit and manage than individual, identifiable, charismatic leaders would have been (Howard et al., 2011; Khondker, 2011). The Idle No More movement in Canada, which began as "teach-ins throughout Saskatchewan to protest impending parliamentary bills that will erode Indigenous sovereignty and environmental protections" (IdleNoMore, 2018), spread through both media coverage and social media across the country, linking Indigenous and non-Indigenous people together to support their cause. Likewise, the global network of social media and advancing technological capabilities allowed pictures and videos of incidents like those of the death of Michael Brown to circulate and provide unequivocal support to the assertions of #BlackLivesMatter. Black Feminists have also intervened in digital spaces to make visible the lesser known lives and violent deaths of Black women through the hashtag #sayhername (Mohrman & Fischer, 2016). Now a "member-led global network of more than 40 chapters", BLM is a "Black-centered political will and movement building project" started by three Black women and propelled by technology and sharing (Black Lives Matter, 2018).

Technology, and in particular social media, presents an open platform for the development and dissemination of ideas and the challenging of social norms (issues of gender, sexual identity, race, and privilege to be presented in this book notwithstanding for the moment), where movements, which begin as small ways of protest can catch larger public attention and help usher in public discourse to make gender inequity visible in new, collectivized ways.

The #everydaysexism and #metoo movements are perhaps the most quintessential example of this power in this contemporary moment.

#metoo was created in 2007 by civil rights and sexual abuse activist Tarana Burke as a way to help victims understand that they were not alone in their sexual victimization. The movement was popularized by actress Alyssa Milano in October 2017 when she encouraged women to tweet "me too" as a way of demonstrating the extensive and pervasive nature of the problem (Garcia, 2017). Since October 2017, countless women and men, celebrities and not, have used the hashtag, as well as the collective power of the movement to express, sometimes for the first time, their experiences with sexual violence (me too movement, 2018). The movement, and those who have broken their silence about sexual misconduct, were named TIME magazine's 2017 person of the year (Zacharek, Dockterman, & Sweetland Edwards, 2017). It has facilitated victimized women and men to come forward and has brought to light persistent and egregious sexual violence committed by very powerful players in Hollywood and elsewhere, including most notably Harvey Weinstein and Kevin Spacey.

The #metoo movement, even as young as it is, has created some dilemmas of its own. After the initial flurry and subsequent steady flow of accusations and support, whispers of backlash appeared. Not long after the strong support shown at the 75th Golden Globe awards with a near-uniform adoption of Black fashion and the donning of "Time's Up" pins (in support if the Time's Up Legal Defence Fund, which pledges to provide support to women and men who have experienced sexual harassment, abuse, or assault in the workplace (Time's Up, 2018)), conversations in some circles have turned to whether the #metoo movement has gone "too far". This accusation teems with a type of aggrieved entitlement Kimmel (2013) attributes to the powerful facing change, where those who have had and maintained privilege in a space (like men in Hollywood, or the arts more broadly) begin to lose the absolute power they once enjoyed and respond by claiming that the work being done to limit that privilege is itself prejudiced (e.g. reverse racism). It does beg the question of how we manage the power and potential of digital movements with wide uptake, especially in the face of critiques like having "gone too far".

At the same time that new digitally integrated reality provides so many opportunities, it presents challenging personal and cultural dilemmas. The gender and power relationships we live with offline have supplanted the utopic visions of a new cyber social order, and in their move online, they have become even more complex. This complexity emerges from the anonymity and personal disconnection available on the web, and although it provides positive self-expression opportunities for some, it permits a new kind of destructive rhetoric and leveraging of gender and power dynamics by others. The same mechanisms that might allow for production and dissemination of educational materials about gender expression for trans-high schoolers (Singh & Johnson, 2018), also permits the transmission and dissemination of anti-feminist or alt-right messaging (Schmitz & Kazyak, 2016), as in the case of extreme men's rights activist (MRA) websites where "women and homosexuals are discouraged from commenting" (Return of Kings, 2017). Where the internet, and particularly social media, permits the dissemination of ideas and critical social commentary, it also permits comments in response, which might include sexual assault or death threats. Such is the case with the now-famous #GamerGate, where the thinly veiled accusations of a jilted ex-partner caused a surge of near-anonymous and vitriolic backlash against female journalists and developers in games (Braithwaite, 2016; Burgess & Matamoros-Fernández, 2016; Massanari, 2017). What complicates the issue of #GamerGate even further is that discussions of the incident in an academic context were quickly and easily roped into discourses and conspiracy theories about the changing landscape of game and game development culture, because of the academic use of technology as a tool for theorization and scholarship (Chess & Shaw, 2015).

Where our new digital reality allows for grassroots social organization in the face of injustice or tyranny (see examples above from #BLM, #metoo, #idlenomore), it also provides the means to monitor, police, or influence the maintenance of the status quo by governments, corporations, and even individuals (Roberts, 2016). For instance, much of the discourse around the release of sexually explicit materials from celebrity cloud accounts (Marwick, 2017; Massanari, 2017), has been about how the female celebrities in question should have "known better", or that it "serves them right" for taking the photos at all. A discourse of ownership and "rights" emerges in the online conversations about these illegally obtained pornographic images, which place the women in question as both lacking agency and intelligence about who should possess the photos, and their rights to privacy as celebrities who are also women. The context of the discussions are important because they centre on affected women celebrities and remind us of cultures of sexual and personal ownership over women's bodies—even women who command large sums of money for the use of those bodies as paid actresses, athletes, or models (Marwick, 2017). Celebrity aside, questions of ownership, leverage, blackmail, and extortion reach women of all ages and statuses in cases where former partners threaten to, or do, release intimate images of former partners or friends—so-called revenge porn. With several entire websites dedicated to this idea of intimate images of women made in private and exposed for public consumption, revenge porn has led to quickly enacted policy and law banning the practice and establishing penalties for perpetrators (Cyber Civil Rights Initiative, 2018).

The Contribution and Organization of this Book

Adopting an interdisciplinary approach, chapters in this book will draw upon different theories, methodologies, and applied (policy and practice-related) perspectives to examine the interrelationships of gendered leisure, advocacy, and civic engagement. In doing so, we seek to advance new approaches to understanding, critiquing, and mobilizing action within the complex gendered relations that are entangled in leisure spaces and digital practices.

Section One: Theory in Digital and Leisure Contexts

The book is divided into three major sections. The first focuses on the application of theory to the digital and leisure contexts as discussed in this introduction. Along with deep theoretical perspectives on how the inclusion of digital media and social spaces have changed feminist activism, this section explores some of the intersections of digital media, race, gender, and (counter)narratives present in our dynamic digital landscapes—beginning with the work of Aimée Morrison, who explores the use of viral Twitter hashtags. These hashtags utilize humour, as well as the speed of information sharing and dissemination in the age of social media, to work at destabilizing the framing imposed on situations by dominant groups. In her exploration of #DistractinglySexy, #StayMadAbby, and #BeckyWithTheBadGrades, Morrison presents the micro-counter-narratives that can be created in the Web 2.0 culture of participant-created media.

Morrison's chapter is followed by a discussion and theorization of the roles that Black Feminism has played in the ongoing fight for social justice on behalf of Black women, girls, and their communities by Ashley Love. Love explores the ways that a Digital Black Feminism is changing and enhancing that work, delving into the ways that Black women have actualized foundational elements of feminism; even at times when their unique voices and perspectives were silenced in the larger feminist movement. Love then moves to demonstrate how Black women and girls are accessing and using social media and other digital communities to modernize and further the mission of Black Feminism in the digital age.

Section Two: Methodological Discussions and Guideposts

The second section of the book moves into methodological discussions and guideposts. Trussell, Apgar, and Kovac analyse and use critical reflection on a community-based research project that shifted from in-person, semi-structured interviews to an online asynchronous forum to help readers understand the opportunities and potential difficulties of employing traditional research methods with diverse and digitally curated social groups. They explore how the intersection of online spaces and feminist research opens up new opportunities for qualitative inquiry through asynchronous online discussion groups. The critical reflection on their research experience also allowed for an analysis of the research process, and how the introduction of digital spaces and research problematizes our traditional notions and approaches to research ethics, methods, and knowledge mobilization.

This chapter is followed by Cousineau, Oakes, and Johnson, who propose a queering of ethnography in online environments, particularly those of fast-moving mobile applications. Providing a methodological approach to exploring and using geo-social networking applications (GSNAs) in research, this chapter examines the fast-changing environment of mobile applications, and the fickle nature of the modern digital consumer, suggesting that research strategies that were once "state of the art", even on digital platforms, no longer meet the needs of some contemporary research venues. Cousineau, Oakes, and Johnson provide a set of directional markers that can help researchers interested in user experiences with mobile apps, and particularly GSNAs, create robust and appropriate research strategies; strategies which remain flexible enough for application in the digital landscape, but theoretically grounded and methodologically sound.

Section Three: Dilemmas at the Intersection of Gender, Gender Identity, and Digitality

The third section of the book shifts focus to particular dilemmas faced at the intersection of gender, gender identity, and digitality. These dilemmas of digital presence, health, and embodiment extend from research exploring mental health, sport, and social conceptions of women's embodiment. Fullagar and Small, in a project framed through an academic-arts collaboration and the *Mindshackles* website, explore the cultural representations of women recovering from depression. Using photographs, film, and audio, the website aims to document stories and the diversity of experiences of women struggling with mental health. Fullagar and Small use theoretically guided feminist questions to explore the ways in which we document, and subsequently experience, the hardship of others allows for the exposition and erasure of gender issues. The chapter touches on issues of medicalized assessment and treatment regimens and the culturally differential way in which mental health is addressed by gender, race, and other marginalized identities.

Swist and Collin continue this focus on mental health with their work on the mobilization of playful modalities in working with young people to develop digital campaigns that engage with the issue of emotional well-being and gender (masculinity) in new ways. Swist and Collin draw on the participatory design of one youth mental health campaign to illustrate the creative possibilities of digital campaigns, as well as illuminate the gendered positions presented and perpetuated by these digital engagements. They also explore how these can change their focus from predetermined expectations of gender and behaviour in mental health to a more complex interplay of digitality, gender, and playfulness.

The next chapter also explores the intersections of the digital, play, and gendered spaces, but Lebel, Pegoraro, and Harman discuss the interaction of women in sport with their social media platforms, examining the complex issues which form at the intersection of digitality, gender, sport participation, and open public interaction online. Aggregating analysis from several studies, they discuss the impacts of social media interactions on women in sport and how these interactions change their negotiation of gender and personal identity as athletes.

The influence of gendered notions of acceptable body image and performance are further discussed by Depper, Fullagar, and Francombe-Webb in their chapter examining the *This Girl Can* campaign in the UK. Depper, Fullagar, and Francombe-Webb present a critical examination of the gendered assumptions presented by the Sport England campaign and explore the intense reactions on social media generated by the portion of the campaign aimed at celebrating natural bodies. They ask whether the ways in which women's bodies are digitally enacted might problematize or undermine the campaign, and how the campaign is, or is not, actualized online and offline.

In the last chapter of this section, Emma Rich moves the discussion to focus on the technologies that mediate the relationship between health and fitness, digitality, and gendered embodiment. Rich explores the co-contingent relationship between the influential and growing area of digital health technologies and the gendered discourses implicated in their production and consumption. She discusses the possibilities available for teaching healthy lifestyle behaviours through these digital health technologies, and how gender and gendered understandings of health and fitness are simultaneously taught and reinforced. She also contends that the pedagogical opportunities created by these digital health technologies have the potential to enact social and individual change.

The purpose of this text is to foster further discussion about the changing formation of leisure and technology in our lives as they continue to intermingle, reproduce, and often challenge gendered ways of being. The speed at which these changes are taking place means that as we are creating or theorizing new technological opportunities, we are simultaneously creating new dilemmas which require different ways of researching gender-power relations. Part of the call in this book is for readers and researchers to critically explore the gender relations that implicitly and explicitly shape technological artefacts, platforms, regulatory mechanisms, and civic spaces as they are experienced in the ubiquity of everyday life. Exploring their influence and implications for gender justice and public life requires intellectual inventiveness to move beyond the normative assumptions of techno-utopia or the moral panic of dystopic fears.

The movements and tools currently available to us are strong because of, and contested by, the technologies which have driven their development and proliferation. #metoo is able to spread and effect massive change because of the always-on nature of digital communication and our need to be in constant contact with the world. But this same need places the movement in the crosshairs of short news cycles and politicized rhetoric, and those same channels which propel a movement for social justice also carry its detractors and critiques. We hope that this book will provide its readers with practical knowledge about methodological and theoretical approaches to working with technologies and their inherent dilemmas, and can serve as a guidepost for continued theorization and practical work on these important issues.

References

Bivens, R. (2017). The gender binary will not be deprogrammed: Ten years of coding gender on Facebook. *New Media & Society, 19*(6), 880–898. https://doi.org/10.1177/1461444815621527.

Bivens, R., & Haimson, O. L. (2016). Baking gender into social media design: How platforms shape categories for users and advertisers. *Social Media Society, 2*(4), 2056305116672486.

Black Lives Matter. (2018). *Black Lives Matter: Herstory*. Retrieved from https://blacklivesmatter.com/about/herstory/

Braithwaite, A. (2016). It's about ethics in games journalism? Gamergaters and geek masculinity. *Social Media Society, 2*(4), 2056305116672484.

Burgess, J., & Matamoros-Fernández, A. (2016). Mapping sociocultural controversies across digital media platforms: One week of# gamergate on twitter, YouTube, and Tumblr. *Communication Research and Practice, 2*(1), 79–96.

Carstensen, T. (2014). Gender and social media: Sexism, empowerment, or the irrelevance of gender? In C. Carter, L. Steiner, & L. McLaughlin (Eds.), *The Routledge companion to media & gender* (pp. 483–492). New York: Routledge.

Chess, S., & Shaw, A. (2015). A conspiracy of fishes, or, how we learned to stop worrying about# GamerGate and embrace hegemonic masculinity. *Journal of Broadcasting & Electronic Media, 59*(1), 208–220.

Cyber Civil Rights Initiative. (2018). *Revenge Porn Laws*. Retrieved from https://www.cybercivilrights.org/revenge-porn-laws/

D'Ignazio, C. (2016). *A primer on non-binary gender and big data.* Retrieved from https://civic.mit.edu/blog/kanarinka/a-primer-on-non-binary-gender-and-big-data

Daniels, J. (2009). Rethinking cyberfeminism(s): Race, gender, and embodiment. *WSQ: Women's Studies Quarterly, 37*(1), 101–124.

Dobson, A.S. (2015). *Postfeminist digital cultures: Femininity, social media, and self-representation.* New York, NY: Palgrave Macmillan.

Durham, A., Cooper, B. C., & Morris, S. M. (2013). The stage hip-hop feminism built: A new directions essay. *Signs: Journal of Women in Culture and Society, 38*(3), 721–737.

Eisenstein, Z. (1998). *Global obscenities: Patriarchy, capitalism, and the lure of cyberfantasy*. New York: NYU Press.

Everett, A. (2004). On cyberfeminism and cyberwomanism: High-tech mediations of feminism's discontents. *Signs: Journal of Women in Culture and Society, 30*(1), 1278–1286.

Fullagar, S., Pavlidis, A., & Francombe-Webb, J. (2018). Feminist theories after the post-structuralist turn. In D. C. Parry (Ed.), *Feminisms in leisure studies: Advancing a fourth wave*. New York: Routledge.

Gajjala, R. (2003). South Asian digital diasporas and cyberfeminist webs: Negotiating globalization, nation, gender and information technology design. *Contemporary South Asia, 12*(1), 41–56. https://doi.org/10.1080/0958493032000123362.

Garcia, S. E. (2017, October 20). The woman who created #MeToo long before hashtags. *The New York Times.* Retrieved from https://www.nytimes.com/2017/10/20/us/me-too-movement-tarana-burke.html

Goldin, I., & Kutarna, C. (2016). *Age of discovery: Navigating the risks and rewards of our new renaissance*. London: Bloomsbury Publishing.

Harvey, A., & Shepherd, T. (2017). When passion isn't enough: Gender, affect and credibility in digital games design. *International Journal of Cultural Studies, 20*(5), 492–508.

Howard, P. N., Duffy, A., Freelon, D., Hussain, M. M., Mari, W., & Mazaid, M. (2011). Opening closed regimes: What was the role of social media during the Arab spring? *Available at SSRN 2595096.*

IdleNoMore. (2018). *IdleNoMore: The story*. Retrieved from http://www.idlenomore.ca/story

Johnson, C. W., & Parry, D. C. (2016). *Fostering social justice through qualitative inquiry: A methodological guide*. Abingdon, UK: Routledge.

Jones, S., & Hughes-Decatur, H. (2012). Speaking of bodies in justice-oriented, feminist teacher education. *Journal of Teacher Education, 63*(1), 51–61.

Keller, J. (2016). *Girls' feminist blogging in a postfeminist age*. London: Routledge.

Khondker, H. H. (2011). Role of the new media in the Arab spring. *Globalizations, 8*(5), 675–679.

Kimmel, M. S. (2013). *Angry white men: American masculinity at the end of an era*. New York: Nation Books.

Lupton, D. (2016). Foreword: Lively devices, lively data and lively leisure studies. *Leisure Studies, 35*(6), 709–711. https://doi.org/10.1080/02614367.2016.1216582.

Lupton, D., & Thomas, G. M. (2015). Playing pregnancy: The ludification and gamification of expectant motherhood in smartphone apps. *M/C Journal*, (5), 18.

Marwick, A. E. (2017). Scandal or sex crime? Gendered privacy and the celebrity nude photo leaks. *Ethics and Information Technology, 19*(3), 177–191.

Massanari, A. L. (2017). # Gamergate and the fappening: How Reddit's algorithm, governance, and culture support toxic technocultures. *New Media & Society, 19*(3), 329–346.

me too movement. (2018). *me too*. Retrieved from https://metoomvmt.org

Mohrman, K., & Fischer, M. (2016). Black deaths matter? Sousveillance and the invisibility of black life. *Ada: A Journal of Gender, New Media, and Technology*, (10), 1–13. https://doi.org/10.7264/N3F47MDV.

Morrison, A. (2014). Compositional strategies of conflict management in personal mommy blogs. *Feminist Media Studies, 14*(2), 286–300.

Noble, S. U. (2016). A future for intersectional black feminist technology studies. *Scholar & Feminist Online*, (13.3–14.1). Retrieved from http://sfonline.

barnard.edu/traversing-technologies/safiya-umoja-noble-a-future-for-intersectional-black-feminist-technology-studies/0/
Norris, P. (2001). *Digital divide: Civic engagement, information poverty, and the internet worldwide*. Cambridge: Cambridge University Press.
O'Riordan, K. (2006). Gender, technology, and visual cyberculture. In D. Silver & A. L. Massanari (Eds.), *Critical cyberculture Studies* (pp. 243–256). New York: NYU Press.
Pavlidis, A., & Fullagar, S. (2014). Women, sport and new media technologies: Derby grrrls online. In Bennett & Robards (Eds.), *Mediated youth cultures* (pp. 165–181). London: Palgrave Macmillan.
Retallack, H., Ringrose, J., & Lawrence, E. (2016). "Fuck your body image": Teen girls' twitter and Instagram feminism in and around school. In J. Coffey, S. Budgeon, & H. Cahill (Eds.), *Learning bodies: The body in youth and childhood studies* (pp. 85–103). Singapore: Springer.
Return of Kings. (2017). *Return of kings: About*. Retrieved from http://www.returnofkings.com/about
Rheingold, H. (1993). *The virtual community: Finding connection in a computerized world*. Reading, UK: Addison-Wesley Longman Publishing, Inc.
Rich, E. (2018). Healthism, girls' embodiment, and contemporary health and physical education: From weight management to digital practices of optimization. In L. Mansfield, J. Caudwell, B. Wheaton, & B. Watson (Eds.), *The Palgrave handbook of feminism and sport, Leisure and Physical Education* (pp. 523–536). New York: Springer.
Roberts, S. T. (2016). Commercial content moderation: Digital laborers' dirty work. In S. U. Noble & B. Tynes (Eds.), *The intersectional internet: Race, sex, class and culture online*. New York: Peter Lang Publishing.
Rose, J., & Spencer, C. (2016). Immaterial labour in spaces of leisure: Producing biopolitical subjectivities through Facebook. *Leisure Studies, 35*(6), 809–826.
Sassen, S. (2002). Towards a sociology of information technology. *Current Sociology, 50*(3), 365–388.
Schmitz, R. M., & Kazyak, E. (2016). Masculinities in cyberspace: An analysis of portrayals of manhood in men's rights activist websites. *Social Sciences, 5*(2), 18. https://doi.org/10.3390/socsci5020018.
Shepherd, T. (2013). Gendering the commodity audience in social media. In C. Carter, L. Steiner, & L. McLaughlin (Eds.), *The Routledge companion to media & gender* (pp. 157–167). New York: Routledge.

Singh, A. A., & Johnson, C. W. (2018). Using collective memory work to create safer schools for queer and trans students: A story of love, liberation, and transformation. In C. W. Johnson (Ed.), *Collective memory work: A methodology for learning with and from 'others'* (pp. 151–174). London: Routledge.

Smith-Prei, C., & Stehle, M. (2016). *Awkward politics: Technologies of popfeminist activism*. Montreal, QC: McGill-Queen's press-MQUP.

Spencer Schultz, C., & McKeown, J. K. L. (2018). Introduction to the special issue: Toward "digital leisure studies". *Leisure Sciences*, 1–20.

Spracklen, K. (2015). *Digital leisure, the internet and popular culture: Communities and identities in a digital age*. New York: Palgrave Macmillan.

Time's Up. (2018). *Time's up: The clock has run out on sexual assault, harassment and inequality in the workplace. It's time to do something about it*. Retrieved from https://www.timesupnow.com/

Turkle, S. (1996). Virtuality and its discontents searching for community in cyberspace. In J. Turow & A. L. Kavanaugh (Eds.), *The wired homestead: An MIT press sourcebook on the internet and the family* (pp. 385–402). Cambridge, MA: MIT Press.

United Nations. (2016). *Human rights council thirty-second session agenda item 3 promotion and protection of all human rights, civil, political, economic, social and cultural rights, including the right to development*. (No. A/HRC/32/L.20-1610802). New York: United Nations General Assembly, Human Rights Council. Retrieved from https://www.article19.org/data/files/Internet_Statement_Adopted.pdf

Wajcman, J. (2000). Reflections on gender and technology studies. *Social Studies of Science, 30*(3), 447–464. https://doi.org/10.1177/030631200030003005.

Wajcman, J. (2010). Feminist theories of technology. *Cambridge Journal of Economics, 34*(1), 143–152.

Warf, B., & Grimes, J. (1997). Counterhegemonic discourses and the internet. *Geographical Review, 87*(2), 259–274.

Whitson, J. R. (2014). Foucault's fitbit: Governance and gamification. In S. P. Walz & S. Deterding (Eds.), *Gameful world: Approaches, issues, applications* (pp. 339–358). Cambridge, MA: MIT Press.

Williams, S. (2015). Digital defense: Black feminists resist violence with hashtag activism. *Feminist Media Studies, 15*(2), 341–344.

YouTube. (2018). *Bethany Mota: About*. Retrieved from https://www.youtube.com/user/Macbarbie07/about

Zacharek, S., Dockterman, E., & Sweetland Edwards, H. (2017, December 18). The silence breakers: TIME person of the year 2017. *Time Magazine*. Retrieved from http://time.com/time-person-of-the-year-2017-silence-breakers/

Section I

Theory in Digital and Leisure Contexts

Laughing at Injustice: #DistractinglySexy and #StayMadAbby as Counternarratives

Aimée Morrison

The viral Twitter hashtag campaigns #DistractinglySexy, and #StayMadAbby and #BeckyWithTheBadGrades, respond to structural oppression in higher education and public culture by producing micro-counternarratives to stereotyped characterizations of women in science and race-based affirmative action in admissions, respectively. These campaigns exemplify an emerging mode of online resistance by marginalized subjects: the use of social media platforms to gain wide visibility, the creation of hashtags to allow for grass-roots collective participation and viral spread of content, and, crucially, the use of humour to destabilize the institutional framing of these conflicts by dominant groups. This chapter will address the productive social justice work that can come from this sometimes uncomfortable context collapse between humour and seriousness, between pop culture and matters of law and politics. The digital dilemma is precisely in belonging to a silenced and deprecated minority, but finding a way to be heard: through hashtags, these Twitter

A. Morrison (✉)
University of Waterloo, Waterloo, ON, Canada
e-mail: ahm@uwaterloo.ca

D. C. Parry et al. (eds.), *Digital Dilemmas*,
https://doi.org/10.1007/978-3-319-95300-7_2

users circumvent lines of power and authority, employing consumer services and pop cultural practices and references to speak truth to power, hilariously.

#DistractinglySexy, from June 2015, responded to British Nobel Laureate Sir Tim Hunt's very public remarks about his "problem with girls" in labs by flooding Twitter with thousands of drolly captioned images of actual women working in a fantastical variety of lab and field settings in academic science. The tweets employ various strategies of irony and absurdity to undercut Hunt's description of weepy, lovesick, juvenile female scientists. #StayMadAbby and #BeckyWithTheBadGrades were launched on each of the two occasions in which the US Supreme Court considered the case of a rejected white female applicant to the University of Texas, Austin who claimed discrimination on the basis of race. Tweets using these tags countered stereotypes of African American students "mismatched" to high status schools by offering waves of images of smiling graduands, with captions relating professional degrees, graduate work, career prospects, and job offers. The hashtags in this instance achieve their comic effect by clapping back at the white woman who did not claim these successes, but felt entitled to take her troubles to the highest court in the land.

Hashtag activism as evidenced in #DistractinglySexy, #StayMadAbby, and #BeckyWithTheBadGrades privileges new types of literacy and new types of social action (Noble & Tynes, 2015). Twitter is an essential platform for such action: hashtags organize content and people against the grain of social media's foundational social graphs, which, by and large, are organized along the lines of *who you know* over *what you're saying*. Our current social media ecosystem is predominantly based in personal or institutional relationship networks: trades in mutual friendship connections and moderated newsfeed (Facebook, Snapchat), literal professional networks (LinkedIn) or interpersonal networks (WhatsApp), or user-curated streams of "follows" (Twitter, Instagram). Hashtags, by contrast, radically recentre content over networks, linking disparate information thematically in searchable and followable ways through a folksonomic practice in which the main currency is not the user name or mutual connections but rather the topic of the post. Hashtags are a very effective way to create a new network, to hop existing networks boundaries, and to rapidly trend emerging topics outside of interpersonal connections. Hashtags are thus particularly effective at organizing, promoting, and making visible political actions in marginalized communities (see also Bonilla & Rosa, 2015). They assemble publics that in the collective can speak more strongly against normative modes. Also unlike mass media, social media, reorganized through emergent hashtag communities, are radically non-hierarchical: anyone can add a tag and join the conversation on an equal technical footing, at the very least. Further, tweets under the hashtags under consideration in this chapter are marked not just by their humour but by their bent towards the colloquial, the vernacular, and the anecdotal, ultimately privileging the very subjects and voices that have been excluded.

The Trouble with Girls in Labs: #DistractinglySexy

"Let me tell you about my trouble with girls," Nobel Prize-winning scientist Tim Hunt opined to an audience of female science journalists in South Korea on June 8, 2015: "Three things happen when they are in the lab: you fall in love with them, they fall in love with you, and when you criticise them they cry." His leaden "joke" was transcribed and tweeted by Connie St. Louis, at the time director of the MA in Science Journalism at City University, London (St. Louis, 2015a). Her tweet was rapidly and widely shared and discussed on Twitter, quickly garnering more than 600 retweets and 160 replies. The associated online commentary split between, on the one hand, agreeing that the statement was egregiously sexist and a harm to women's advancement in science and, on the other hand, calling St. Louis a science-hating humourless feminist while stridently defending Hunt. The first mainstream news article on the issue appeared in the *Guardian* early in the day on June 10, and quoted St. Louis's tweet (Ratcliffe, 2015). The Royal Society, of which Hunt is a member, issued a statement "distancing" itself from his remarks and affirming its commitment to women in science (Royal Society, 2015). University College London let it be known that Hunt had resigned his honorary research professorship there (Sir Tim Hunt FRS and UCL, 2015). Outlets from the BBC, the *Observer*, and the *Independent* to the *Daily Mail UK* rapidly produced news articles and opinion pieces on Hunt's remarks, on the online reaction to them on Twitter, and on the dramatic consequences to his career. Hunt himself gave interviews in which he apologized for offending people, but then stood by the content of his remarks, and ultimately asserted that he had been "hung out to dry" unfairly (McKie, 2015a). Public figures, including then-mayor of London Boris Johnson, journalist Jonathan Dimbleby, and prominent scientists Richard Dawkins and Brian Cox, proffered statements supporting Hunt and decrying what they described as an online "witch hunt" against him (e.g., BBC, 2015a; BBC, 2015b; Johnson, 2015; McLelland, 2015; McKie, 2015a; McKie, 2015b; Press Association, 2015; Quinn, 2015; Ratcliffe, 2015; Whitnall, 2015).

St. Louis returned to the story with an op-ed in the *Guardian* on June 23 after most of the fray had subsided. She considered the progress of the controversy: "The Tim Hunt story has followed a typical pattern of oppression. First there is a hollow apology. Then there is claim about being misunderstood. Next there is an outcry from the establishment" (St. Louis, 2015b). The *Observer* profile, for example, explicitly framed the controversy as an exemplary case of "academic self-harm" as though the main victim were Hunt himself (McKie, 2015a). As St. Louis and others pointed out, the broader public discussion of Hunt's remarks devolved into binary positions on whether he should face this or that consequence, or not; how great a scientist he was; how unfair the backlash was. It remained *all about Hunt*, and not at all about the underlying question of women in science.

But, there was another reaction to Hunt's remarks. Around the time the *Guardian*'s first story appeared, early on June 10, the online feminist magazine *The Vagenda* put a call on Twitter, asking female scientists to share images of their work under the hashtag "#DistractinglySexy" (The Vagenda Team, 2015) (see Fig. 1). What resulted was the crowd-sourced creation of a powerful counternarrative that put the lie both to Hunt's characterization of "girls in labs" and to the media framing of the online reaction as violent, disproportionate, and mob-like. Science and culture blogger Helen Cahill argued that in much of the coverage of the joke and its aftermath, "the most important people in the story have been drowned out: the women scientists who are living proof of just how wrong Hunt

Fig. 1 @vagendamagazine 10 June 2015

is" (2015). She continued, "Unless we acknowledge the stories of women [Hunt] has forgotten, a negative portrayal of women once again takes centre stage" (Cahill, 2015). This is the work of #DistractinglySexy. Tweets using the hashtag began appearing nearly immediately after *The Vagenda* launched the call. Thousands of tweets appeared in the ensuing days, and many were widely reprinted in mainstream media, in addition to being virally shared online, filling in that crucial gap Cahill identified (e.g., Chappell, 2015; Kohli, 2015; Healy, 2015; Wendling, 2015). The tag continues to be used, more than two years later, as I write this. It has produced offshoot projects such as that by graduate student Eden Hennessey, who used the tag as the basis for a series of photographic portraits of female scientists in the Waterloo Region who had faced sexism in their careers, naming her show #DistractinglySexist (Wilfrid Laurier University, 2015).

The hashtag took off because it was an exemplary viral meme: fun to browse, easy to participate in, humorously ironic, very shareable, and sometimes laugh-out-loud funny. Twitter user @rat_spit (an article later identifies her as Zoé Vincent-Mistiason, a PhD student in the UK [Kohli, 2015]) captioned her image thus: "Stopped crying long enough to upload this #distractinglysexy #TimHunt @VagendaMagazine" (see Fig. 2). Vincent-Mistiason's image is staged for maximum foreground and background absurdity, and references Hunt's claim that women cry in labs. It gained 725 retweets and over 1250 likes. Many more images rapidly appeared, individually obscure with minimal shares and commentary perhaps, but ultimately creating a massive and traversable set of represen-

Fig. 2 @rat_spit 10 June 2015

tations that populated the hashtag overwhelmingly with simultaneously goofy and sarcastic female scientists, alone and in groups, at the bench, in the field, at conferences, and everywhere else science takes place. Part of the power of the tagged tweets was their incredible variety, but nearly all who participated employed one or more of the following techniques: structural irony, visual or verbal irony, intertextuality, physical comedy, and absurdity.

Here are several more tweets that show the variety of ways female scientists took up the call. Most posts play up the hashtag's fundamental structural irony: that women's presence and participation in the daily work in science could be objectively, systematically construed as distractingly sexy. This irony is both visually and textually encoded: nearly all the tweets exploit the pervasive mismatch between the visual content of the images they share and their being tagged as "#distractinglysexy." Users very commonly employed ironic self-deprecation, like Vincent-Mistiason's assertion that she only "stopped crying long enough" to take and upload a photo. This strategy is shown as well by other participants who stage images in which they "fall in love" with pieces of lab equipment, for example. Others hook into broader internet and youth culture, referencing popular culture and popular memes powered by irreverence and silliness, rather than seduction. Yet others counter the implicit minority status of female scientists by depicting groups of women working together. Finally, a very large number of the images depict women actually performing science: calibrating expensive lab equipment, digging in holes, up to their hips in creeks, scraping poop samples into tubes.

Twitter user Bailey Rose (@baileysutton), a student based in the US, pictures herself draped distractingly over lab equipment (see Fig. 3). Her caption, "Chain me up like one of your gas tanks," marks this user's internet fluency and flags her youth: she is referencing a meme, "Draw me like one of your French girls," which overlays the phrase on images of pets and people in "seductive" poses that fail to be seductive, a meme which draws its text from the movie *Titanic* (1997), in which Rose enjoins Jack to draw her nude (Tibbetts and deertysanchez, 2017). Its register and rhetorical strategies are native to the internet, and it succeeds as a funny tweet in the more general sense, as well as a canny instance of #distractinglysexy in particular. Bailey Rose's tweet has layers of irony and of intertextuality and is pitched to most amuse internet-savvy, younger female scientists or science students. Her tweet, furthermore, cannily uses two tags: #DistractinglySexy and #womeninscience, yoking a trending and specific hashtag to a longer-standing more general one, linking two communities and promoting broader reach. The large public already gathered around the established #womeninscience is a desirable audience for #distractinglysexy, while those casual readers who follow the trending hashtag

Fig. 3 @baileysutton 17 June 2015

#distractinglysexy can learn more about the existing networks and practices of #womeninscience.

User Mallori Joseph (@gracefulbeauty1) staged a group shot, a sort of *tableau vivant* illustrating Hunt's expressed fears. It shows three women in the foreground and mid-ground in full lab gear, smiling at the camera. Their flirty facial expressions are counteracted by the lab context: all three wear dark and boxy lab coats, safety glasses, and latex gloves. The caption reads:

> We were just too disruptive in in the lab #womenofscience #distractinglysexy.

The tweet's text, "We were just too disruptive in the lab" refers to the two figures in the background, male scientists in white lab coats, one sliding his glasses down his nose, and the other tilting his body, his head, and his eyebrows, to leer more effectively at the women in the foreground. This image makes clear that it is not the *women* who are distracted and unprofessional, but rather the *men*. The composition of the visual field of this image, and its deployment of stereotyped poses (for both the men and the women) that are easily recognizable from television advertisements (cheesy smiles, broad telegraphing of mood through exaggerated gesture, befuddled men and flirty women), add to the irony of the hashtag. This set of scientists represents a set of comedic stereotypes, not reality. It's sitcom funny, or cleaning product advertisement funny, which is to say, fake and ridiculous—the implication is that of course Hunt's conception is fake and ridiculous in just the same ways. Outmoded as well: it's *Benny Hill* in lab coats. The image is also compelling because of the obvious collaborative feeling in the lab, the willingness of male colleagues to participate, and the demonstration that white women are not the only "girls in labs." This tweet, too, is double-tagged #womeninscience and #distractinglysexy.

One final example, from Colette Mesher (@csmesher), is representative of the large number of tweets depicting the daily working conditions of a wide variety of field and lab scientists (see Fig. 4). Mesher is depicted supine, lifted up on one elbow across some boxes arranged on a flat-bed truck. Her gender is not immediately discernible from the image, as she is wearing boxy and oversized work pants, sweater and gloves, work boots, and a beekeeping helmet. The pose is reminiscent of babes-on-cars calendars, but this woman's body is completely hidden, and she is lying on top of what we infer, from the caption, to be nine boxes of bees. As "the only woman on the beekeeping crew," she writes, "clearly all the guys are in love with me."

The #DistractinglySexy tweets punctured the self-serious rhetorical posturing evident in so much of the media coverage and official press releases following the publication of Hunt's remarks. They avoided being tarred with the brush of "internet outrage" that directed so much mainstream coverage of the controversy. The human-interest profile of Hunt in the *Observer*, for example, asserted that, whatever retrograde gender assumptions his "joke" revealed, "[h]is treatment also demonstrates the

Fig. 4 @csmesher 19 June 2015

innate cruelty of social media, and in particular the savage power of Twitter" (McKie, 2015a). Even Brian Cox, who in a lengthy BBC radio interview decried the Internet mob out to ruin Tim Hunt's career (BBC, 2015b), had nothing but praise for this particular Twitter movement, replying to user Karen James on the platform that he found that the "#distractinglysexy campaign … is a superb response to [Hunt's] daftness" (Cox, 2015). Many others online were also keen to make the point that if there was a braying internet mob seeking some sort of cultural death penalty for Hunt, it was not to be found on this hashtag. But mostly, instead of discussing the controversy, they kept producing, tweeting, and sharing their own #DistractinglySexy images.

As St. Louis observed: "Hunt had a chance when there was a lot of attention focused on him to use that moment for good. He could have apologised properly; he could have talked about the brilliant work carried out by women scientists" (St. Louis, 2015b). But he didn't, of course, and neither did most of the press coverage. On June 9, the Royal Society released a public statement, that read in part: "The Royal Society has acted to distance itself from reported comments by Sir Tim Hunt FRS about women in science [....] Hunt was speaking as an individual and his reported comments in no way reflect the views of the Royal Society" (Royal Society, 2015). Readers are then encouraged to "visit our diversity webpage" (Royal Society, 2015, 2017) as evidence of this commitment to equity in science. Sara Ahmed observes that diversity statements perform work more rhetorical than material: they assert inclusive values, not as a precursor to changes in institutional practices, but rather as the alternative to such changes (Ahmed, 2012). Indeed, academic science remains stubbornly unreflective of general demographics: in 2015, according to the US National Science Foundation, 70% of academic scientists are men and 67% of them are white. Indeed, *white men make up fully half the sample* (49%) (National Science Foundation, 2017). The Royal Society itself, a 2014 report noted, saw its proportion of female fellowship winners drop steadily and unequivocally from a high of 36% in 2010 (which the society itself called as a "blip") to a low of 4.6% in 2014 (Else, 2014). Female scientists continue to report chilly climate issues, workplace sexual harassment, and pervasive structural sexism (e.g., as reported in Barthelemy, McCormick, & Henderson, 2016): Hunt's joke is all too real in its casual reference to the supposed sexual availability, emotional volatility, and intellectual weakness women in science are assumed to embody.

The #DistractinglySexy tweets were funny rather than cruel, individual, and clever but achieved important and serious goals: #DistractinglySexy recentred the female scientists as active agents in their own narratives; reframed the media narrative around the controversy; and slyly pointed out the absurdity and inaccuracy of Hunt's claims, without attacking him directly. In short, the "Tim Hunt" story became instead, through their own efforts, the story of working female scientists. These tweets present female scientists as adult women, not girls. Rather than crying, they're making arch jokes about "tear-proof" headlamps for field work. Female scientists, often isolated in their own labs, find common identity as well as common cause through their participation in the hashtag. All of this without asking for Tim Hunt's head on a pike.

The #Distractingly Sexy hashtag foregrounds the existence and work of female scientists and insists that we see them in their numbers and in their variety, in their non-crying, non-falling-in-love, presumably open-to-criticism yet capable work. The hashtag was funny viral clickbait of the highest order, tweeted and retweeted very widely on Twitter itself, of course, but with several of the best instances reprinted over and over again in journalistic media. It succeeded, then, in shifting the agenda of media coverage both of "girls in labs" and of the power of grass-roots participatory media. As against one very prominent—knighted!—white male scientist and his powerful (white, male) allies in politics, journalism, and science all loudly asserting that Hunt is at worst a poor humourist, female scientists in their obscure thousands joined their voices together and told a different story and insisted we hear it.

#StayMadAbby and #BeckyWithTheBadGrades

Abigail Fisher wanted to attend the University of Texas, Austin, but was not admitted to the Class of 2012. Claiming racial discrimination, Fisher took her complaint all the way to the US Supreme Court—twice. The hashtags #StayMadAbby and #BeckyWithTheBadGrades respond directly to the titular complainant in Fisher v. University of Texas (1) and Fisher v. University of Texas (2), and take on widely circulating negative characterizations of race-conscious affirmative action in higher education. The tags were started by African American students at University of Texas at Austin (UT) but spread to students at other schools, then to the broader online space known as "Black Twitter" (Brock, 2012; Lee, 2017; Manjoo and Glaser, 2010; Monk-Payton, 2017, 26), and then to more general and diffuse audiences on that platform. They were collected, glossed, and reprinted in online black-focused and progressive media (e.g., Naasel, 2015; Stokes, 2015; Whaley, 2015) to support narratives of black academic excellence against racist and counterfactual public narratives of "unfair advantage" and "reverse racism" (Goldstein Hode & Meisenbach, 2017, 1). As with #DistractinglySexy, the corpus of linked images-and-caption became a news story in its own right, and received broad and direct coverage in mainstream media (e.g., Feldman, 2015;

Harris, 2016; Harvard, 2016). This participation in reframing is important, as the African American Policy Forum specifically indicts mainstream media as "a central source of the misrepresentation of [affirmative action admissions] policies and in creating public perceptions that affirmative action is fundamentally unfair" (n.d). Catherine Knight Steele agrees, asserting that "the use of personal narrative combats dominant discourse and provides the opportunity for Black women [in particular] to use their own voices in resistance of marginalization" (2016, 80). #StayMadAbby and #BeckyWithTheBadGrades offer sharp counternarratives against stereotypes deployed to undermine race-conscious affirmative action policies in American universities and colleges, making use of culturally specific pop culture references and modes of humour, to develop in-group cohesion as well. Brandy Monk-Payton notes the development and use of a post-satire mode of sass and shade as a mode of "ridicule [...] tethered to Black vernacular in attitude and tone," which both assert and sustain "Black structures of feeling" that are denigrated in the popular framing of the Fisher case (2017, 17).

The stakes are very high. The Fisher case was universally understood as an assault on race-conscious affirmative action in admissions on a national scale (e.g., Barnes, 2012; Bazelon, 2012; Hannah-Jones, 2016; Jaschik, 2013; Ocen & Beydoun, 2015; Sidhu, 2013). By the time the case was first heard in 2013, Fisher had matriculated at a different institution and was nearing graduation. Indeed, in an interview after the court's final ruling against her in June 2016, she asserted that she never intended the lawsuit to secure her admission to Austin but rather to serve a larger cause (Edwards, 2016). As she relayed to the BBC: "The day she received her rejection letter from UT, Fisher picked up the phone and called [lawyer] Edward Blum [....] A friend of her father's, Blum had spent years looking for a plaintiff to take on affirmative action" (Edwards, 2016). And so, Fisher offered herself as a figurehead to this movement. As Nikole Hannah-Jones argued in a deeply sourced piece for ProPublica in 2013, Abigail Noel Fisher was the perfect plaintiff for such a case. The narrative circulated in the press (but not in the legal arguments) painted Fisher, as Hannah-Jones puts it, as a hardworking UT Austin legacy candidate, who had "her dream snatched away by a university that closed its doors to her because she had been born the wrong color: White" (Hannah-Jones,

2016). Every newspaper article, every TV segment, featured images of the complainant, foregrounded and alone at a microphone or on the court steps, backgrounded by a veritable phalanx of lawyers and interveners. Her story was told again and again—legacy applicant, hard worker, life-long dream, good student—and her image widely publicized. These types of representation matter: as Hannah-Jones reminds us, the strategy of seeking exemplary plaintiffs for lawsuits that aimed to force courts to address civil rights was developed by the National Association for the Advancement of Colored People (NAACP). Ruby Bridges was not the first child to desire school integration; Rosa Parks not the first woman to wish to sit nearer the front of the bus. An exemplary plaintiff is one who adheres to "the politics of respectability" in looks, deportment, and personal history (White, 1990, 76, 2001); an exemplary plaintiff will not distract from the legal or policy goals with a messy personal story that is in any way distasteful to newspaper readers or other normatively conceived American mainstream public.

Upon review of the facts, it is hard to see where Fisher was discriminated against on the basis of race. Her grades and test scores, actually, were middling. Also, among admitted applicants "with lower test scores than Fisher, five were black or Latino applicants. Forty-two were white. The University also noted that 168 black and Latino students with better academic and personal achievement records than Fisher were rejected" (Massie, 2016). Instead of outright rejection, too, Fisher was offered the compromise option of beginning her studies at another UT campus and then transferring to Austin in her sophomore year, which she refused on principle, such as it was. On simple merits, then, Fisher's case was very weak—but the case was less about Fisher's admissibility than chipping away at the legality of race consciousness in admissions. The flip side of the demand for Fisher's admission, of her characterization as exemplary plaintiff, of course, is the implication that minority candidates have not earned their own places, that they are unqualified, undeserving, not hard working, unmeritorious, certain to fail. Late Justice Antonin Scalia actually made the following argument in court: "There are those who contend that it does not benefit African Americans to get them into the University of Texas, where they do not do well, as opposed to having them go to a less-advanced school, a slower-track school where they do well" (qtd. in Mencimer, 2015). He continued: "I'm just not impressed by the fact the University of Texas may have fewer [blacks]. Maybe it ought to have fewer" (qtd. in Mencimer, 2015). Clarence Thomas voiced similar thoughts on another affirmative action case in higher education, Grutter. v. Bollinger, in 2003: his dissenting opinion purports that "[t]he Law School tantalizes *unprepared students* with the promise of a University of Michigan degree and all of the opportunities that it offers. These *overmatched students* take the bait, only to find that they *cannot succeed* in the cauldron of competition" (qtd. in Grutter vs Bollinger, 2003; emphasis added). "Mismatch theory" relies on two pernicious and widespread myths about affirmative action: first, that unqualified (African American) students are gaining admission to selective colleges and "taking the place" of white students, and, second, that these unqualified students do not succeed in these programs, when faced with (presumably meritocratic) competition from standard admissions (Crenshaw, 2006).

#StayMadAbby and #BeckyWithTheBadGrades work on two fronts. First, to counter the favourable individuation of Fisher as exemplary plaintiff pitted purposefully against a faceless mass of unfairly advantaged minority applicants, tweets using the tags show image after image of particular and specific African American students succeeding—wave after wave, if you will, of exemplary defendants. Second, in tagging her "bad grades" Twitter users foreground the factual baselessness of Fisher's complaint, at the same time that they de-invididualize her by making her stand for a type of entitled "basic" white woman, a "Becky." #StayMadAbby launched and peaked in early December 2015, in response to Scalia's comments. Joy Stokes on *XO Necole* describes the tag's origins thus: "So Black Twitter clapped back [to Scalia] in the most beautiful way possible, and from it we saw the #StayMadAbby hashtag, where black college graduates from UT, and beyond, showed their educational excellence in all of its finest glory". An article in *USA Today*'s College section also draws this causative line, describing Scalia's ideas "being drowned out by a tremendous surge of support for UT, including a new hashtag: #StayMadAbby" (Bernstein, 2015). 2014 Vanderbilt graduate Patrick Sutton, an early user of the tag, explained to the BBC: "It is like saying, 'We know you're mad and upset with our success or current situation but we're letting you know it's not going to change anytime soon.' We are not phased by her disgruntled attitude or other people's negative thoughts and actions" (Gold, 2015). Sutton is describing as well the more general black Twitter tag #StayMad, already well established at that point but repurposed here to specify Fisher as a collective target. #StayMadAbby tweets thus taunt Fisher over her rejection from UT Austin and put the lie to mismatch theory. It offers social critique in the form of a diss and a clapback.

Many of the #StayMadAbby tweets consisted of an image of a black student in cap and gown, or of a group of students, or of diplomas, a straightforward refutation of Scalia's invocation of mismatch theory and a clapback at Fisher's failure to make the grade. Here are some paradigmatic examples of this type of tweet, from the day it launched (see Fig. 5). User Kinya Harte (@Next_of_KinYA) lists her GPA, degree, and academic honours, and includes a smiling selfie in academic regalia:

Fig. 5 @Next_of_KinYA 10 Dec 2015

#StayMadAbby. User Vagney Bradley (@VagneyBradley) is a bit more direct in her taunting of Fisher, depicting herself in graduation cap, flipping her hair over her shoulder as she strides in front of the UT Austin logo. The caption reads:

> I'm a proud #Longhorn who earned my degree from the best university ever #UT! #StayMadAbby.

Her post is further tagged with UT Austin-specific hashtags: #Longhorn and #UT assert her membership in the community from which Fisher was excluded, with a knock-on effect of bringing #StayMadAbby into broader visibility in the UT Twitter community. User Gideon (@nollywood_Q) also takes the opportunity to combine celebrating his own academic success with actively dragging Fisher: his image shows him in cap and hood, leaping into the air. He provides this gloss: "When you up high laughing cause Abby couldn't get in." He creates his own hashtag to reinforce the point: #iearnedMyhorns, again a reference to the school's football team, the Longhorns (see Fig. 6).

As these instances aver, not only did Fisher *not* get into UT, but many black Twitter users *did* get into UT, and not only did they *get in*, they also *graduated*. Not only did they happily celebrate their own graduations, but now they're using their graduation photos to celebrate Fisher losing her case for admission. These tweets are pleasurable on the level of the diss and the clap back, hearkening to a long tradition of insult humour that has become associated with African American cultural practices (Wald, 2014).Others make the political content more explicit. User Ahsante Bean (@AhsanteB) addresses Scalia directly: "Thanks Scalia, but this is more our speed." "This" is an image of a group of eight African American graduates in caps and gowns, tagged #Harvard. The post is also, of course, tagged #StayMadAbby, but Ashante Bean adds two further tags #ByeScalia and #blackexcellence, explicitly addressing mismatch theory (see Fig. 7).

The tag and concept of a positively framed #blackexcellence recurs in the corpus, a celebration to counter overwhelmingly negative portrayals of black youth in mainstream media (see Lee 2017 for a broader analysis of this phenomenon). Positive and supportive depictions of black stu-

Fig. 6 @nollywood_Q 10 Dec 2015

dentship are essential survival tools, as user FreeingMindsBW (@ FreeingMindsBW) asserts in a tweet, writing: "If you're a black woman and you're struggling in school and trying to stay sane, take a look at #StayMadAbby and get your life!" To "get your life" is to be refreshed by the positivity and solidarity expressed by tag users. Other users employed the tag to simply drag Fisher directly. User Guwopele (@ladyblovebytes) tweets: "If Abigail Fisher put as much effort into her studies as she's put into defending her mediocrity, she might've gotten in #StayMadAbby." Many wrote tweets that, rather than adding content to the tag, aimed to bring it to the attention of their own follower community, boosting the tag's viral dissemination, in the same vein as @FreeingMindsBW. These tweets focused on the pleasures of the tag's consumption: the hotness of

Fig. 7 @AhsanteB 10 Dec 2015

the "tea" (the snark or gossip level), exclamations that "this hashtag is everything" in its affirmations of black excellence, and describing the tag as "the best thing on the internet" for its skill in crafting memes, disses, and clapbacks. Such tweets employ language that reinforces in-group status for members of the deprecated outgroup who are the focus of Scalia's remarks and Fisher's suit: African American youth. Indeed, mass participation populated the hashtag with an incredible set of representations of black excellence. To browse the tag is to get the impression that all black youth go to selective colleges and thrive and that selective colleges are heavily populated with black students.

On the occasion of the Supreme Court's final decision against Fisher in early summer 2016, another hashtag sprang up. #BeckyWithTheBadGrades also builds from an existing hashtag on Black Twitter, namely #BeckyWithTheGoodHair. That hashtag, of course, refers to a line in Beyoncé's then-recently released *Lemonade*, that seems to both name and dismiss a husband's cheating with a white woman, "Becky with the good hair"—"Becky" here standing as some generic white girl name, a term that has since that time come into fairly wide usage in that sense. #BeckyWithTheBadGrades thus both marks Fisher as an uninteresting cardboard cutout of white femininity and denies Fisher her own individual name, rendering her both much less important than she would seem to want to be, and, crucially, making her a member of a class and thus open to structural critique. One of the insidious ways that white supremacy perpetuates itself is by making Whiteness itself invisible, and the tag counters that invisibility in naming Fisher as "Becky." It speaks as well to Fisher's academic mediocrity and the lack of grounds for her court challenge.

What happened on Twitter was a thorough takedown of the issues at the heart of the public understanding of the case, which is based not on the merits of Fisher's application in particular but on the *merits of affirmative action itself*. Particularly, the hashtags worked to name, ridicule, and counter Fisher's own personal mediocrity, but also, and crucially, to generalize out from this to the white entitlement undergirding the whole case, and to offer a counternarrative of black scholarly excellence and achievement. Monk-Payton marks the doubled work of anger and pleasure, noting, "the dynamic aggression of such online content generates a common joy among Black folk that is constitutive of the ways in which race and race relations are processed in digital culture" (Monk-Payton, 2017, 28). The hashtags use humour to express outrage, to assert group identity, to promote black excellence, to shift a narrative, to dislodge stereotypes—the tags are embedded in a rich Black Twitter context, devised and circulated for the pleasures and creativity and consumption of cultural insiders, set to the tune of Beyoncé.

Collective/Laugh

To focus on tweet-length humour, on brief hashtags, is neither to deny the seriousness of the issues being addressed, nor to suggest that the online humourists are themselves unserious. It is, instead to describe and examine yet one more vector along which social justice might be pursued, a viral means by which the unrepresented and misrepresented can write themselves back into the story, can write their own stories. #DistratctinglySexy, #StayMadAbby, and #BeckyWithTheBadGrades counter a lack of representation that invisibilizes, and misrepresentations that demonize, scapegoat, or caricature marginalized academic subjects. They do so by creating mass-participatory movements that flood public space with images that move beyond the default view, the clip art, the out-of-date stereotype, images that in their variety of subjects, locations, framing, and focus flag intersections and complexities, producing celebrations and critiques simultaneously. This is an important and difficult kind of social justice work. It is not an easy thing to craft a hashtag that will take off, to nurture and support it with media appearances or essays or concerted collective action. Often this labour is performed, uncredited, by women of colour particularly, whose contributions are often costly to them, erased, or downplayed. Consider Connie St. Louis tweeting Tim Hunt's sexist remarks about "girls" in science, and being harrassed, doxxed, and discredited in the tabloid and online press for her trouble (Bradley, 2015, Fernandez, 2015, Yiannopolous, 2016): Google suggests autocompleting a search on her name with "fired," "apologizes," "fabricated CV," and "retraction." Consider Twitter user @SheBeShonuff crafting #BeckyWithTheBadGrades mostly uncredited, while many advertising-supported sites repackage tagged images into clickbait (Dionne, 2016, Ng, 2016, stevekindof, 2016). Consider longstanding Black Twitter modes of humour that were so easily transferred to the Fisher case without their history and context being acknowledged.

Rhiannon Cosslett, journalist and co-founder of *The Vagenda*, took to the op-ed pages to counter assertions that #DistractinglySexy aimed to ruin Tim Hunt's careers (Cosslett, 2015). Connie St. Louis, also a journalism professor, similarly wrote an op-ed to counter the backlash against her own tweet (St. Louis, 2015b). I acknowledge and applaud these women's labours to shift representation to match reality and to promote joyful, positive frames to lighten the burdens of oppression faced by participants, as well as the risks they take in leading collective actions that expose them to hostile public and institutional cultures.[1] In any case, in both campaigns, the repeated, collective assertion of one's own self and everyday realities, from small joys to microaggressions, counters the silencing and erasures that a rigid distinction of "public" from "private" culture, of serious from non-serious, where whatever is cast as a joke can never be seriously critiqued, and serious critiques can never take the form of jokes. Both hashtag campaigns respond to structural, institutional harms, issuing from the seats of power and privilege and esteem: universities, courts, politicians, learned societies. They aim at these loftiest of targets with the most informal of means: Twitter jokes. This is a powerful technique, but not all powerful. Cosslett asserts:

> In voicing their genuine frustrations about sexism, women are providing media outlets with "clickbait" content, largely for free. And it will continue, at least until the media start taking women's stories seriously by hiring them and allowing them to shape the news agenda in more profound ways. Until then, going viral is often our only recourse. But ask how much power it really wields, and the answer is probably much less than you think (2015).

You can't, as Audre Lorde put it, take down the master's house using the master's tools. Statements by individual Supreme Court judges, doubting

[1] Black cultural labour is erased and appropriated enough already: as Evelyn Atieno notes, there's got to be some reason that Daniel Lara, the handsome white teenager who is back at it again with the white Vans has a name we know and several endorsements deals, while "Peaches Monroee" (Kayla Newman), whose eyebrows have always been on fleek, goes uncredited and uncompensated for her lexical innovation. There is a further danger of appropriating these labours, of repacking them for a different audience in a totally alien context and then profiting from them—it's great that images from both campaigns are heavily reprinted in mainstream media, but the campaigns are not always credited to their creators, or, when acknowledged, these creators face harassment campaigns and backlash.

black excellence and espousing a racial politics of utopian colour blindness, never mind accumulating case law that chips away at the fundamental purposes and practices of affirmative action in admissions, prompt little faith that the court accepts that historically excluded groups continue to be disadvantaged today. Even as universities and the filers of *amicus* briefs nominally defend affirmative action, they too move away from the concept of social justice or equity to frame affirmative action as promoting a "diverse" educational experience for *normative (white, privileged) students*—that is, affirmative action is desirable because it exposes white students to diversity that makes them more successful in an increasingly globalized work environment (Crenshaw, 2006; Goldstein Hode & Meisenbach, 2017). The Royal Society affirms its commitment to women in science on its "diversity" webpage, but sees a precipitous drop in the number of women to whom it awards major prizes (Else, 2014; Royal Society, 2017). It "distances" itself from Tim Hunt's remarks, but then, months later, quietly reappoints him to a working group on UK science research, describing him as "a leading expert" and "an obvious choice" for membership (qtd. in Tonkin, 2015). University College London trumpets its early, equitable admission of female students but pays its female science faculty less than the male faculty (Cohen, 2015). With friends like these, why show up to the party, even if they do sometimes deign to invite you? Even when you win in these institutional contexts, it seems, you still lose. In taking to Twitter, and using humour, hashtags, captions, and images, female scientists and African American undergraduate and graduate students create *their own tools* that work to change the venue, change the participants, change the focus, and change the script on these debates. They aim at different outcomes: visibility, diverse and inclusive representation, solidarity, and laughter. Official channels are untrustworthy and largely closed: they take the fight instead to their own turf, setting the agenda and reframing discussion, laughing the whole way.

References

Ahmed, S. (2012). On being included: Racism and diversity in institutional life. In *Durham*. London: Duke University Press.

Atieno, E. (2016, February 26). Damn, Daniel: White mediocrity wins again. Retrieved August 9, 2016, from http://www.huffingtonpost.com/evelyn-atieno/damn-daniel-white-mediocrit_b_9328438.html

Barnes, R. (2012, September 27). Supreme Court may limit use of race in college admissions – The Washington Post. The Washington Post. Retrieved from https://www.washingtonpost.com/politics/decision2012/supreme-court-may-limit-use-of-race-in-college-admissions/2012/09/27/3d9c69fa-065a-11e2-afff-d6c7f20a83bf_story.html?utm_term=.40814124e17e

Barthelemy, R. S., McCormick, M., & Henderson, C. (2016). Gender discrimination in physics and astronomy: Graduate student experiences of sexism and gender microaggressions. Physical Review Physics Education Research, 12(2). https://doi.org/10.1103/PhysRevPhysEducRes.12.020119

Bazelon, E. (2012, October 11). The Supreme Court wrestles with affirmative action in Fisher v. University of Texas-Austin. Retrieved August 1, 2017, from http://www.slate.com/articles/news_and_politics/supreme_court_dispatches/2012/10/the_supreme_court_wrestles_with_affirmative_action_in_fisher_v_university.html

BBC. (2015a, June 10). Sir Tim Hunt "sorry" over "trouble with girls" comments. BBC News. Retrieved from http://www.bbc.com/news/uk-33077107

BBC. (2015b, June 16). Tim Hunt should not have quit over "sexist" remarks—Brian Cox. BBC News. Retrieved from http://www.bbc.com/news/uk-33152345

Bernstein, R. (2015, December 13). U. of Texas Supreme Court fight gets hashtag: #StayMadAbby. Retrieved August 9, 2016, from http://college.usatoday.com/2015/12/13/u-of-texas-supreme-court-fight-gets-hashtag-staymadabby/

Bonilla, Y., & Rosa, J. (2015). #Ferguson: Digital protest, hashtag ethnography, and the racial politics of social media in the United States: #Ferguson. American Ethnologist, 42(1), 4–17. https://doi.org/10.1111/amet.12112

Bradley, R. (2015, August 1). Connie St Louis: Delusional or dishonest? Retrieved August 8, 2017, from http://www.skepticink.com/lateral-truth/2015/08/01/connie-st-louis-delusional-or-dishonest/

Brock, A. (2012). From the blackhand side: Twitter as a cultural conversation. Journal of Broadcasting & Electronic Media, 56(4), 529–549. https://doi.org/10.1080/08838151.2012.732147

Cahill, H. (2015, June 12). The unseen women scientists behind Tim Hunt's Nobel prize. *The Guardian*. Retrieved from https://www.theguardian.com/science/blog/2015/jun/12/the-unseen-women-scientists-behind-tim-hunts-nobel-prize

Chappell, B. (2015, June 12). #Distractinglysexy tweets are female scientists' retort to "disappointing" comments. Retrieved July 21, 2017, from http://www.npr.org/sections/thetwo-way/2015/06/12/413986529/-distractinglysexy-tweets-are-female-scientists-retort-to-disappointing-comments

Cohen, C. (2015, September 2). University in Tim Hunt sexism row admits paying women less. *The Telegraph*. Retrieved from http://www.telegraph.co.uk/women/womens-life/11838761/Tim-Hunt-sexism-UCL-university-admits-paying-women-less.html

Cosslett, R. L. (2015, June 17). My #distractinglysexy hashtag is not to blame for Tim Hunt's resignation. *The Guardian*. Retrieved from http://www.theguardian.com/commentisfree/2015/jun/17/hashtag-distractinglysexy-not-blame-tim-hunt-resignation

Cox, B. (2015, June 3). @kejames Thanks. I wasn't referring to the #distractinglysexy campaign, which I think is a superb response to his daftness! [Tweet].

Crenshaw, K. (2006). Framing affirmative action. *Michigan Law Review First Impressions, 105*(1), 123–133 Retrieved from http://repository.law.umich.edu/mlr_fi/vol105/iss1/4.

Dionne, E. (2016, June 24). Black Twitter's latest hashtag trend has the best responses to Abigail Fisher's affirmative action fail. Retrieved August 8, 2017, from http://www.revelist.com/viral/becky-bad-grades-hashtag-abigail/3221

Edwards, G. (2016, July 29). Abigail fisher: Affirmative action plaintiff "proud" of academic record. Retrieved August 9, 2016, from http://www.bbc.com/news/world-us-canada-36928990

Else, H. (2014, September 25). Success rate for women on Royal Society fellowship tumbles. Retrieved July 20, 2017, from https://www.timeshighereducation.com/news/success-rate-for-women-on-royal-society-fellowship-tumbles/2015983.article

Feldman, B. (2015, December 10). 'Stay Mad Abby': Black College Graduates Ridicule SCOTUS Affirmative-Action Case. NYMag. Retrieved from http://nymag.com/selectall/2015/12/black-graduates-ridicule-affirmative-action-case.html

Fernandez, C. (2015, June 30). Connie St Louis who accused Tim Hunt keeps job despite her dubious career claims. *Daily Mail Online*. Retrieved from http://www.dailymail.co.uk/news/article-3143945/Lecturer-accused-sexist-Nobel-Prize-professor-keeps-job-despite-Mail-revealing-dubious-claims-career-told-update-CV.html

FreeingMindsBW. (2015, December 1). If you're a black woman and you're struggling in school and trying to stay sane, take a look at #StayMadAbby and get your life! [Tweet]. Retrieved August 3, 2017, from https://twitter.com/search?l=&q=%23staymadabby%20since%3A2015-12-10%20until%3A2015-12-11&src=typd

Gold, A. (2015, December 11). #StayMadAbby: How black graduates responded to a key Supreme Court case. Retrieved August 5, 2016, from http://www.bbc.com/news/blogs-trending-35065014

Goldstein Hode, M., & Meisenbach, R. J. (2017). Reproducing whiteness through diversity: A critical discourse analysis of the pro-affirmative action amicus briefs in the Fisher case. Journal of Diversity in Higher Education, 10(2), 162–180. https://doi.org/10.1037/dhe0000014

Grutter v. Bollinger et al. 539 U.S. 516 (2003).

Hannah-Jones, N. (2016, June 23). What Abigail Fisher's affirmative action case was really about. Retrieved August 9, 2016, from https://www.propublica.org/article/a-colorblind-constitution-what-abigail-fishers-affirmative-action-case-is-r

Harris, H. (2016, June 23). Twitter responds to Supreme Court ruling with #BeckyWithTheBadGrades. Retrieved August 9, 2016, from http://www.refinery29.com/2016/06/114851/becky-with-the-bad-grades-twitter

Harvard, S. (2016, June 23). Abigail fisher lost her anti-affirmative action case and the internet is roasting her | mic. Retrieved August 9, 2016, from https://mic.com/articles/146985/abigail-fisher-lost-her-anti-affirmative-action-case-and-the-internet-is-roasting-her#.n5eqCDNRZ

Healy, B. (2015, June 11). 16 on-point responses from female scientists to Nobel winner's sexist comments. Retrieved July 21, 2017, from http://mashable.com/2015/06/11/female-scientists-responses-tim-hunt-distractinglysexy/

Jaschik, S. (2013, June 25). Lawyers analyze Supreme Court decision on affirmative action. Retrieved August 1, 2017, from https://www.insidehighered.com/news/2013/06/25/lawyers-analyze-supreme-court-decision-affirmative-action

Johnson, B. (2015, June 14). Male and female are different: Hardly earth-shattering news. Retrieved from http://www.telegraph.co.uk/news/society/11674257/Male-and-female-are-different-hardly-earth-shattering-news.html

Kohli, S. (2015, June 12). Women scientists fight sexism with #distractinglysexy pictures on Twitter. Retrieved July 21, 2017, from https://qz.com/426894/women-scientists-fight-sexism-with-distractinglysexy-pictures-on-twitter/

Layout 1 – Affirmative-Action-Primer-Focus-on-Affirmative-Action.pdf. (n.d.). Retrieved from http://static.squarespace.com/static/53f20d90e4b0b80451158d8c/53f399a5e4b029c2ffbe26cc/53f399c7e4b029c2ffbe2aad/1408473543120/Affirmative-Action-Primer-Focus-on-Affirmative-Action.pdf?format=original

Lee, L. (2017). Black twitter: A response to bias in mainstream media. Social Sciences, 6(1), 26. https://doi.org/10.3390/socsci6010026

Manjoo, F., & Glaser, A. (2010, August 10). How black people use twitter. *Slate*. Retrieved from http://www.slate.com/articles/technology/technology/2010/08/how_black_people_use_twitter.html

Massie, V. M. (2016, May 25). White women benefit most from affirmative action—And are among its fiercest opponents. Retrieved July 20, 2017, from https://www.vox.com/2016/5/25/11682950/fisher-supreme-court-white-women-affirmative-action

McKie, R. (2015a, June 13). Tim Hunt: 'I've been hung out to dry. They haven't even bothered to ask for my side of affairs'. The Observer. Retrieved from https://www.theguardian.com/science/2015/jun/13/tim-hunt-hung-out-to-dry-interview-mary-collins

McKie, R. (2015b, June 20). Sir Tim Hunt: My gratitude to female scientists for their support. *The Observer*. Retrieved from https://www.theguardian.com/world/2015/jun/20/sir-tim-hunt-gratitude-female-scientists-support-joke

McLelland, E. (2015, June 20). Nobel prize winners defend sexism-row scientist Sir Tim Hunt. Retrieved July 21, 2017, from http://www.dailymail.co.uk/news/article-3132413/Eight-Nobel-prize-winners-attack-lynch-mob-forced-sexism-row-professor-Sir-Tim-Hunt-job.html

Mencimer, S. (2015, December 9). Justice Scalia suggests blacks belong at "slower" colleges. Retrieved August 9, 2016, from http://www.motherjones.com/politics/2015/12/justice-scalia-suggests-blacks-belong-slower-colleges-fisher-university-texas

Monk-Payton, B. (2017). #LaughingWhileBlack: Gender and the comedy of social media blackness. Feminist Media Histories, 3(2), 15–35. https://doi.org/10.1525/fmh.2017.3.2.15

Naasel, K. R. (2015, December 11). #StayMadAbby in 9 Amazing Tweets [Text]. Retrieved August 9, 2016, from http://www.colorlines.com/articles/staymadabby-9-amazing-tweets

National Science Foundation. (2017). Women, minorities, and persons with disabilities in science and engineering (No. NSF 17–310). Arlington, VA: National Center for Science and Engineering Statistics. Retrieved from https://www.nsf.gov/statistics/2017/nsf17310/digest/about-this-report/

Ng, A. (2016, June 23). Abigail Fisher is now Becky with the bad grades. Retrieved August 8, 2017, from http://www.nydailynews.com/news/national/abigail-fisher-becky-bad-grades-article-1.2685865

Noble, S. U., & Tynes, B. M. (Eds.). (2015). *The intersectional Internet: Race, sex, class and culture online*. New York: Peter Lang Publishing, Inc.

Ocen, P., & Beydoun, K. A. (2015, March 30). Taking affirmative action off the table. Retrieved August 1, 2017, from http://www.aljazeera.com/indepth/opinion/2013/03/201332919345912 8484.html

Press Association. (2015, June 16). Brian Cox criticises "disproportionate" reaction to Tim Hunt's comments. *The Guardian*. Retrieved from http://www.theguardian.com/uk-news/2015/jun/16/brian-cox-criticises-disproportionate-reaction-to-tim-hunts-comments

Quinn, B. (2015, June 11). Nobel laureate Tim Hunt resigns after "trouble with girls" comments. *The Guardian*. Retrieved from https://www.theguardian.com/education/2015/jun/11/nobel-laureate-sir-tim-hunt-resigns-trouble-with-girls-comments

Ratcliffe, R. (2015, June 10). Nobel scientist Tim Hunt: Female scientists cause trouble for men in labs. *The Guardian*. Retrieved from https://www.theguardian.com/uk-news/2015/jun/10/nobel-scientist-tim-hunt-female-scientists-cause-trouble-for-men-in-labs

Royal Society. (2015, June 9). Science needs women. Retrieved July 20, 2017, from https://royalsociety.org/news/2015/06/tim-hunt-comments/

Royal Society. (2017). Diversity in science. Retrieved July 20, 2017, from https://royalsociety.org/topics-policy/diversity-in-science/

Sidhu, D. S. (2013, February 18). A critical look at the "critical mass" argument. The Chronicle of Higher Education. Retrieved from http://www.chronicle.com/article/A-Critical-Look-at-the/137369

Sir Tim Hunt FRS and UCL. (2015, June 10). Retrieved July 17, 2017, from http://www.ucl.ac.uk/news/news-articles/0615/100615-tim-hunt

St. Louis, C. (2015a, June 12). Nobel scientist Tim Hunt FRS @royalsociety says at Korean women lunch "I'm a chauvinist and keep 'girls' single labpic.twitter.com/Z9NhykaTPv [Tweet].

St. Louis, C. (2015b, June 23). Stop defending Tim Hunt. *The Guardian*. Retrieved from http://www.theguardian.com/uk-news/2015/jun/23/stop-defending-tim-hunt-brian-cox-richard-dawkins stevekindof. (2016, June 23). #BeckyWithTheBadGrades: The Tweets you need to see. Retrieved August 8, 2017, from http://heavy.com/news/2016/06/beckywiththebadgrades-becky-with-the-bad-grades-abigail-fisher-supreme-court-affirmative-action-decision-pictures-gifs-memes/

Stokes, J. (2015, December 10). The #StayMadAbby hashtag was the best thing on the Internet this week. Retrieved August 9, 2016, from http://xonecole.com/the-staymadabby-twitter-hashtag-is-the-best-thing-on-the-internet-this-week/

Team, T. V. (2015, June 10). Call for all female scientists to upload pictures of themselves at work with the hashtag #distractinglysexy [microblog]. Retrieved August 4, 2016, from https://twitter.com/VagendaMagazine/status/608584030032945152

Tibbetts, S., & deertysanchez. (2017). Draw me like one of your french girls. Retrieved August 9, 2017, from http://knowyourmeme.com/memes/draw-me-like-one-of-your-french-girls

Tonkin, S. (2015, December 19). Scientist back working for Royal Society six months after sexism row. Retrieved August 8, 2017, from http://www.dailymail.co.uk/news/article-3366843/Sexism-row-scientist-working-Royal-Society-just-six-months-forced-complaining-problem-women-labs-fall-love-you.html

Wald, E. (2014). Talking 'bout your mama: The dozens, snaps, and the deep roots of rap (First issued as an Oxford University Press paperback, 2014). Oxford, NY: Oxford University Press.

Wendling, M. (2015, June 11). Female scientists post "distractingly sexy" photos. BBC News. Retrieved from http://www.bbc.com/news/blogs-trending-33099289

Whaley, N. (2015, December 10). #StayMadAbby goes off on white woman who sued against affirmative action policy. Retrieved August 3, 2017, from http://www.bet.com/news/national/2015/12/10/staymadabby-calls-out-white-woman-who-wants-to-bring-down-affirmative-action.html?cid=facebook

White, E. F. (1990). Africa on my mind: Gender, counter discourse and African-American nationalism. Journal of Women's History, 2(1), 73–97. https://doi.org/10.1353/jowh.2010.0246

White, E. F. (2001). *Dark continent of our bodies: Black feminism and the politics of respectability*. Philadelphia, PA: Temple University Press.

Whitnall, A. (2015, June 11). Sir Tim Hunt loses university job after comments on "trouble with girls" in laboratories | The Independent. Independent. Retrieved from http://www.independent.co.uk/news/uk/home-news/sir-tim-hunt-loses-university-job-after-comments-on-trouble-with-girls-in-laboratories-10312086.html

Wilfried Laurier University. (2015, September 10). #DistractinglySexist exhibit challenges gender discrimination in Canada's tech triangle. Retrieved September 19, 2017, from https://www.wlu.ca/news/news-releases/2015/sept/distractinglysexist-exhibit-challenges-gender-discrimination-in-canadas-tech-triangle.html

Yiannopolous, M. (2016, January 17). Lying Liar Connie St. Louis Just Accused Me Of Calling For An Assassination! Retrieved August 8, 2017, from http://www.breitbart.com/tech/2016/01/17/someone-just-accused-me-of-plotting-an-assassination-attempt/

Digital Black Feminism

Ashley Love

What has Black Feminism done for Black women and girls? Black Feminisms have existed even when the official historical record assigned the birth of feminist ideologies to white women and Black women felt it strategic or reasonable to align their interests with their white counterparts. From the moment pioneering Black Feminists Maria W. Stewart became one of the first Black women to publicly speak on women's rights and the abolition of slavery, Frances Harper addressed the Brooklyn Literary Union, or Sojourner Truth took center stage at the Women's Rights Convention in Akron, Ohio in 1852, and even before then, Black Feminism has been the platform on which Black women (activists) have stood to call attention to the injustices endured by Black women, girls, and oppressed people everywhere. These women are a few members of the inaugural group of Black women talking back to white supremacist patriarchy. They made use of the technologies of their time; writing books, periodicals, and speaking at public gatherings. Their use of public

A. Love (✉)
University of Georgia, Athens, GA, USA
e-mail: allove@uga.edu

D. C. Parry et al. (eds.), *Digital Dilemmas*,
https://doi.org/10.1007/978-3-319-95300-7_3

pedagogy when school was prohibited for Black people created Black Feminist intellectual traditions before Collins (1990) eloquently articulated it as such in her book. Black Feminism is a means by which Black women are able to create and define their own agency while educating others and fighting for acknowledgement of their humanity. The connections between the work of Maria Stewart, Frances Harper, Sojourner Truth, Ida B. Wells, Harriet Tubman, to the more contemporary work of Audre Lorde, bell hooks, Patricia Hill Collins, Angela Davis, Barbara Hill, Alice Walker, and many others is not disparate; it is connected through the articulation of related experiences Black women share. Digital Black Feminism (DBF) rests on the foremothers who embodied activism, community building, public pedagogy, and spiritual fortitude. This chapter calls attention to hallmarks of the concept of more contemporary manifestations of Black Feminism using digital means, thus the name Digital Black Feminism.

DBF, predicated on Black Feminisms and Womanisms, is taken up by Black women and girls who seek to collaborate, mobilize, and nullify misrepresentations of Black women and people using digital and social means. Thus, in order to better understand the foundations of DBF, it is important to posture conversations of history, place, and power in relationship to social justice and change. The idea of Black Feminism being digital challenges popular culture, current events, and politics to address critical issues in the Black community at local and global levels. Furthermore, the ideas of organization and mobilization are central to understanding the breadth and depth of DBF, its audiences, and its facilitators and leaders. DBF enables educators, politicians, social figures, and everyday people to bring critical conversation into the classroom and everyday life in order to highlight the counternarratives and excellence of Black women and girls. By calling attention to individual and collective truths via digital/online forums, DBF offers real-time critique of overarching institutions that seek to perpetuate oppression and inequality. Additionally DBF provides opportunities for Black women, girls, and their allies to engage in narrative-shifting and truth-telling conversations that place Black girlhood and womanhood at the center of said conversations.

This chapter will open with a definition for DBF that situates it within the historical and political contexts of Black Feminism and intellectual and social activism. This chapter will also delve into the historical figures and their contributions to Black Feminist activism while highlighting common threads and causes with their contemporary descendants. The third topic this chapter presents is the Black Feminist voices of the diaspora and the ways in which DBF has engaged global communities. The final and most important section of this chapter addresses the advantages and allowances digital spaces afford Black Feminism in conversation with potential (digital) dilemmas Black Feminism has faced with sustainability, organization, and mobilization and how Black Feminism in the digital realm may offer viable solutions or present new challenges. In closing, the chapter will elaborate on the current scholarship and critique surrounding digital activism, media, and ways Black Feminism is a form of public pedagogy and praxis for communities of Black women and girls to create, consume, and recreate globally.

What's in *This* Name? On Defining Digital Black Feminism

What does it mean to be Black and feminist? Shirts with the word "Feminist" are available for purchase at Macy's, but does anyone really know what it means *in real life*? Black Feminism is a term that describes the particular vantage points of Black women. This section's title pays tribute to activist-scholar Patricia Hill Collins' (1996) *What's in a Name? Womanism, Black Feminism and Beyond.* In her work Collins acknowledges the merit in the work of Black Feminists, intellectuals, and scholars who tirelessly seek to maintain visibility and space for Black women and girls to educate, organize, and sustain themselves and their communities. Like other Black Feminists foremothers this task of defining DBF reiterates the importance of narrative telling and truth telling to establish the Black Feminist voice and the ongoing intellectual and pedagogical investments required to sustain Black Feminism in digital environments. One of the most notable Black Feminist manifestos was that of the Combahee River Collective (CRC). The Combahee River was an actual body of water in South Carolina that Harriet Tubman traversed in order to lead Black people to freedom.

The CRC is a proclamation that seeks to center Black Feminism as a viable political movement to empower women of color and combat oppression. The CRC was a group of feminist and womanist activist-scholars who collectively established the genesis of Black Feminism by organizing their politics and objectives in order to establish a clear direction for the future of Black Feminism. Black Feminism as articulated in the CRC resides at the intersection of theory and practice and foregrounds the articulation of Black Feminism as a sociopolitical movement.

The CRC also identifies the arduous task of taking on a range of oppressions as one issue in the CRC Statement. Additionally, much like Hill Collins will mention later, Black women do not have the racial, sexual, heterosexual, class privileges, or resources to rely on in the same way as white feminists (p. 54). Thus, per the CRC "the material positions of the Black woman would hardly lead them to upset both economic and sexual arrangements that seem to represent some stability in their lives, thus Black women cannot risk struggling against the broader range of oppressions all at once (p. 55). This statement is powerful because it establishes expectations on behalf of the CRC and is clear about the power Black women hold when left to their own devices. Another concurrent theme with Hill Collins is the open confrontation of racism in mainstream (white) feminism. These confrontations take place in academic, political, and social spaces that enable Black Feminists to "name" the oppression they experience in the name of feminism and denounce them as aspects of true feminist praxis. The ability for Black women to pinpoint contradictions and shortcomings on the axes of white feminism based on their own experiences is the most crucial differentiation between white feminism and Black Feminism.

The CRC also provides insight as to what happens when groups take up revolutionary tasks such as assuming responsibility for the safeguarding of the cultural, economic, political welfare of Black people while displaying the reality of their politics through the writing and distribution of their work. The CRC was not just a group of women who met to discuss things. It was a group of Black women from various walks of life, varying levels of education and lived experiences providing a benediction for future Black Feminists as they embrace the real work of activism deeply tethered to Black Feminist intellectual traditions. So why are the guiding principles and foundational tenants of Black Feminism so important to understand prior to examining longevity and sustainability for Black Feminism in digital spaces?

Let's be clear. Black Feminism is first and foremost the understanding that Black women and girls are inherently invaluable and their contributions are enumerable. Black Feminism is anti-racist, anti-sexist, and anti-oppression in general. Rather than placing Black women and people in opposition to white people and white standards of living, Black Feminism seeks to uplift and affirm Black women for the sake of their ability to uplift humanity. Naming can be associated with narrative telling and truth telling, which are both common threads in Black Feminism. *When and Where I Enter* is Giddings thoughtful and thorough attempt to "strike balance between the subjective and the objective" in the meaning making process of writing about Black women and being a Black woman (p. 5).

The major objective of this text was to establish a historical timeline of Black Feminist activist and intellectual traditions and hallmark the contributions Black women have made to every cultural, economic, educational, political, and social movement that has taken place for the advancement of all people but largely those that impact Black people since Reconstruction. This is not dissimilar from this current chapter in its attempt to expound on Black Feminism and broaden/extend Black Feminism into digital communities. Like the work of other Black Feminists such as Davis (1981a, 1981b, 1989), Hill Collins (1990), Giddings grounds the early formation of Black Feminist organizing in the discontent of Black women during and immediately following slavery with the conditions under which they lived and work being the springboard into action. In these chronicles about early Black Feminist organizing, Giddings credits (Shadd) Cary's efforts in 1880 to assert equal rights of women, including suffrage in her creation of the Colored Women's Progressive Association. Giddings notes that, given the cultural, educational, political, and social climate of the 1880s, Black women found themselves in a pivotal moment, making substantial gains in education and the professions and wanted to make institutional claims to economic, social, and political rights (p. 75).

Giddings (1984) provides depth and clarity on some of the most famous Black social justice campaigns and organizations formed to attend to, in some cases, the specific needs of Black people at key periods in time. Traditionally, Black Feminist intellectuals lead movements by establishing the objectives of Black Feminist-activists and intellectuals who sustain each organization and endeavor. This is an important task for two reasons: first, it foregrounds my understanding of the ongoing, unrelenting efforts of Black women in *every* struggle for Black liberation and people. Second, it sheds light on a large-scale social movement in the history of the United States that has been cultivated and maintained by Black women (irrespective of whether or not they are acknowledged to mainstream audiences) and allows me to examine the long-standing predicament of Black women in the United States and the perpetual contentions we have with being exploited as it relates to our labor and production of any and everything.

The idea that Black women are the captains of their own ships and able to tell their own stories from their vantage point(s) is a powerful counternarrative to the white, male dominant ways established and maintained here in the United States. DBF also requires a critical lens. Critical media literacy is one way for individuals to filter and consume information (MacArthur 2016). Using digital mediums, Black women and girls can create content and stories in order to express themselves across platforms, quickly organize for a cause, and cultivate communities online. #BlackLivesMatter #Blackgirlmagic, and #Sayhername are some of the most visible manifestations of DBF.

Black Lives Matter (BLM), Black Girl Magic (BGM), and Say Her Name were founded by Black women who used digital environments to define and determine issues plaguing Black communities such as police brutality (BLM), and erasure of positive images (BGM) and raise awareness in spaces curated by Black people. BLM, which was founded by Alicia Garza, Patrise Cullors, and Opal Tometi, is a call for action in response to the death of Trayvon Martin and other innocent Black youth who have been killed. BLM aims to call attention to the value of Black life and seek justice for Black people who are victims of anti-blackness related violence. BGM is an online campaign that also began as a hashtag on social media. Initiated by CaShawn Thompson in response to Black

Entertainment Televisions's Black Girls Rock campaign, Thompson was showing appreciation for the Black women honored at this annual event and television special and highlight the accomplishment of Black women and girls for everyone to see. Both digital campaigns gained momentum and influenced online and offline events. Say Her Name was triggered by ongoing violence against Black women advocating for justice and visibility of issues of abuse, brutalization, and sexual violence. Say Her Name is a digital manifestation of Crewnshaw's (1991) previous work in intersectionality, identifying the multiple intersections of oppression faced by black women: class, gender, and race.

By applying either hashtag to a person, place, or event, followers were able to "name" and place tags (geographical and chronological), which influence activism and participation at local and global levels. By acknowledging the power of digital Black communities online, Black people are provided with opportunities for Black women and girls to (re) generate their ideas of intellectual and community work of Black women and girls, and also define what activism, education, and excellence mean for Black communities. Collins (1990) asserts that Black Feminism was established to afford Black women the opportunity to self-define, self-determine, and self-regulate when and where they choose to invest and divest their efforts to uplift their communities, humanities, and themselves.

#BlackLivesMatter, #BlackGirlMagic, #BlackWomenLead, #CurlyGirlCollective are ways in which Black women and girls both define and make themselves accessible to others. But the Black (Feminist) Internet is not for the faint of heart. This is true of what Cooper deems percussive feminism where power is regulatory and resistant and the collective ideas of Black women are privileged over hegemonic ways of thinking. The Internet, as previously mentioned, is this free-range space for creativity and cultivating community; another powerful use of digital spaces is for contestation and talking back. This is where #hashtags prove themselves as useful tools for communication, organization, and mobilization among Black Feminists and other activists. #BlackLivesMatter #SayHerName, #Staymad, and other personalized hashtags have been used to articulate and push back against intersecting issues plaguing Black women such as classism, racism, or sexism. #SayHerName was a result of the intersectional work of Kimberlé Crenshaw to heighten the world's awareness of the brutalization and sexual violence endured by Black women and girls. #SayHerName has even provided enough rich data for research such as that of Brown, Ray, Summers, & Fraistat (2017). This empirical study makes viable connections between digital technologies and how it engages political protest and real world action (p. 1831). By highlighting micromobilization, that is, linking individual and sociocultural issues and motives, this study highlights intersectionality and collective identity for sociopolitical progress. One major finding of this particular study is the notion of solidarity among participants using the hashtag. Additionally, the findings reveal that community activists and individuals who were neither celebrities nor academic employed the hashtag more than any other group. This is important to note when reflecting on the original premise of Black Feminism which privileges lived experiences over high culture academic elitism. Black Feminism and this study of #SayHerName both demonstrate the importance of narratives and the power that collective narratives have in influencing true change.

Furthermore, any hashtag affiliated with the advancement and uplift of Black women and girls further prove that Black women and their body of knowledge are diverse and immovable and unreplicable. Black women and their experiences cannot be painted with a broad brushstroke. People, places, and things are always put in conversation with one another, which fortifies coalitions and relationships. Hill Collins' work seeks to place Black Feminism on a nonlinear continuum that provides space, time, and power for Black women to engage and reconceptualize Black womanhood and girlhood and the activism that springs forth as a result of DBF.

Sites of Digital Black Feminist Activism and Knowledge

One major contribution DBF offers social justice efforts is its ability to unite women of the Diaspora using digital communities and technologies. From the inception of the Black press to Black digital spaces, public intellectuals have significantly held and do hold power as sites of rhetorical education in the twenty-first century. Black women are literally the "sites" of knowledge as it originates in them and allows them to hold space for other women. There is a geographic resonance to their intellectual work but the inability to quickly unite causes and mobilize for action and change. DBF changes the digital, pedagogical, and political landscapes, as information is readily available for people using technology and means they already possess. DBF also expounds the idea that public pedagogy and public intellectualism are not unique or exclusive to the academy but all are very important in sustaining the field of knowledge (re) production and research for Black women (Collins 1990). This chapter provides historical and contemporary examples of Black Feminist organizing using technological advancements and what said advancements mean in terms of public pedagogy and education, politics, social justice, and social entrepreneurship.

So why not just call DBF, Black Feminism that takes place on the Internet? This question is central to understanding the roots of Black Feminism and the future of DBF. The former is a tradition of scholarly, community, and activist work (often all three) that has addressed the marginalization of Black women under white supremacy, anti-blackness, and patriarchy (also known as *misogynoir*). The latter is a manifestation of Black Feminism that resides at the intersections of Black culture, gender, geography, history, race, and technology. In order to understand DBF, it is important to note that Black Feminism has always been an adaptive, ever-evolving movement that advocates for Black women and girls while creating spaces for imagination and possibility. Black Feminism provides this space irrespective of the negative portrayals and treatment of Black women and girls. It has also taken advantage of the technologies readily available to its subscribers as a means to disseminate information, educate communities, or influence change. DBF offers opportunities for contestation of the aforementioned negative portrayals of Black women and girls while simultaneously providing space for intergenerational and intercultural dialogue. It expounds on the breadth and depth of Black Feminism by its inclusive nature.

DBF holds philosophical and rhetorical power irrespective of where, when, and how it is being deployed. DBF also has linguistic and analytical strengths and connects Black women and girls from all over the world. It makes local struggles and movements globally visible in real time and enables coalition building and community organizing readily available. That being said, DBF can be as liminal, intangible, and ever changing as it is powerful and concrete. None of this aims to discount what Black Feminism has done in order to arrive at its digitized offspring but rather to explain that Black Feminism gave way to DBF so there is no need to make a departure from its origins. The relationship can be equated to that of a very well-educated mother or grandmother and the "woke" innovative daughter/granddaughter. The mother and grandmother know times are changing and they've taught the granddaughter everything they know so the granddaughter has the cultural and technological aptitude to carry the torch. The granddaughter has one task and one task alone: do it for the culture.

Do It for the Culture: Digital Black Feminism and Digital Dilemmas

Digital Black Feminist Jessica Byrd has been utilizing social media and digital communities to empower Black women and girls, increase the Black vote, and train a new generation of Black women to lead in politics and policy:

> *If our jobs are always convincing people of our humanity, we'll never get to do our work. I want to do my work. People with "identities" deserve for us to do our work.*—Jessica Byrd (personal communication, July 7, 2017)

Alongside her pioneering digital, Black, activist-peers Garza, Thompson, and Cooper, Byrd's relentless efforts to express both passion and urgency about Black education, policy, and social justice can be documented on social media. Because these conversations do not take place in a closed boardroom, DBF faces its fair share of opposition. Opposition is necessary in order to have multiple perspectives. One major dilemma DBF faces are Internet trolls who seek to negate anything being said on the topics of race, class, gender, economics, politics, and sexuality. The Internet can be a space where everyone knows everything, something, or nothing at all. Black women have always been silenced and challenged by anti-blackness and sexism. The limitlessness of the Internet can pose as a problem for causes of social justice because of the pervasiveness of anti-blackness and anti-intellectualism. Coupled with class and gender struggles it can be a complicated and frustrating experience. One prevalent example is #AllLivesMatter used by white supremacists to mock and silence the #BlackLivesMatter movement.

All Lives Matter decenters blackness and the Black experience. This retaliatory response undermines the attention Blacks are trying to call to state-sanctioned violence and presents Black contestation of said violence as extremist and un-American.

The cultural specificity of DBF is necessary, as it is known of Black women to fight for the humanity of Black people and other oppressed communities. However, it is important to note that the work of Black women is accessed through their intersecting oppressions and experiences as individuals who identify as both Black and female. Black women fight anti-racism in real and meaningful ways, irrespective of the level of education they have obtained or their socioeconomic status. Anti-racism is not specific to Black academics or intellectuals and social media demonstrates how much more readily accessible announcements and manifestos can be in digital spaces and, to some extent, how much more consumable the information is for people who do not engage in Black Feminism at the academic or political levels but subscribe to its beliefs.

Other dilemmas pertaining to feminisms, mainly Black Feminism, in digital and non-digital spaces are the issues of organization and mobilization, invisibilization (oppression), and sustainability. The past has proven that feminism strikes a chord with many, energizing them and calling them to action. The dilemma is simple; action typically takes place immediately, and longevity is often left out of the discussion. Thus, there is a stark difference between using digital and non-digital means to organize groups and call them to action versus maintaining energy within groups to continuously organize and mobilize. Additionally, digital media allows for users and viewers to call and be called to action, but it is not necessarily the most effective way to maintain relationships with followings for the sake of sustainability.

Similarly, Wallace & Dent (1992) in *Black Popular Culture* state the following dilemma as it pertains to Black popular culture; "Tragically, even though black folks have historically unprecedented access to the realm of material acquisition (by fair means or foul), we have been systematically losing ground when it comes to making political interventions that would fundamentally transform the lives of African American and the society as a whole" (p. 49). Wallace & Dent (1992) then suggest that only by systemic resistance to the existing social order, which denies our worth, can we, as African Americans, fully affirm ourselves as a people or as individuals. Thus, DBF, then, is a viable solution for making Black Feminism central in digital interactions and engaging academic and communal audiences in order to systemically counter oppression and fully affirm families, communities, and us.

Per Jewel Amoah, Black Feminist Thought cannot challenge hegemony and oppression without empowering Black women (1997, p. 4). Empowerment, then, is a necessary constant (theme) in DBF. Thus, #BlackGirlMagic, #BlackWomenLead, and #BlackExcellence are necessary in order to cultivate #BlackJoy.

The more lighthearted side of Black digital spaces have allowed for Black people to send (and revoke) invites to the proverbial cookout, broadcast real-time updates to award ceremonies and popular television shows, partake in the memification that canonizes relatable blackness by way of memes, or clapback on (Black) Twitter. Lightheartedness in critical spaces is necessary to maintain balance and reinforce Black comedy and joy as important aspects of Black survival.

Oppression can happen within the confines of Black digital popular culture and DBF calls for Black men to do better and aide in the process of dismantling systems of oppression alongside Black women. *Misogynoir,* which was named by Moya Black, speaks to the perpetuation of negative images of Black women in popular and visual cultures. Black's use of misogynoir relates back to Hill Collins' (1990) four controlling images, in that it talks back to anti-Black sexism directed towards Black women. Taking down the master's house cannot be done by using his tools, thus DBF, in order to be sustainable and successful, must reject false claims that digital connections are superficial and per Kalonji Nzinga, a digital scholar-activist, "we must never let them convince us that our bonds are shallow. Never let them slander our kinship" (2017). Nzinga (2017) also noted that "Black people [in digital communities] are building a movement; a network of hope". This is of the utmost important when we as Black people think about how we engage in digital communications and communities online and what they mean specifically for promoting Black enjoyment, expression, and empowerment. The work of DBF is centered on the idea that social media can be a site of teaching and learning. Said teaching and learning is vital to the survival and livelihood of Black people. Education has been a contentious topic since the earliest Africans were brought to the United States as slaves. Education has its place and value in all societies and because of fervent efforts to deny Black people have access to education, oral histories and public pedagogies have been very consistent way in which Black people can educate and learn about their communities, conditions, and potential. Public pedagogy as a general concept is the belief that education should be free and accessible to anyone willing to listen and learn in public and open spaces. By using social media as a site for education, information, and idea sharing, Black women are engaging in what King and Ferguson (2011) refer to as tracing the mother line and remaining cognizant of the ways in which the past informs the present and future. Digital forms of public pedagogy that are displayed by Digital Black Feminists such as Drs. Gloria Ladson-Billings, Ruth N. Brown, Brittany Cooper, Cynthia B. Dillard, Venus Evans-Winters, Treva Lindsey, Bettina L. Love, Sherrell MacArthur, and Elaine Richardson are not dissimilar to that of Maria W. Stewart and Sojourner Truth, who spoke to their communities and sought to educate Black women and girls by use of narrative and truth telling. This mother line has historical roots but also engages multiple generations of Black women and girls. The work of the aforementioned scholars provides tangible and relatable contexts for Black women and girls outside of the academy to contribute to the ongoing conversation about Black womanhood and girlhood using digital communities. Notable examples include critical and social commentary pieces by Digital Black Feminists Brittany Cooper and Treva Lindsey who both contribute to digital editions of Complex and Cosmopolitan Magazines, Huff Post Live, in addition to their own digital sites. By publishing work in multiple, far-reaching outlets, Cooper and Lindsey empower other Black women activists and scholars to write think pieces in traditionally white-dominant digital spaces, making issues facing Black women and communities central.

Another very recent example of DBF was Candice Benbow's (2017) response to Jay-Z's newest album *4:44* with her widely received blog entry entitled *4:43*. The popularity of Candice Benbow's (2017) *4:43* shows how quickly information can be disseminated and the voices of Black women can be heard. Benbow's work is in response to a rap album by Jay-Z also known as Shawn Carter, who is married to self-proclaimed feminist and superstar Beyoncé, where he admits his past shortcomings and wrongdoings and encourages other (Black) men to heighten their level of economic, emotional, spiritual, and romantic growth and openness. The album was released and the digital (Black) spaces erupted in response; those who liked it said it was a strong addition to an already revered body of work from Carter. Benbow's (2017) response, however, was not all praise but rather a provocative example of DBF and how inclusive conversations about relationships, health and well-being, and popular culture in Black communities:

> I wonder if you realize the cost we pay for loving men like you. My anxiety. Bey's miscarriages. My cousin's hair loss. Your homegirl's weight gain. Depression. Suicidal ideation. Substance abuse. Retail therapy and maxed credit cards. Entertaining n----s we don't even like just to feel wanted. So many forms of self-harm. We pay with our bodies. Sometimes our lives. And even in that trauma, we still find ways to sow deeper into the love we have for you, hoping it will get better.

This unabridged emotion called for Black women and men to quickly reconsider their reasons for accepting Carter's work from his vantage point (which is arguably still valid) rather than from the perspective of the women who were on the receiving end of his shortcomings and wrongdoings. Benbow's work confronted the real complexities of Black love and relationships and initiated a conversation about love, respect, and reciprocity between Black men and women about often-overlooked forms of abusive relationships. Additionally, members of the LGBTQ community were able to name their experiences and identify with both Carter and Benbow, which invited other members of the Black community to this ongoing discussion about Black love. DBF is the tool Benbow used to captivate, educate, and disseminate information about her lived experience(s) while evoking a more inclusive conversation about Black relationships and popular culture. But Benbow is not alone. There are activist-scholars like Brittney Cooper who also use digital communities as a platform to educate Black women, girls, and all who follow digitized magazines such as *Cosmopolitan* on Black popular culture, policy, and social justice.

In Cooper's (2017) most recent post for *Cosmopolitan,* she also discusses Jay-Z's *4:44* while elucidating the ways Jay-Z's latest album is as much an economic and political act as it is a romantic plea to his wife and life partner, Beyoncé, to make amends for his wrongdoings. Cooper (2017) discusses the long-standing trauma of being Black and dispelling assumptions about the impossibility of Black love, marriage, and success.

> Relationships are hard. Black relationships are harder. This is not because black people are more broken or pathological than any other group. We are not. But we grow up in a world that says we are. Shaped by racism and its multigenerational assault on black families, black people often have had steep mountains to climb to find our way to each other.

Cooper's work then draws a vivid picture for readers, outlining the turmoil performed in Beyoncé's *Lemonade* album coupled with stories projected by gossip columns and speculative reporting to demonstrate the vulnerability present in interactions between Black men and women. This is necessary in order to address a tenant of Black Feminism which is to combat racism and sexism inflicted upon Black women and people form the outside world but also to address its internal struggles with gender inequality and relationships. Cooper (2017) said it best when she said that Black women "do what we need to do in order to survive and sometimes that looks like being respectable, but we should never buy into the idea that we are at fault for the violence we are experiencing".

But Cooper's work is not limited to her provocative pieces with *Cosmopolitan.* Cooper is also one of the founders of the *Crunk Feminist Collective* (CFC), which is one of the pioneering online communities for

Black Feminists and people to follow, receive, share, and revisit (if/when necessary). In a post from January 23, 2017, the topic of vaginas and the Women's March on Washington created space for a new way of thinking about how pussy hats and vagina monologues marginalize "womenfolk who don't have those parts".

The accessibility and consumability of CFC make it unique and special as Black women are able to express themselves freely, disseminate information in ways that do not exclude Black women who do not run in academic or political circles but who are impacted by the goings-on of the world. All of the examples provided are a few examples of Digital Black Feminist spaces where Black women and girls can affirm one another, promote Black joy and possibility, organize, and mobilize for social justice. Combahee paved a way for Black women to think critically about the importance of their role in Black liberation, namely how to act on political realizations based on the lived experiences of Black women and people and maintaining political consciousness without the fatigue associated with being in a constant state of oppression.

Back to the Future: Why Do Black People Need Digital Black Feminism?

Previous sections of this chapter speak to the long-standing traditions of Black Feminism and how activism and critical community dialogues can be shared across digital mediums in real time. Digital interactions can be curated but largely enable people of varying backgrounds and interests to express themselves freely and discuss economic, political, and social topics in open forum. Shirley Wilson Logan outlines sites of rhetorical education in African American communities in the United States during the nineteenth century and mentions self-education as an intentional act to equip oneself with oratory and written skills to engage in civic activism (p. 29). This is an example of public pedagogical practices that Black communities adopt in order to disseminate information and organize themselves for social and political movements, run churches, and overall community education. DBF gives way to a new way to similarly organize and educate oneself and others using digital resources and connecting from one digital community to another digital community.

One thoughtful observation that should be made from this chapter is cultivating an understanding that Black women and girls have paid and continue to pay the ultimate price in order to uplift themselves, their families, their communities, and humanity, and their role in society is invaluable even when the masses refuse to acknowledge said contributions. Sealey-Ruiz makes this assertion when retracing the lineage of anti-Blackness and anti-Black womanhood throughout the duration of chattel slavery.

The overall goals of Black Feminism and thus DBF are to dispel assumptions that Black women are monolithic or generalizable. In order for Black women to discredit the prevailing images of Black womanhood such as the mammy, the matriarch, the jezebel, and the Janus-faced welfare queen, Black women must first become aware of their own ability to find themselves inside and outside of larger communal and societal terms (Collins 1990). This is an arduous but not impossible task. DBF employs the tenets of Black Feminism while engaging a generation of Black women and girls that have more access to technology than ever before. DBF is an inclusive community resisting colonization and homogeneity and should not be taken for granted (hence the need to constantly (re) member and (re) visit our definitions of BF and (re) assess our goals and objectives). DBF makes space for new voices that may be marginalized by or within the academy, voices that are often silenced in academic spaces due to lack of tenure, exposure, or mentorship. DBF is a (re)cognizing of early Black Feminisms that enable every participant to speak from her own perspective and with their own (personal) authority. That is, through blogging, social media posts, the comment sections on articles and in other digital communities Black women and girls are able to be their own sources of experience, information, and expertise. This is not to be mistaken for anti-intellectual; Black Feminist voices from the academy are necessary in the ongoing fight within the academy to acknowledge Black Feminist intellectual traditions as funds of knowledge and sources worth citing and for making reference. Most important, Black women coupled with digital mediums can serve as a powerful tool to self-determine and self-define narratives and truths for themselves and people of the African Diaspora. If you read this chapter and thought about the ways in which you have witnessed, participated in, and advocated for DBF, then the future is already brighter and you now possess the power to define your own unique experiences within DBF and in real life.

Such power should not be taken for granted but rather carefully observed and mastered in order to strategically organize and mobilize Black communities in ways that educate, empower, and uplift all Black people. In Ziyad's (2017) work *My Gender Is Black,* the author understands that at the basis of all activism is for Black people to be acknowledged and revered as human. The longstanding dehumanization of blackness and black people maintained through exclusion subsumes all nonconforming identities. DBF provides space and opportunities for Black women and girls to define their own humanity and affirm it in one another. In pedagogical terms, DBF is a manifestation of a communal learning space that cultivates knowledge and understanding. DBF allows for Black women to spearhead conversations about beauty (double) standards, class, gender, politics, and race while providing a counterspace to combat issues such as police brutality, misogynoir, anti-blackness, and social injustices. This pedagogical method did not originate in digital spaces but was digitized through the advancement of communication and technology. In summary, digitized stresses the fact that a particular phenomenon wasn't born in the digital environment; it was born in real life and reimagined in the digital environment. Thus, Black communal learning uses elements of storytelling, soul searching, truth-seeking, and fact-finding that make it unique to the experiences and lives of Black people globally. By way of digitization, Black Feminist intellectual traditions have been able to continue to flourish, furthering the mission of Black Feminism as advancing and improving Black women, girls, and communities everywhere.

References

Amoah, J. A. (1997). Narrative: The road to *black* feminist theory. *Berkeley Women's Law Journal, 12*, 84–102.

Benbow, C. (2017, July 4). 4:43. Retrieved from http://www.candicebenbow.com/blog/443

Brown, M., Ray, R., Summers, E., & Fraistat, N. (2017). #SayHerName: A case study of intersectional social media activism. *Ethnic and Racial Studies, 40*(11), 1831–1846. https://doi.org/10.1080/01419870.2017.1334934.

Byrd, J. [Jessica]. (ca. 2017). Timeline [Facebook page]. Retrieved July 7, 2017, from http://www.facebook.com

Collins, P. H. (1990). *Black feminist thought: Knowledge, consciousness, and the politics of empowerment*. New York: Routledge.

Collins, P. H. (1996). What's in a name? Womanism, black feminism, and beyond. *The Black Scholar, 26*(1), 9–17.

Cooper, B. (2017, July 14). *Jay-Z's apology to beyoncé isn't just celebrity gossip—It's a political act.* Retrieved from http://www.cosmopolitan.com/entertainment/music/a10307014/jay-z-444-review-beyonce-apology/

Crenshaw, K. (1991). Mapping the margins: Intersectionality, identity politics, and violence against women of color. *Stanford Law Review, 43*(6), 1241–1299.

Davis, A. (1981a). Reflections on the black woman's role in the community. *The Black Scholar, 6*(2), 2–15.

Davis, A. Y. (1981b). *Women, race, & class*. New York: Random House.

Davis, A. Y. (1989). *Women, culture & politics*. New York: Random House.

Ferguson, S. A., & King, T. C. (2011). *Black womanist leadership: Tracing the motherline*. Albany, NY: State University of New York Press.

Giddings, P. (1984). *When and where I enter: The impact of black women on race and sex in America*. New York: W. Morrow.

MacArthur, S. (2016). Black girls and critical media literacy for social activism. *English Education, 48*(4), 462–479.

Nzinga, K. [Kalonji]. [ca. 2017]. Timeline [Facebook page]. Retrieved July 23, 2017, from http://www.facebook.com

Wallace, M., & Dent, G. (1992). *Black popular culture: Discussions in contemporary culture*. Seattle, WA: Bay Press.

Ziyad, H. (2017, July 14). *My gender is Black*. Retrieved from http://afropunk.com/2017/07/my-gender-is-black/

Section II

Methodological Discussions and Guideposts

Online Qualitative Methods: Confronting New Possibilities and Challenges Within a Social Justice Perspective

Dawn E. Trussell, Jen Apgar, and Laura Kovac

In this chapter, we argue that online spaces should not only be investigated as an object to be studied, but as a context of conducting qualitative inquiry whereby researcher and participant can actively and intentionally co-construct knowledge (Dadas, 2016; de Jong, 2015). Although online spaces bring questions of injustice related to social identities (e.g. gender, sexual identity, race), we also believe that scholars can "reimagine the ways online spaces may be incorporated as sites for

This work was supported by the Social Sciences and Humanities Research Council of Canada, Insight Development Grant #430-2013-001081.

D. E. Trussell (✉)
Faculty of Applied Health Sciences, Brock University, St. Catharines, ON, Canada
e-mail: dtrussell@brocku.ca

J. Apgar
Community Researcher, Guelph, ON, Canada

L. Kovac
Brock University, St. Catharines, ON, Canada

D. C. Parry et al. (eds.), *Digital Dilemmas*,
https://doi.org/10.1007/978-3-319-95300-7_4

methodologies" (de Jong, 2015, p. 212) and as a mechanism for positive social change. In turn, developing online research methods opens up possibilities for challenging social injustices as well as transforming knowledge mobilization strategies into everyday life.

We position this argument through critical reflections of a research project on families of lesbian, gay, bisexual, transgender or queer (LGBTQ) parents and sport that shifted its original research design from in-person, semi-structured interviews to an online asynchronous forum through the use of social network platforms (i.e. Facebook, Twitter). Drawing on this experience, we aim to highlight the complexities of using social media as a data collection tool with qualitative methods traditionally used in offline research (i.e. focus groups). Like many feminist scholars, we align our work with a social justice perspective that goes beyond describing the oppression of different groups to focusing on advocacy and strategies to address power differences in society (Parry, Johnson, & Stewart, 2013). Online spaces and the intersection with feminist and social justice perspectives create new possibilities for innovative methods in qualitative inquiry. As Morrow, Hawkins, and Kern (2015) argued:

> Online spaces present rich and complicated environments for feminist research, as they blur the boundaries between public and private, have the potential to politicize everyday life in new ways, and involve a wide array of authors self-publishing their ideas and experiences. (p. 527)

It is through this lens that we situate our work. We begin the chapter by briefly describing the Team Family Pride Project, which was the context for the research profiled herein. We then examine three key areas where questions emerged for us as the project unfolded and embed our reflections within broader theoretical debates for online research methods. First, we examine traditional methods that are being (re)conceptualized through new digital platforms and the productive possibilities that exist with these new approaches. Second, we analyze the implications of online research methods and social media; in particular problematizing research ethics established through offline research traditions. Third, we examine the concept of citizen researchers and the potential for online research methods and social media to transform knowledge mobilization within the 'slow' academe. Embedded throughout these three key areas are shifts of power between participants and researchers, which underscores a new perspective of how we conceptualize this relationship. Throughout the chapter, we also provide guidance to researchers who would like to incorporate social media as a qualitative inquiry tool.

Project Background

This chapter is based on research reflections from a project that investigated the complexities of diverse family structures within community-based youth sport organizations, notably families of LGBTQ parents. Specifically, we sought to understand the parents' experiences and what initiatives, programs, and/or adaptations organizations should consider to meet the needs of diverse family structures. Organized sport has a long history of a culture of homophobia that prevents "gay men, lesbians, and transgendered people from fully participating in sport" (Davison & Frank, 2007, p. 178). Feminist scholars have challenged the way in which gendered discourses shape the interactions, practices, and structures of sport organizations and maintain sport's patriarchal, heterosexist norms (e.g. Fink, 2016; Shaw & Frisby, 2006). During the gendering process, assumptions of heterosexuality are implicit and sport becomes a context wherein a dominant cultural ideology such as heterosexism acts as an oppressive control mechanism, which reinforces and maintains the disadvantage of minority groups (Cunningham, 2008; Walker & Sartore-Baldwin, 2013).

To examine LGBTQ parents' experiences in youth sport, the research team was composed of three members. Dawn is a heterosexual ally, mother, feminist, and academic whose research focuses on family life and issues of power and social inclusion with an emphasis on the connection to gender and parenting ideologies. Jen is a lesbian mother and avid technology enthusiast, who in her professional life is a technology coach for the curriculum department of a public school board. She also embodies the concept of 'citizen researcher' that we take up in the final section of this chapter. Laura is a graduate student in the Social Justice and Equity Studies program at Brock University whose research focuses on girlhood culture and aesthetic sports.

The original design of this research project was semi-structured face-to-face interviews. After almost six months of failed participant recruitment, Dawn (re)connected with Jen through a mutual friend on Facebook. This moment in time was the perfect storm. Dawn was in the midst of putting together her tenure and promotion materials and it was through this process that she began to question the social value of her research. Seeds of this early research crisis had been germinating. She was relatively successful by measures of academia with what Stokowski (1999) referred to as publishing trophies and several federally funded grants. She wondered, however, if she was *really* making a difference and fostering the positive social change that she claimed guided her theoretical perspective.

As an avid technology enthusiast in her personal and professional life, it was Jen who suggested that the project should move to a digital platform. It was at that moment Dawn 'let go' of traditional offline approaches to data collection with the new and exciting possibilities that Jen's digital knowledge and enthusiasm brought. Consequently, the initial meeting with Jen turned into an engaging conversation related to the possibilities of a new research design on a digital platform.

Over the next six months, there were several disappointments that were endured, including the failure of using Twitter as the data collection platform as well as using a Facebook "page". However, by creating an intentionally designed research space, through a closed group on Facebook, the project finally found success. A total of 73 parents participated in a month-long asynchronous focus group, representing three different countries: twenty-three of the participants were from the United States, 18 from Canada, 16 from Australia, and the remaining 16 did not specify where they resided.

As Krueger and Casey (2015) point out, for an online focus group to be successful, it should have two moderators who are socially present throughout the conversations. Jen and Dawn moderated the digital discussion over the duration of one month. On a weekly basis, Dawn or Jen would post new questions and Laura would follow-up with participants who had not responded to the post through a direct message. Data analysis was guided by an inductive approach to facilitate understanding of the participants' experiences; specifically, a constant comparative analytic framework that is congruent with a focus group method of data collection (Krueger & Casey, 2015; Levy, 2015). For an example of empirical findings from this project, please see Trussell, Kovac, and Apgar (2018).

Yet, traditional, offline research protocols and institutional structures at times clashed with our new dynamic online research design and required much critical thought and ongoing dialogue to resolve. Our chapter takes up this ongoing critical reflection that led to the emergence of three key areas. Aligned with diverse forms of representation found in qualitative inquiry, we also sought creative ways to represent our critical reflections. Toward this end, our chapter is framed by personal narratives from each of the three authors that are represented in the form of vignettes. We used traditional academic writing with theorization as a form of representation. As a method of reflection, Jen also created sketches, and we have included some of them in this chapter. These diverse forms of representation illustrate the complexity of the issues that we confronted as well as strategies employed to help negotiate the challenges.

Traditional Qualitative Methods in New Digital Platforms

As a millennial, technology has been a part of my life since I was in elementary school. When I first began working on this project, all of my friends could not believe that I was actually getting paid to spend time on Facebook, and rightly so – it was an amazing project to work on. There were some difficult moments though. Contacting administrators of LGBTQ Facebook pages to ask if they would be willing to post about the project on their Facebook page left me feeling vulnerable in some ways. While reaching out to strangers via social media might initially seem easier than connecting in person, I was hesitant to share details about my education and work affiliation with people who could view my name, public profile, and photo. We are taught to keep our personal and professional lives separate and using my Facebook account in a work context felt like a deep blurring of these boundaries and exposed my personal life. Yet at the same time, I found it fascinating to virtually meet so many new people. (Laura, Research Assistant)

Researchers centered on issues of social justice have found online methods to be effective for investigating marginalized populations such as LGBTQ communities who may be socially stigmatized, yet digitally active (McInroy, 2016). Evidence suggests that online research methods may be particularly effective to access populations that are hard to reach in offline contexts as they may reduce or temporarily remove barriers associated with groups with less physical mobility (e.g. disabled, in prison, in hospital) or the socially isolated (e.g. illness, gang members) (Madge, 2007). Using traditional methods of data collection such as focus groups or interviews within online spaces may also better facilitate discussion of sensitive or personal issues that may be difficult in conventional face-to-face offline methods. The online focus group was not only effective for reaching a large group of people, but it also created a unique space where participants could connect with others with similar experiences.

"Facebook has the potential to allow for different ways of knowing that cannot be ascertained in more orthodox research spaces" (de Jong, 2015, p. 211). As Jen's sketch illustrates (see Fig. 1) a key ongoing concern we had to consider in the research design process was: "How can we adapt established research methods to better meet the needs of such dynamic spaces" (Dadas, 2016, p. 61)? For the focus group, we chose to use an

Fig. 1 *New Tricks.* (Jen Apgar)

online asynchronous format that allowed people to participate across geographic distances and time zones and to participate at any point throughout the day (Comley & Beaumont, 2011; Krueger & Casey, 2015). Upon reflection, we believe that this might be one of the reasons that our earlier attempt to facilitate discussion via the Twitter platform ultimately failed. As McGeeney (2015) noted, the temporality of Twitter is experienced "as instantaneous, fast and ephemeral" (p. 312). The limitations of the Twitter platform meant that the tweets resembled more of a synchronous conversation, and it became difficult to identify what time zone we should host the chats even within Canada. Facebook also became a good tool whereby the majority of participants had maximum familiarity with the platform and could easily access the discussion forum in their everyday lives; a difficulty that Genoe, Liechty, Marston, and Sutherland (2016) identified when their participants used a specialized platform that they found intimidating and unfamiliar.

An online asynchronous forum provides participants with "more opportunity to think about the topic" and has "the potential to be more in-depth and reflective than those in either the chat room or in a face-to-face focus group" (Krueger & Casey, 2015, p. 212). We agree with Krueger and Casey that the asynchronous discussion provided the opportunity for the participants to do so; and yet, it also provided enhanced moments of reflexivity for the research team. Reflexivity is an important aspect of social justice research "to ensure that our work is subjected to continual internal scrutiny … and an appreciation of the situatedness of what we study" (Long, Fletcher, & Watson, 2017, p. 5). Through an asynchronous discussion, we were able to not only reflect and follow up on individual posts, but we were able to reflect on the data collection as it unfolded. Although eight thematic questions were developed at the start of the project, each week they were slightly refined as we learned what to ask or follow-up on within the collective Facebook group posts. The use of social media also meant that participants could incorporate alternate forms of data such as personal photographs and Internet links to other sites to help illustrate their meanings and experiences.

Aligned with a social justice feminist perspective, the forum was created in a way that would build a sense of community and create a space whereby the participants could learn from one another. That is, participants were also encouraged to ask questions of other participants and share their stories and experiences through the online forum. On a few occasions, the discussion among participants wandered from the initial research questions; however, we saw this as an important aspect of building community and embraced the use of our research space as such.

An ongoing tension that we encountered was that not all participants responded to all questions—and some never made a single post. The 'messiness' of the social media platform and the inability to control algorithms that curates users' feeds (Bivens, 2015) left us to wonder how many questions were missed along the way. Aligned with social media platforms and user experiences, we also recognize that some participants could be framed as 'lurkers' (someone who reads posts, but does not contribute to it) (Horrell, Stephens, & Breheny, 2015). At first, this brought us much anxiety and disappointment about the inherent value of the research design. Upon reflection, however, we came to resolve this tension through framing this phenomenon as an act of 'listening' (see de Jong, 2015) rather than lurking. Feminist traditions advocate for social change and praxis and alternate forms of participation in ways that are not valued in conventional knowledge production. The potential for participants to listen and learn from each other was clearly evident (as well as important to them) with some of the comments and feedback posted as well as direct messages we received upon completion of the focus group. Many participants expressed gratitude for the opportunity to learn from each other and bring the insights back to their own family and/or community.

Problematizing Offline Research Ethics for Online Methods

I have always had a keen interest in the methodological and ethical issues in the research process. The decision to conduct this project within online spaces seemed to heighten the complexities that I felt in every step of the process. I was navigating unfamiliar terrain with little guidance to turn to, whether it be the Institutional Review Board or the scant literature that discussed using social media as a constructed research space with participants. I was stumbling in the dark. I was excited, but with little guidance to draw on, I was also afraid of making a mistake that could potentially place a member of the research team or a participant in harm's way. I was avidly mindful of the power of social media as a space of empowerment, but also of malicious and ill intent. (Dawn, Principal Investigator)

Although opinion is divided whether online research methods are potentially more harmful than those associated with conventional offline methods (Fox, Morris, & Rumsey, 2007), there are important ethical issues to consider. Many professional bodies and university ethical review committees are well established in offline social research, and in turn, online research is heavily influenced by these existing guidelines (Eynon, Schroeder, & Fry, 2009). Madge (2007) identified five key issues of ethical conduct that are identified in the literature related to procedural ethical guidelines for online research. These included informed consent, confidentiality, privacy, debriefing, and netiquette. Clearly, many of these principles are found within offline research; however, using online research methods on a social media platform meant that we were confronted with the inability for traditional offline strategies to work within the digital context of the research process. For example, as Jen's sketch (see Fig. 2) illustrates, traditional information letters and consent forms that needed to be signed and returned to the researcher did not align well

Fig. 2 *Are you a Robot?* (Jen Apgar)

with our research design. We were disappointed to learn that online research projects by other researchers used email or web attachments or even conventional mail (Madge, 2007), all of which we thought to be counterintuitive to an online digital platform framed by Web 2.0 interactional tools.

As such, we believed that typical offline ethics protocols did not align with novel online methods. Dawn contacted her research ethics board to help work through issues of consent, confidentiality, and privacy that would be congruent with an online focus group for our (future) Facebook site. As it turned out, our novel methods were reaffirmed with our Social Science Research Ethics Board (SREB) contact having no precedent on how to handle this type of data collection. Working with our SREB contact, we were able to digitize the ethical guidelines for this project via creating a 'clickthrough' on the Facebook page to Dawn's independent professional website as her institutional webpage did not provide such flexibility in its structured design. It was here that in-depth content was created, outlining issues of confidentiality, anonymity, privacy, and the opportunity to withdraw from the project.

We hoped that creating an intentional research space via a new Facebook group centered on the research project would minimize the issue of privacy and the public/private debate that is often found in research that mines data from existing individual or group postings. (Cleland, 2014; Madge, 2007). We were transparent in every phase of the research project—that the Facebook group was intentionally created for the purpose of research. A post was 'pinned' to the top of the page to indicate as such so it would not become buried in the groups' collective posts. We were also flexible with the research design to accommodate various participants' level of comfort. For example, for each of our posted discussion topics, participants could respond to the closed group and/or via a direct message to any member of the research team if they did not feel comfortable in 'publicly' doing so.

Throughout the entire research (re)design process, we had heightened sensitivity to ethical issues of *netiquette*, and Jen's experience in navigating and facilitating digital forums was instrumental to the leadership of the project in this regard. Madge (2007) describes netiquette as

> the term used to describe the code of conduct between those communicating on the internet. It is concerned with internet courtesy and protocols and is directed at preventing aggressive and insulting behavior. It includes often unspoken rules about what is considered appropriate, polite and respectful behavior online. (p. 663)

Indeed, as a research team we were intentional from the outset of the digital aspect of the project to create a safe and inclusive space. As such, we outlined guidelines related to respectful participation through the 'click-through' to Dawn's professional website. In turn, not only were ethical issues surrounding netiquette clearly stated on her website but it was an ongoing process that meant we were continually examining the data through a lens of inclusivity and the construction of a safe and respectful space.

Netiquette also involves "the researcher being familiar with common language including jargon, abbreviations, acronyms, emoticons and common grammatical rules" (Madge, 2007, p. 663). Once again, Jen's leadership in the areas of LGBTQ community, digitality, and social networking platforms was instrumental in creating this rapport with the participants. Our commitment to being 'up front' about the purpose and nature of the research and Facebook group as outlined earlier also aligns with principles of researcher netiquette (Halls et al. 2004 as cited in Madge, 2007).

Our self-identification as researchers was critical to research practices and issues of ethical conduct (Halls et al. 2004 as cited in Madge, 2007). By indicating that this was a university project and providing the logo and a link to an institutional website on our Facebook page and group, it increased the credibility of the researcher and project (Madge, 2007). Moreover, we saw the convergence of netiquette with feminist offline espoused values of transparency, the personal as being political, as well as challenging the public-private binary. With Facebook "there is an assumption that personal information will be shared" (de Jong, 2015, p. 218), thus, this approach was congruent with the research culture that we hoped to create and the platform that we used. For example, Dawn was intentional in being transparent with her positionality as a heterosexual, mother, and academic with her professional website as well as Facebook posts to the group. She used these forums to explain her personal interest in the research project and why this particular topic was important to her. Jen was also transparent with her positionality, identifying as a lesbian, mother, and educator.

Researchers and participants were engaged in overlapping research practices by recording, selecting, and interpreting comments provided by fast-moving data that were instantaneously indexed through a time/date stamp (McGeeney, 2015). In contrast to conventional research methods such as interviews or in-person focus groups, participants were able to 'access' the raw data and draw their own analyses from it in real time. The research teams' contributions to the online forum also meant that the researcher became the researched whereby participants could determine the intention, authority, and integrity of the research team. That is, the temporal affordances of the social media platform and the digital archive of all posts also meant that the participants could take prolonged time to reflect and evaluate the research teams' comments, in a way that is not provided in face-to-face synchronous research.

Related to this point, it is not only completed research and knowledge dissemination that benefits from social media but also the analysis process of knowledge construction (Hays, Spiers, & Paterson, 2015). Unlike any former research project that Dawn had been a part of, the public transparency of the entire data set meant that we felt increased accountability that sensitized us to "detailed accounts of how and why the fragments of data presented have been carefully selected as emblematic of the archive of material from which they are taken" (McGeeney, 2015, p. 312). Simply put, we felt nervous with the implications of having the raw data for all members of the Facebook group to access, and in turn, evaluate our interpretations of the collective posts. Yet, we believe that this enhanced the 'trustworthiness' of the findings, as we felt greater accountability with the transparency of the raw data to the research participants.

Feminist research has a long history of challenging institutional ethics, and as these examples illustrate, ethics approval was seen as a process that was continuous and organic within the digital medium. Similar to Fox et al. (2007) the evolving nature of the project required several amendments to the original application. It was through trial and error and collective problem solving with our institutional SREB that we were able to reimagine what ethical protocols should look like within this forum. This aligns with a key guiding principle that the ethics working committee of the Association of Internet Researchers (see Markham & Buchanan, 2012) refers to as a case-based framework: "Rather than one-size-fits-all pronouncements, ethical decision-making is best approached through the application of practical judgment attentive to the specific context" (p. 4). Moreover, it also emphasizes that online research methods have not merely blurred conventional ethical guidelines but are transforming them.

Citizen Researchers and the Temporality of Knowledge Mobilization

> *As the community facilitator of this project, I was excited to support a line of inquiry with a diverse group of participants. When first approached by Dawn, I was very excited about the topic but felt that the community/cohort that she could curate in person would be very small and relatively local. When Dawn shared some of the earlier (yet limited) work in the area of LGBTQ parents and family leisure, I wondered whose experiences did it really reflect? It appeared to me that it was a pretty 'homogenous' group. This wondering, combined with my interest and experiences in social media platforms as educational spaces, led me to suggest that Dawn should consider the possibility of moving the project to Twitter, and then later Facebook. I was excited to be actively and meaningfully engaged in formal and funded academic research, something that is not usually accessible to learners who are not involved in post-graduate studies. As a life-long learner, I am interested in using qualitative data to affect positive social change and saw this a rich and unique opportunity to be involved in research more than just being a participant. (Jen, Community Engagement Facilitator)*

The concept of *citizen researcher,* Fielding (2014) ascertains, is on the rise due to increased access and ease of information that can be found via new digital media. The advancement of digitization has complicated and blurred the boundaries between researcher and researched and has given rise to the citizen researcher. Digitization has facilitated social change through a "proliferation of digital devices and online social media platforms that enable non-professional researchers to engage in everyday research practices – recording, documenting, and sharing details of the social world (Marres, 2012)" (McGeeney, 2015, p. 310). Digitization has also blurred the boundaries between research/researched and data collection, analysis, representation, and knowledge mobilization.

Citizen research has always existed through the "amateur scientist" or "social reformer" (e.g. Jane Addams in the United States) (Fielding, 2014). But it is the rise of citizen research via online media that is "likely to entail unpredictable changes in the practice and purposes of social research … Citizen researchers largely do research for purposes other than adding to academic knowledge" (Fielding, 2014, p. 1066). Moreover, "people are no longer passive receivers of information distributed by experts but are actively using the Internet to find information" (Hays et al., 2015, p. 1577). Through this process, Hays et al. (2015) suggest that people are able to connect with others with similar experiences, share personal stories, and gain insights while fostering meaning making.

Perhaps the greatest potential for social media and citizen researchers are the new possibilities for knowledge exchange that have temporal implications and blur the boundaries between researcher/researched. As McGeeney (2015) argues:

> [I]n the context of digitization social research becomes a 'distributed accomplishment', with online platforms, social media users and digital devices actively contributing to the performance of digital social research. This prompts reconsideration of what is meant by 'research', 'data' and 'method' and the role, value and authority of the social researcher. Although social research has always been a shared accomplishment between different actors (researchers, participants, institutions, organizations), digitization has made this visible and possible in new, exciting and troubling ways. … How might the intensification and 'speeding up' of time afforded through digitization shape research practices and writing craft? (pp. 310–311)

The temporal affordances of using social media platforms as an online research tool were perhaps the most exciting yet challenging tensions we had to reconcile. Indeed, as alluded to earlier, although the complexities of consent, privacy, and control of the data were problematized throughout the research process, we believed that the social media platform was one step toward meeting our social justice research goals of asking important questions "to change the material conditions of women's (and other marginalized groups) everyday lives" (Parry & Johnson, 2015, p. 29). As Jen's sketch (see Fig. 3) illustrates, social media platforms provided the opportunity for the participants in our project to learn from each other and mobilize knowledge exchange in real time.

This is in contrast to conventional research methods that are defined by a "slow cyclical movement between data collection analysis, writing" (McGeeney, 2015, p. 312). McGeeney (2015), drawing on Gill's (2009) term 'fast academia', argues that social media may provide one way in which researchers are able to quickly distill and access ideas and information. Indeed, one benefit of using online research methods was the opportunity to maintain a prolonged engagement with the Facebook group through the social media platform, in that, long after the formal data collection period was over, we were able to post materials related to the project (i.e., preliminary summary of the findings, press releases, published manuscripts). Indeed, a considerable benefit of digital media for knowledge dissemination

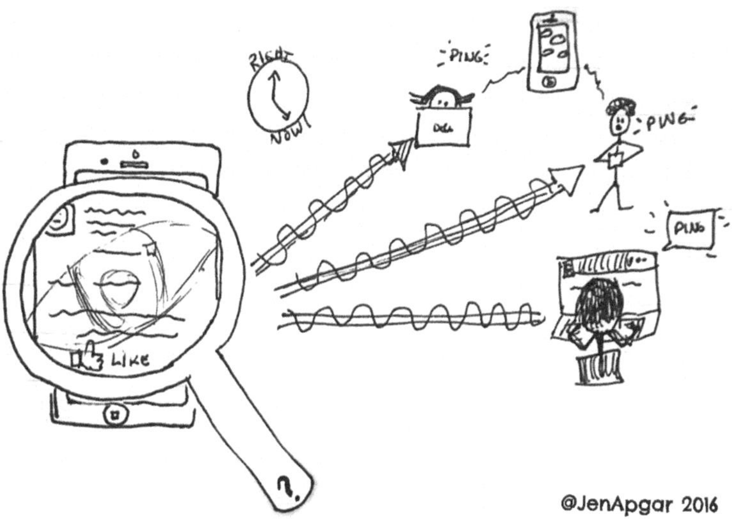

Fig. 3 *The mobile network.* (Jen Apgar)

that is not realized by traditional means (e.g. journal articles) is that it "significantly widens the audiences that have ready access to the research findings" (Hays et al., 2015, p. 1578). Moreover, when people are able to interact and provide comments and opinions to the research findings, they are more apt to learn more about the findings as well as develop attitudinal change (Prisline et al. 2011 as cited by Hays et al., 2015).

There is growing regulatory pressure to ensure open access of knowledge with all publicly funded research using online and offline methods. With the temporal affordances of the social media platform, we believed that this aligns with the spirit of this movement and the opportunity to create shared archives of knowledge (McGeeney, 2015). However, critics of this type of research governance have alluded to the tensions that arise when doing so that fail to acknowledge the labor of research production (McGeeney, 2015).

One tension that Dawn had to reconcile was the accessibility of the raw data and what that meant for intellectual property and the development of future publications within academia. Although such challenges may exist when individuals attend a scholarly presentation (Hays et al., 2015), or are collaborators on research projects, the ease with which digital data may be captured left us with pause. In some ways, this ongoing tension was resolved when the shift of the online platform was moved from Twitter whereby anyone could potentially access the raw data to an online closed group on Facebook where the data was only readily accessible to those who were 'approved' members. Moreover, upon reflection, this tension was reconciled when it became evident that the collection of online texts did not represent our labor wherein the difficult work lies in the analysis as well as creation of academic outputs such as conference presentations and journal manuscripts.

Conclusion

The critical reflections that were highlighted in this chapter emphasize the importance of understanding online qualitative research methods and social media and make several contributions to the literature. Although issues of temporality, power, privacy, ethics, and representation are not unique to online research, we were confronted with the inability of traditional offline strategies to work within the digital context. Instead, we forged different ways to reconcile some of these existing tensions that arose during the research process. In doing so, we believe that we were able to build an online community that shared insights and experiences, that ultimately became a form of knowledge dissemination, throughout the research process.

Although further work is required to gain a more complete understanding of conducting qualitative inquiry in online spaces, our critical reflections indicate that the possibilities of these spaces and the intersection with feminist research can create novel insights into the issues of social justice and everyday meanings and experiences. Throughout the online asynchronous focus group, we attempted to reconcile the tensions we felt ultimately viewing the issues "as opportunities to work toward new understandings" (Dadas, 2016, p. 68). Moreover, in both Dadas (2016) study and the present study, we learned to embrace research activity as a nonlinear entity that

> does not necessarily progress through sequential stages of (private) data collection and analysis and then on to a (public) presentation of the findings when the reader is ready. Refusing this linear progression is one way that we might adapt established research methods to better meet the needs of dynamic online spaces. (p. 71)

Finally, despite the documented difficulties, we argue that in many ways being able to experience failure with the (initial) offline research design and reimagine an online qualitative project strengthened the very creation of knowledge for this area of inquiry. It provided the opportunity to 'let go' of traditional research methods used in academia and seek out new ways to build research collaborations with citizen researchers as well as construct and mobilize knowledge into everyday life.

References

Bivens, R. (2015). Under the hood: The software in your feminist approach. *Feminist Media Studies, 15*(4), 714–717. https://doi.org/10.1080/14680777.2015.1053717.

Cleland, J. (2014). Racism, football fans, and online message boards: How social media has added a new dimension to a racist discourse in English football. *Journal of Sport & Social Issues, 38*(5), 415–431. https://doi.org/10.1177/0193723513499922.

Comley, P., & Beaumont, J. (2011). Online research: Methods, benefits and issues – Part 2. *Journal of Direct, Data and Digital Marketing Practice, 13*(1), 25–39.

Cunningham, G. B. (2008). Creating and sustaining gender diversity in sport organizations. *Sex Roles, 58*(1–2), 136–145. https://doi.org/10.1007/s11199-007-9312-3.

Dadas, C. (2016). Messy methods: Queer methodological approaches to researching social media. *Computers and Composition, 40*, 60–72. https://doi.org/10.1016/j.compcom.2016.03.007.

Davison, K., & Frank, B. (2007). Sexualities, genders, and bodies in sport: Changing practices of inequity. In K. Young & P. White (Eds.), *Sport and gender in Canada* (2nd ed., pp. 178–193). Toronto, ON: Oxford University Press.

de Jong, A. (2015). Using Facebook as a space for storytelling in geographical research. *Geographical Research, 53*(2), 211–223. https://doi.org/10.1111/1745-5871.12095.

Eynon, R., Schroeder, R., & Fry, J. (2009). New techniques in online research: Challenges for research ethics. *Twenty-First Century Society, 4*(2), 187–199. https://doi.org/10.1080/17450140903000308.

Fielding, N. G. (2014). Qualitative research and our digital futures. *Qualitative Inquiry, 20*(9), 1064–1073. https://doi.org/10.1177/1077800414545237.

Fink, J. S. (2016). Hiding in plain sight: The embedded nature of sexism in sport. *Journal of Sport Management, 30*(1), 1–7. https://doi.org/10.1123/jsm.2015-0278.

Fox, F. E., Morris, M., & Rumsey, N. (2007). Doing synchronous online focus groups with young people: Methodological reflections. *Qualitative Health Research, 19*(4), 539–547. https://doi.org/10.1177/1049732306298754.

Genoe, M. R., Liechty, T., Marston, H. R., & Sutherland, V. (2016). Blogging into retirement. Using qualitative online research methods to understand leisure among baby boomers. *Journal of Leisure Research, 48*(1), 15–34. https://doi.org/10.18666/JLR-2016-V48-I1-6257.

Gill, R. (2009). Breaking the silence: The hidden injuries of neo-liberal academia. In R. Flood & R. Gill (Eds.), *Secrecy and silence in the research process: Feminist reflections* (pp. 228–244). London: Routledge.

Hays, C. A., Spiers, J. A., & Paterson, B. (2015). Opportunities and constraints in disseminating qualitative research in Web 2.0 virtual environments. *Qualitative Health Research, 25*(11), 1576–1588. https://doi.org/10.1177/1049732315580556.

Horrell, B., Stephens, C., & Breheny, M. (2015). Online research with informal caregivers: Opportunities and challenges. *Qualitative Research in Psychology, 12*, 258–271. https://doi.org/10.1080/14780887.2015.1040318.

Krueger, R. A., & Casey, M. A. (2015). *Focus groups: A practical guide for applied research* (5th ed.). Thousand Oaks, CA: SAGE.

Levy, D. L. (2015). Discovering grounded theories for social justice. In C. W. Johnson & D. C. Parry (Eds.), *Fostering social justice through qualitative inquiry* (pp. 71–99). Walnut Creek, CA: Left Coast.

Long, J., Fletcher, T., & Watson, B. (2017). Introducing sport, leisure and social justice. In J. Long, T. Fletcher, & B. Watson (Eds.), *Sport, leisure and social justice* (pp. 1–14). New York: Routledge.

Madge, C. (2007). Developing a geographers' agenda for online research ethics. *Progress in Human Geography, 31*(5), 654–674. https://doi.org/10.1177/0309132507081496.

Markham, A., & Buchanan, E. (2012). Ethical decision-making and internet research: Recommendations from the AoIR Ethics Working Committee (version 2.0). Retrieved from the Association of Internet Researchers website: http://www.aoir.org/reports/ethics2.pdf

Marres, N. (2012). The redistribution of methods: On intervention in digital social research, broadly conceived. *The Sociological Review, 60*, 139–165.

McGeeney, E. (2015). Live tweeting and building the digital archive; #NFQLR – Who and what is it for? *International Journal of Social Research Methodology, 18*(3), 307–319. https://doi.org/10.1080/13645579.2015.1017898.

McInroy, L. B. (2016). Pitfalls, potentials, and ethics of online survey research: LGBTQ and other marginalized and hard-to-access youths. *Social Work Research, 40*(2), 83–93. https://doi.org/10.1093/swr/svw005.

Morrow, O., Hawkins, R., & Kern, L. (2015). Feminist research in online spaces. *Gender, Place and Culture, 22*(4), 526–543. https://doi.org/10.1080/0966369X.2013.879108.

Parry, D. C., & Johnson, C. W. (2015). Theoretical perspectives for social justice inquiry. In C. W. Johnson & D. C. Parry (Eds.), *Fostering social justice through qualitative inquiry* (pp. 23–41). Walnut Creek, CA: Left Coast.

Parry, D. C., Johnson, C. W., & Stewart, W. (2013). Leisure research for social justice: A response to Henderson. *Leisure Sciences, 36*(4), 349–364. https://doi.org/10.1080/01490400.2013.739906.

Shaw, S., & Frisby, W. (2006). Can gender equity be more equitable? Promoting an alternative frame for sport management research, education, and practice. *Journal of Sport Management, 20*, 483–509.

Stokowski, P. (1999). Trophy hunting in the shadow of the castle keep. *Journal of Leisure Research, 31*(2), 189–191.

Trussell, D. E., Kovac, L., & Apgar, J. (2018). LGBTQ parents' experiences of community youth sport: Change your forms, change your (hetero) norms. *Sport Management Review, 21*(1), 51–62. https://doi.org/10.1016/j.smr.2017.03.003

Walker, N. A., & Sartore-Baldwin, M. L. (2013). Hegemonic masculinity and the institutionalized bias toward women in men's collegiate basketball: What do men think. *Journal of Sport Management, 27*(4), 303–315. https://doi.org/10.1016/j.smr.2014.02.004.

Appnography: Modifying Ethnography for App-Based Culture

Luc S. Cousineau, Harrison Oakes, and Corey W. Johnson

It had only been a full week since he arrived at his parents' small bungalow in Mexico, but to Jeremy it felt like a year. Nestled in a small village several kilometers outside a small city, Jeremy's parents belonged to a conservative sect of Evangelical Christians. He saw them once a year and the visit was always pleasant enough, but he could not shake the feeling that he was a stranger to them.

A gay atheist attending graduate school in the US, Jeremy could hardly be more different from his family and the culture he grew up in. While he experienced a sense of comfort from the familiarity of his family's customs, it clashed with the stark isolation he felt in his relationships with his parents and older brother. Desperate to talk to someone who was like him, he went into his room, closed the door, and opened Grindr on his iPhone.

L. S. Cousineau (✉) • C. W. Johnson
Department of Recreation & Leisure Studies, University of Waterloo, Waterloo, ON, Canada
e-mail: Luc.cousineau@uwaterloo.ca; corey.johnson@uwaterloo.ca

H. Oakes
Department of Psychology, University of Waterloo, Waterloo, ON, Canada
e-mail: hoakes@uwaterloo.ca

D. C. Parry et al. (eds.), *Digital Dilemmas*,
https://doi.org/10.1007/978-3-319-95300-7_5

There, on the screen before him, were the familiar rows of users, arranged in order of geographical proximity. He scrolled through the rows as he sat down on his bed, noting the differences in the user profiles from those he saw back home. Fewer men included their faces in their profile picture, and a lot of profiles mentioned "activo" and/or "passivo". Curious, he pulled up his translator and began to translate users' Spanish profile descriptions into English.

Seconds later, his iPhone vibrated and he saw that ballar35 had sent him a message. "hola", it read, and Jeremy smiled to himself. Even in Mexico, gay guys still used the same lackluster openings. "Hola", he typed back. "Cómo estás?" He smiled again. He had exhausted the extent of his knowledge of Spanish, but it felt good to interact with someone who was like him. Somehow, he felt a little less alone.

Jeremy's experience exemplifies one of the key aspects of digitality in today's world: the hybridization of digital and physical spaces. Hybrid space allows sexual minorities to be as visible as desired (virtually), regardless of the physical space they inhabit (Roth, 2014). Jeremy's ability to queer the staunchly heterosexual space his physical body was situated in by logging in to Grindr highlights just one way (of infinite possibilities) in which digital and physical spaces interact to create hybrid spaces that shape people's experience of life.

In this chapter, we will explore the world of apps like Grindr and how we might study them and their users. In providing guideposts for studying these apps, we will draw on feminist and queer theory to inform our articulation of a new digital ethnography. Less a prescriptive list of how-to's, we instead outline theoretical considerations for incorporating apps like Grindr into digital ethnographies. We do this in recognition of, and in response to, the dilemmas in digital research. These dilemmas arise from quickly changing social and technological environments—where updates, competitors, and user preferences can dramatically change the site of one's research at any time—and from the need for research processes that are strongly grounded in theory, yet flexible enough to adapt to the rapid fluctuations in digital environments. Though not an easy task, we attempt to address some of these dilemmas in our proposal for digital ethnographies of apps like Grindr.

The language we use throughout this chapter warrants special mention. We use the term "digital" interchangeably with virtual, online, and computer-mediated (see: Kollock & Smith, 1999; Law & Singleton, 2000; Turkle, 1996) because we perceive these terms to be synonymous with each other for our purposes. However, in certain fields (e.g., new media studies, internet studies) terms like Internet, internet, web, and so on, mean different things, and we have done our best to reflect those meanings here. For example, "web" refers specifically to the content of the World Wide Web or what might be colloquially called the internet (lower case i). When people say they "went online" or "found it online", they are generally referring to the web, although it is possible to have online interactions without being on the web (e.g., Internet Relay Chat—IRC). Use of the term "the Internet" (capital I) is generally reserved for discussion of the infrastructure and content of the global network, including underground/water cabling which connects continents, data centers, server farms, and your cloud email account. Although most of what we discuss in this chapter references internet interaction, some of it does not (e.g., SMS is not Internet-based—although that line is blurred by Apple's use of data for iMessage), and we do our best to distinguish between the two accurately.

Geo-Social Networking Apps

Geo-social networking applications (GSNAs)[1] use mobile technologies to create computer-mediated interactions whereby users participate in different relational activities exclusively through mobile, internet-connected, global positioning system (GPS)–enabled devices. Despite their relatively recent appearance on the technological scene, they have quickly become a locus in the social lives of their users, with several GSNAs boasting millions of users (Grindr, n.d.-a; Perry Street Software,

[1] Though we adopt the term "geo-social networking apps", other scholars have used a variety of different terms to denote the same object of study (e.g., "location-based real-time dating apps", Blackwell et al. 2015; "location-based social networking applications", Brubaker et al. 2016; "GPS-enabled networking site", Gudelunas 2012, p. 348; "gay-targeted geosocial networking services", Roth 2014, p. 2118).

Inc. n.d.; Tepper, 2017). The basic design of GSNAs is simple: users log on and are presented potential matches that are curated based on geographical proximity and user preferences. The user can choose to interact (or not) with their potential matches, and the apps facilitate electronic communication (e.g., text, virtual gifts, photo, video).

One of the first GSNAs released, Grindr launched in March 2009 (Kincaid, 2009) as a virtual space in which "gay, bi, curious, and queer men" (Grindr, n.d.-a) could connect and spend time with each other. Grindr is "the largest all-male social network in the world, with over 3 million daily active users in 234 countries and territories" (Grindr, n.d.-b). On average, users log in to Grindr 18 times per day and spend 54 minutes actively logged in across each day (Grindr, n.d.-b). Woo (2015) argues Grindr has become the central "lens through which we may examine the quickly changing Western queer culture, and the values and beliefs of the men in it" (p. 63). Of course, Grindr is not the only mainstream GSNA for sexual minority men (e.g., SCRUFF, Jack'd, GROWLr, Hornet), nor are GSNAs solely geared toward sexual-minority men.

The most popular GSNA catering to heterosexual users is Tinder[2] (Tepper, 2017). Released in late 2012, Tinder's popularity quickly exploded, becoming the most popular app of its kind. By spring 2014, the app had reached one billion matches between users (Stampler, 2014). Currently boasting over ten billion matches made (Tinder Inc., 2017), Tinder not only includes the ability to connect with individual users, but also featured "Tinder Social," the ability for groups to connect with other groups to coordinate social gatherings (Tinder Inc., 2017)[3]. Recently, Tinder also expanded users' options for identifying their gender, allowing them to self-define and select whether their profile should be shown in searches for men, women, or both (Tinder Blog, 2016).

Beyond Grindr and Tinder, a host of dating and hookup apps aim to cater to more specific niche markets in an effort to address particular users' needs and desires. For example, Feeld was designed for singles or couples to meet other "kinky, curious and openminded humans" (Feeld

[2] Tinder also caters to non-heterosexual users, but it is currently the most popular app for heterosexual users.

[3] The "Tinder Social" feature is no longer available in the app. Even though Tinder claims it was successful, they decided it did not best "meet their brand goals" as a service. This is also an excellent example of the important temporality of studying apps and app-based technology spaces (discussed below), as this change occurred between the writing of this chapter and the proofing process.

Ltd., 2017), Sizzl was designed by Oscar Mayer for bacon lovers (Matney, 2015), and Sweatt was designed for fitness lovers (SWEATT Inc., 2017). While many of these niche apps are bound to go the way of most new startups (indeed, Sizzl already appears to have done so), they highlight the growing diversity among GSNAs and challenge the mainstream GSNAs to diversify their design and services to meet the unique needs of their members.

Despite the prevalence and diversity of GSNAs around the world, relatively little work has examined their implications for users and social cultures. Of the work that exists, much of it focuses on sexual minority men. As such, there is a dearth of research on GSNA use among gender minority, female sexual minority, and straight populations. This lack of research belies the many rich opportunities for novel theorizing and insights into human behavior that we believe GSNAs offer. Among these opportunities are topics related to the overlay of physical and virtual spaces, identity and identifiability (Blackwell, Birnholtz, & Abbott, 2015), user profiles, and user interactions. As we move on to consider the theoretical implications of queer and feminist theory for the study of GSNAs, we will highlight several ways in which researchers can address these (and other) topics in meaningful ways.

Feminist Theory, Queer Theory, and Digital Cultures

With the introduction of what has been called a "fourth wave" of feminism in North America, feminist theory has refocused to include new social domains (e.g., the web) and the potential for new allied voices (e.g., men) (Johnson & Cousineau, 2018). It is through this development that we, as three White men, are able to both participate in, and contribute to, the discourses developing in this volume. In doing so, we must acknowledge that we engage with feminist theory from a positionality that is indeed "locat[ed] within shifting networks of relationships" (Maher & Tetreault, 2001, p. 164), but is inherently different from that of our female colleagues. We also engage with queer theoretical perspectives as they interrogate the assumed naturalness of binary identities and allow us to be sensitive to "the complicated and multilayered lived experiences and subjectivities of individuals" (Valocchi, 2005, p. 767), including our own.

Feminist and queer theoretical orientations provide tools to identify and examine the structural and discursive elements of social phenomena that otherwise are often overlooked. This expository quality makes both theories particularly valuable for our adaptation of digital ethnography to GSNAs because they position the elements of digital space for deep critique, both in approach and in the "who" these spaces claim to represent. This positionality allows us to understand the digital and digitality as extensions of—not separate from—the social power relations that permeate our everyday lives.

Both feminist and queer perspectives on the early web adopted the prefix "cyber" (cyberfeminism, cyberqueer) as they shifted their focus to this new social space. Although "cyber" evades thorough specification, its junction to either theoretical perspective reflected the symbiotic relationship between theory and digital space, and each perspective's initial celebration of the potential for the Internet to queer social life and realize new and utopic digital cultures (Daniels, 2009; Gross, 2007; Paasonen, 2011; Rodat, 2014; Wakeford, 2000). To early cyberfeminism and cyberqueer theorists, the Internet was an opportunity to dissolve the embodied self through anonymity and opportunities to adopt and perform multiple identities (e.g., Rheingold, 2000).

Over time, and particularly with the rise of Web 2.0 user-generated profit models (Parks, 2015; Shade, 2013; Star, 1999), hegemonic social cultures and power relations from the physical world largely supplanted those which pre-existed online (Rodat, 2014). In some cases, the manifestations of these power relations became even more problematic (e.g., consider the common practice of sending unsolicited "dick pics" (i.e., pictures of men's penises)); see Barlett (2015); and Barlett, Gentile, & Chew (2016) for discussions of anonymity in cyberbullying; see Omernick & Sood (2013) for a discussion of anonymity in reader comments on a news site), forcing both theoretical perspectives to shift their focus to addressing discrepancies of representation and power as they extend into the digital. Simultaneously, cyberfeminism and cyberqueer theory maintain the ideological perspective that online experiences need not be gendered, powered, oppressed, or actualized in the same ways that physical ones currently are. It is with these lenses that we explore how we might queer digital ethnographic research to better represent the experiences of users and the social, power, technological, and infrastructural settings of those experiences.

Digital Ethnography

Ethnography is a methodology that has deep roots across a variety of disciplines, especially in anthropology, but also in sociology, communications studies, cultural studies, and leisure sciences. Although the practice of ethnography is slightly different between disciplines and paradigms, Karen O'Reilly (2012) summarizes their commonalities by describing ethnography as

> [a] practice that evolves in design as the study progresses; involves direct and sustained contact with human beings, in the context of their daily lives, over a prolonged period of time; draws on a family of methods, usually including participant observation and conversation; respects the complexity of the social world; and therefore tells rich, sensitive, and credible stories. (p. 4)

Although her definition is broad in scope, it has not been without its detractors, particularly from researchers applying ethnography to digital spaces, also known as digital ethnography. Pink et al. (2016), along with other scholars researching the digital world, contend that O'Reilly's insistence that researchers have direct and sustained contact with human beings during the course of their research is mostly impossible for digital contexts. O'Reilly's implication, they claim, is that researcher contact must be in-person, ruling out digital contact as "true" ethnography. This has led some researchers to propose a separate space for ethnography in the "digital" (e.g., *netnography*; (Kozinets, 2010)), or, like Pink et al. (2016), digital ethnography.

We contend that digital contact (e.g., through blogs, massively multiplayer online environments [MMOs], online chat rooms, social media,

GSNAs) does indeed meet the standard for O'Reilly's direct and sustained contact if we first reject the premise that a person's online actions and representations are separate from their offline self (sometimes referred to as their "real" self). Scholars across various fields have established the non-separation of the digital and the "real" (e.g., in anthropology, see Boellstorff, 2016; for a queer perspective, see Mowlabocus, 2010), and we rely on their theorizing to help frame a new digital ethnography that eschews a digital/"real" divide and is a robust and appropriate way to undertake the study of GSNAs specifically, and other contexts more generally.

Borrowing from Pink et al. (2016), as well as theories on the multiplicity of subjectivities (Pavlidis & Fullagar, 2013), and the queering of digital spaces (Keeling, 2014; Lupton, 2015), we argue that a digital ethnography of GSNAs must (a) incorporate the many ways users intersect and interface with the digital; (b) be transparent and reflexive about the how and why of the ethnographic project and in communicating with and involving participants; and (c) acknowledge the non-centrality of the digital spaces or media objects within the ethnographic study, recalling the intersections of individual, social, technological, personal, and public that interpolate the user. We situate these ethnographic elements in feminist and queer theory to remain conscious of the social power dynamics that are critical for understanding the false dichotomy of digital/"real", user profiles, digital space and place, contextuality, and temporality of GSNA interactions.

Taking up a queer approach to research begins with recognizing that queer exists within (Ahmed, 2006). To "queer" ethnography (or any other methodology), then, involves a process of finding what within it is queer, identifying those "queer moments" that lead to an "intellectual experience of disorder" (Merleau-Ponty, 2002, p. 296)[4] and embarking with that insight in mind. These realizations also serve to identify and expose power relationships and inequities to be explored and challenged from a feminist perspective.

[4] We borrow Ahmed's (2006) reading of Merleau-Ponty's (2002) work on the phenomenology of perception for its ability to evoke a phenomenological image of what it means to "queer" ethnography.

Next, proper contextualization of the research object/phenomenon and the locality and temporality of the research are necessary for a feminist/queer-influenced digital ethnography. Mowlabocus (2010) argued that to study digital culture, we have first to step back from the digital to look at the sociohistorical "contexts, discourses and structures that frame" (p. 21) the broader cultural and sociopolitical contexts. Only in understanding the relevant sociohistorical contexts can one fully appreciate the current manifestations of digital culture and the pre-existing conditions of knowledge production that have shaped them. Contextualization can, among other things, help to do "justice to the ways that people live their sexual identities with complexity and [to question] the conditions of knowledge production when theorizing queer lives" (Rooke, 2009, p. 157) or complex power structures in social and sexual relationships. Finally, we must carefully consider the ethical implications of our methodologies and how we implement them, acknowledging and engaging with the inherent power we gain as researchers, and using this awareness in our reflexive practice.

What follows is an exploration of each of these elements of GSNA study, guided by feminist and queer theoretical perspectives, and including our recommendations for this methodological approach. This exploration will create a set of guideposts that other researchers can utilize when contemplating and planning digital ethnographies of GSNAs or other digital contexts.

Methodological Considerations

The uniqueness of GSNAs requires that we consider carefully the approach that we take in choosing to study them. What follows are considerations that we propose for the queering of digital ethnography to meet the needs of this particular research space, beginning with how we must understand the intertwined nature of digital and "real". This is followed by a discussion of the power and influence of profiles on users and researchers, the importance of space and place when engaged with GSNAs, and, finally, the significance of both context and temporality on research decisions and practices.

The Digital Versus the "Real"

Early web research often contextualized online/digital and offline/"real" as separate and distinct within the social, physical, and emotional manifestations of the people involved (see Rheingold, 1993, for a well-known example). The binary nature of this distinction allowed for theoretical considerations of digital space as new, fresh, open, and void of latent social influence in its development (ward, 1999). Although the lines between "digital" and "real" increasingly blurred as computer technology began to infiltrate all aspects of life (e.g., Gross, 2007; Gudelunas, 2012; Manovich, 2006), notions about the distinct separation between "digital" and "real" selves continue to be employed in research (cf. Mishna, McLuckie, & Saini, 2009; Riebel, Jaeger, & Fischer, 2009) and colloquial understandings of self (nobullying.com, 2016).

This perceived digital/"real" divide is softened some by the increasingly ubiquitous nature of personal technologies like mobile devices, and has prompted the emergence of a discourse around "hybridized" bodies and spaces (e.g., Gudelunas, 2012; Kozinets, 2010; Nayar, 2010). Roth (2014) described this hybridization as "[u]sers [being] at once constructed as data [online] and physically engaged in social and sexual interactions [offline]" (p. 2128). Rather than a digital/"real" identity binary, then, these personifications are interwoven in a fundamental way, a matrix of the physical body with the digital manifestations of the self (Roth, 2014).

GSNAs provide a tangible representation of this matrix. As one example, in-app (i.e., "digital") interactions are predicated on the visually personified elements of the profile and frequently geared toward securing in-person (i.e., "real") meetings for social and/or sexual purposes (Tikkanen & Ross, 2004; Rodat, 2014). The "digital" and "real" elements of these interactions are interwoven with each other, both determining the course and outcome(s) of the connection between users. It is crucial, then, for a new digital ethnography to deconstruct the online/offline, virtual/real binaries in a way that recognizes the virtual as the extended, constructed self (or selves), while remaining mindful and respectful of the fact that, for some users, a multiplicity of representations might be necessary for the emotional (and at times physical) safety of the user.

Profiles

Perhaps no aspect of GSNAs is better suited to cyberqueer or cyberfeminist analysis than "the profile;" the nexus of social interaction on GSNAs. Profiles are the point at which users render themselves visible, assert their identity(ies), and position themselves as part of (or not) a digital community (Horne & Lewis, 1997; Mowlabocus, 2010). Coupland (1996) described such visibility as "involved not only with the promoting or 'selling' of selves but [also] with the attracting or 'buying' of others" (p. 191). In a sense, profiles grant users membership into a buyer's club while simultaneously functioning as an advertisement aimed at garnering potential buyers' interests. Of critical importance is the image of a user's brand—the "profile pic". Many considerations go into selecting the right image and no wonder, considering users must contend with a saturated market in which disconnection is easy, rejection is easier still (to dish out and to accept), and where users frequently "rebrand" their profile to increase their perceived attractiveness (Brown, Maycock, & Burns, 2005; Woo, 2015). Self-presentational concerns dominate users' experiences and—regardless of individual users' politics or queerness—create powerful incentives to curate attractive profiles so as to increase their odds of generating other users' interest (Blackwell et al., 2015).

When curating a profile, users must contend with the limitations of GSNA designs for quantifying and categorizing users. Opting out of these reductive signifiers results in exclusion from filters and searches based on them, weakening users' integration into the space of a GSNA (Roth, 2014). However, by quantifying identity, GSNAs create "credentials against which individuals can (and frequently do) assess themselves" (Roth, 2014, p. 2125). Therefore, digital ethnographies of GSNAs must recognize these hetero/homonormative simplifications of user identity and interrogate users' potential for queering their profiles and/or participation in the digital space.

For the digital ethnographer, the profile is the gateway to accessing participants and the compelling data we seek. Beyond simply collecting the photos, categorical identifiers, and open-ended descriptions on users' profiles, we must use interviews to discuss the considerations that go into profile creation. From staging the perfect profile picture (e.g., considering lighting, angle, facial expression, body posture, clothing (or lack thereof), setting, background) to choosing (or avoiding) certain categorical identifiers, we should explore users' understanding of the function of the profile in their presence in GSNAs. One way in which this is (sometimes) achieved is by having a user take us through their profile and explain the thought process behind their profile decisions. This approach is similar to the guided tour method used by Manago (2013) and extends the user-centered walk-through method of apps research suggested by Light, Burgess, and Duguay (2016). In this way, we are able to distinguish, for example, between the user who does not fill out their profile because they are resisting identity categorization and the user who does not do so because they believe most other users will not read what they have written.

With these considerations in mind, researchers may use their own profiles (if they already have one) as a setting to document their interactions with other users. In this case, the researcher will likely have an established familiarity with the currency and valuations within that particular GSNA interface, and can leverage that knowledge to generate data. Another option is to recruit research assistants (RAs) who are already users of the GSNA(s) of interest, thereby relying on the same insider knowledge (and hopefully diversity of representation) in data gathering. It is worth acknowledging, however, that using personal profiles—the researcher's or the RAs'—has the potential to be problematic because of the profile's initial aim toward the personal goals of the researcher or RA (relationship, social, or sex) and not the ethnographic project. This goal incongruence may inhibit the researcher from connecting with users on a personal level (e.g., for sex or dating) or could lead to undesired contact and/or harassment from participants post-participation. At the same time, we employ queer theory to challenge the culturally constructed binary of personal/professional and suggest using personal profiles as a way to bring academia to the GSNA and vice versa (Levy & Johnson, 2011). If we further read the profile as marketing material, membership access, and specific representation of a multiple self, we can understand its power in the cultural representation and presentation of bodies and beings. Thus, the cultural power of the profile must necessarily interact with the inherent power relationships created by being researchers on GSNAs. A queering of digital ethnography must engage directly with these power relationships and immerse the researcher in their complexities.

Space and Place

For the purposes of this discussion, we adopt Massey's (1994) conceptualization of space as dynamic "social relations" (p. 3) inherently bound up with time and place as "the specificity of the mix of links and interconnections to [the] 'beyond'" (p. 6) that make up each articulation of the spatial. Users create space in GSNAs through their virtual presence and profile curation. Simultaneously, GSNAs create place by informing users of their (fluctuating) relative proximity to other users and their standing within the sexual field of the GSNA, based on who shows (or does not show) interest and/or who does (not) respond to their messages (Brubaker, Ananny, & Crawford, 2016; Green, 2014). Because the virtual space of GSNAs is organized by geographic proximity, that space is necessarily in flux (Kitchin & Dodge 2011). As people move through physical space, they change the virtual space around them just as that space is changed by others' movement around them (see Massey, 1994).

The spatial flux gives queer people the ability to construct and/or locate gay space anywhere they travel by simply logging in to their GSNA(s) (Mowlabocus, 2010, p. 202), as seen in our opening vignette. Even within traditionally gay spaces (e.g., gay bars), GSNAs change the space by layering the physical with the virtual and creating more complex social interactions (Brubaker et al., 2016). This is also true for non-sexual minority users, modifying the social dynamic of bars and meeting places by opening users up to more potential partners (Tyson, Perta, Haddadi, & Seto, 2016; Ward, 2017). The implications of this overlap involve a necessary rethinking of established theory around location and community in regard to identities, bodies, and sexualities (Roth, 2014).

Whereas it had previously been suggested that virtual connections present new opportunities for community formation (Earl & Kimport, 2011), with GSNAs, connection rarely implies community. Rather, connection tends to be transactional, more in line with consumerism (Linnes, Metcalf, & Shahijan, 2017; Mowlabocus, 2010), and aimed at quickly identifying and connecting with similar others (whether for social or sexual purposes). Over time, this connection—and, we would argue, mode of connecting—leads users to see themselves differently and to act differently (Chua, 2014). Digital ethnographies need to consider the long-term effect of virtual engagement in GSNAs on identity processes, both online and off.

A final consideration of space and place concerns researchers who already use GSNAs outside the ethnographic project. In contrast to researchers who engage with GSNAs only in the context of digital ethnography, researchers as pre-existing GSNA users engage with a space defined by pre-existing social relations. This pre-established spatial structure may grant researchers "insider status" and greater access to participant interactions, from chatting with other users to meeting up for social or sexual purposes. While documenting the erotic subjectivity of the researcher may be contentious, we align ourselves with Rooke (2009) in "bend[ing] the established orientation of … [digital ethnography's] method, ethics, and reflexive philosophical principles" (p. 149), requiring us to "[draw] attention to the erotics of knowledge production" (Rooke, 2009, p. 154).

For the researcher occupying GSNA space for research purposes only, their "outsider status" will be an obstacle to navigate. In this instance, the researcher is ethically compelled to be open and honest about their status within the GSNA and the purpose of their building and displaying a profile. Doing so may negatively affect participant recruitment, but it also protects the researcher against unwittingly exploiting participants through deception (cf. Benbunan-Fich, 2016). By allowing potential participants to choose whether or not they wish to engage with the researcher and/or the research project, researchers invest in a balance of power distribution between themselves and potential participants (Ceglowski, 2000).

Contextualization

The design of GSNAs is an important interactive context and limitation for the researcher, but also the user (Chun, 2006). The limitations (purposeful or subconscious) inherent in all programming designs have the potential to coercively shape interaction just as social norms shape social interaction (Chun, 2006; Connell, 2005). Accordingly, new digital ethnographies must recognize the ways in which interactions on GSNAs are limited by the available technology and developers' design decisions. As technology becomes increasingly complex and advanced, the implications of interacting via GSNAs also change. Woo (2015) hints at this when he contrasts the basic design of Grindr profiles with Jack'd and SCRUFF, both of which provide more room for elaboration in their user profiles, thereby allowing users to develop a greater sense of whom they are interacting with.

In studying digital space/culture, one must consider the unique features of the medium and their implications for users. For example, SCRUFF's landing page presents four 4 × 4 grids of user profiles, including two which feature profiles that have received the most endorsements from other users, as measured through the number of "woofs" received.[5] These profiles are largely homogeneous: mostly White, very muscular, shirtless, and "scruffy" (i.e., have body hair and/or beards).

On the other hand, Tinder has no landing page of this nature and offers no in-app articulation of who receives the most likes or swipes right. In this interface, the user is presented with a series of unique potential matches and is simultaneously entered into the queue as a potential match for others in their area. Two of Tinder's original designers, Sean Rad and Justin Mateen, had the following to say when interviewed about their design choices:

> We always saw Tinder, the interface, as a game," … "Nobody joins Tinder because they're looking for something," Rad said. "They join because they want to have fun. It doesn't even matter if you match because swiping is so fun. (Stampler, 2014)

Because Tinder's creators deliberately treated Tinder as a game, it is of little surprise that users often lament the sense of dehumanization it gives them (e.g., Bailey, 2015; Whitley, 2017). From the app-as-game perspective,

[5] In SCRUFF, users are able to send each other "woofs" as a way of expressing attraction and desire.

one might conclude the user was bound to be dissatisfied because they were using an app designed as a game to look for a romantic partner. But as Woo (2015) argues, it's not an issue of the app; it's an issue of the user using the app to accomplish something the app was not designed to do.

Interrogating design context also creates an opportunity to discuss the limitations of self-expression based on app design. To get at these limitations, one could ask users what feature(s) they wish were available in the GSNA(s) they use. For users who use multiple GSNAs, it may be interesting to explore whether they pursue different goals or user types on the different apps or perceive them as conducive to varying kinds of interaction. In some of our initial research, users report using multiple GSNAs as a way of casting their net wider but favoring one over the others. Often, this preference is tied to a perceived advantage, whether user type, available interactions, or other design features particular to one GSNA.

Temporality

One of the difficulties in studying GSNAs is the speed with which new versions and updates are released, not to mention the frequent releases of altogether new apps. As certain GSNAs gain popularity, others pop up in response to perceived shortcomings in the user experience, social dynamics of the app interface (see the example of Bumble in response to Tinder; (Shontell, 2015)), or accessibility to sexually marginalized groups or subgroups (see the example of the emergence of SCRUFF in response to Grindr (Roth, 2014)). Users may also migrate between apps when seeking out different kinds of interactions (e.g., using Grindr to find hookups and Tinder to seek relationships) or may leave the GSNA landscape altogether. These migrations may be ongoing and may occur during the period of study, and it is important for new digital ethnographies to be aware of these markers of time, context, and user engagement.

When conducting a digital ethnography on GSNAs, it is necessary to document the updates and changes in each new version of the GSNA that is released throughout the study. This may include small changes to the visual characteristics of the app, changes to the app interface, the addition of new features to the app, or major changes that alter the app and target market significantly (e.g., the addition of same-sex matching or varied gender options on Tinder). These changes to the apps that users are already using may promote different kinds of usage and may change the nature of observations and participant data while the project is underway. It is also important, where possible, to document the emergence of new, niche apps that develop in response to perceived shortcomings in industry leaders. Although increasingly difficult with the plethora of GSNAs coming online (a simple Google Play Store search for "dating, gps" yields dozens of results), this practice may provide valuable data about the state of industry, user desires, and technological development that may inform study analysis and findings.

Conclusion

In this chapter, we have provided the theoretical underpinnings for queering digital ethnography using a set of reflections on its application to studying GSNAs. Our purpose for doing so is twofold: the first is that we have yet to come across an ethnographic methodology that can adequately look into the quickly changing world of apps and their users. The two comprise an evolving co-dependence that relies partly on the capitalist nature of social interaction today and on the integration of technology into all aspects of life (e.g., the quantifiable self (Walker, 2014); mobile and wearable infrastructures (Whitson, 2014); the search for sex/romance (Race, 2015)). This technological infiltration invariably changes our everyday lives, and the way we engage in work and leisure pursuits. In an attempt to adequately represent these dilemmas, we propose a digital ethnography for GSNAs that is open, reflexive, malleable, and that employs both feminist and queer theoretical perspectives in its application.

Second, as researchers engaging in digital environments, and particularly GSNAs, we must remain reflexive about our appreciation and analysis of the varied aspects of our research spaces. The GSNA researcher must remain conscious of the false digital-real divide; with the increasingly integrated technological landscape, lives, jobs, and leisure activities can no longer be divided between the "real" and the "virtual". Instead, they must be considered as existing within a hybridized space.

In documenting these hybrid spaces, we must keep several considerations in mind. First, we must remain conscious of the power structures that shape the design, sales, use, and turnover of mobile apps. We need to investigate how these power structures broker what is valued and how these curated spaces normalize narrow understandings of gender, sexual relations, and attractiveness. Especially in user profiles, these understandings mimic and build upon the "traditional" power relationships both queer and feminist theorists have been critiquing for some time. Second, we must also remember that the offline and online romantic and leisure lives of GSNA users are blurred and intertwined, and that these hybrid spaces and corresponding places are unique to each user and in constant flux. Finally, we must remember that the digital spaces we investigate are locked into contextual and temporal frames that are particular to the apps, versions, users, and technologies available at the specific moment in time that we document them but are also connected to the "beyond" of the moment (Massey, 1994).

We hope that this chapter provides theoretical grounding and guide-posts for those who seek to build their own ethnographies of digital spaces and that through this work and the work of those who will follow, we will be able to generate a better picture of the lived experiences of those who are meeting, connecting, dating, and/or having sex through GSNAs.

References

Ahmed, S. (2006). *Queer phenomenology: Orientation, objects, others*. London: Duke University Press.

Bailey, A. (2015, August 11). I became an ice-cold Tinder assassin. *Elle*. Retrieved from http://www.elle.com

Barlett, C. P. (2015). Anonymously hurting others online: The effect of anonymity on cyberbullying frequency. *Psychology of Popular Media Culture, 4*, 70–79. https://doi.org/10.1037/a0034335.

Barlett, C. P., Gentile, D. A., & Chew, C. (2016). Predicting cyberbullying from anonymity. *Psychology of Popular Media Culture, 5*, 171–180. https://doi.org/10.1037/ppm0000055.

Benbunan-Fich, R. (2016). The ethics of online research with unsuspecting users: From A/B testing to C/D experimentation. *Research Ethics*, 1–12. https://doi.org/10.1177/1747016116680664.

Blackwell, C., Birnholtz, J., & Abbott, C. (2015). Seeing and being seen: Co-situation and impression formation using Grindr, a location-aware gay dating app. *New Media & Society, 17*, 1117–1136. https://doi.org/10.1177/1461444814521595.

Boellstorff, T. (2016). For whom the ontology tolls: Theorizing the digital real. *Current Anthropology, 57*, 387–407. https://doi.org/10.1086/687362.

Brown, G., Maycock, B., & Burns, S. (2005). Your picture is your bait: Use and meaning of cyberspace among gay men. *Journal of Sex Research, 42*(1), 63–73.

Brubaker, J. R., Ananny, M., & Crawford, K. (2016). Departing glances: A sociotechnical account of 'leaving' Grindr. *New Media & Society, 18*, 373–390. https://doi.org/10.1177/1461444814542311.

Ceglowski, D. (2000). Research as relationship. *Qualitative Inquiry, 6*, 88–103. https://doi.org/10.1177/107780040000600106.

Chua, L. J. (2014). *Mobilizing gay Singapore: Rights and resistance in an authoritarian state*. Philadelphia: Temple University Press.

Chun, W. H. K. (2006). *Control and freedom: Power and paranoia in the age of fiber optics*. Cambridge, MA: MIT Press.

Connell, R. W. (2005). Change among the gatekeepers: Men, masculinities, and gender equality in the global arena. *Signs, 30*, 1801–1825. https://doi.org/10.1086/427525.

Coupland, J. (1996). Dating advertisement: Discourses of the commodified self. *Discourse & Society, 7*, 187–287. https://doi.org/10.1177/0957926596007002003.

Daniels, J. (2009). Rethinking cyberfeminism(s): Race, gender, and embodiment. *Women's Studies Quarterly, 37*, 101–124. Stable URL: http://www.jstor.org/stable/27655141.

Earl, J., & Kimport, K. (2011). *Digitally enabled social change: Activism in the internet age*. Cambridge, MA: MIT Press.

Feeld Ltd. (2017). Feeld – Dating for couples and single. *iTunes Preview*. Retrieved from https://itunes.apple.com

Green, A. I. (2014). The sexual fields framework. In A. I. Green (Ed.), *Sexual fields: Toward a sociology of collective sexual life* (pp. 25–56). Chicago: The University of Chicago Press.

Grindr. (n.d-a). About. *Grindr*. Retrieved from https://www.grindr.com

Grindr. (n.d-b). Advertise with Grindr. *Grindr*. Retrieved from https://www.grindr.com

Gross, L. (2007). Foreword. In K. O'Riordan & D. J. Phillips (Eds.), *Queer online: Media, technology, & sexuality* (pp. vii–vix). New York: Peter Lang Publishing, Inc.

Gudelunas, D. (2012). There's an app for that: The uses and gratifications of online social networks for gay men. *Sexuality and Culture, 16*, 347–365. https://doi.org/10.1007/s12119-012-9127-4.

Horne, P., & Lewis, R. (1997). Visual culture. In A. Medhurst & S. Munt (Eds.), *Lesbian and gay studies: A critical introduction* (pp. 99–112). London: Cassell.

Johnson, C. W., & Cousineau, L. S. (2018). Manning up and manning on: Masculinities, hegemonic masculinity, and leisure studies. In D. C. Parry (Ed.), *Feminisms in leisure studies: Advancing a fourth wave* (pp. 126–148). New York: Routledge.

Keeling, K. (2014). Queer OS. *Cinema Journal, 53*(2), 152–157.

Kincaid, J. (2009, Mar 25). Gay dating makes its way to the iPhone. *TechCrunch*. Retrieved from https://techcrunch.com

Kitchin, R., & Dodge, M. (2011). *Code/Space: Software and everyday life*. Cambridge, MA: MIT Press.

Kollock, P., & Smith, M. A. (1999). *Communities in cyberspace*. In M. A. Smith & P. Kollock (Eds.), *Communities in cyberspace* (pp. 3–26). New York: Routledge.

Kozinets, R. V. (2010). *Netnography: Doing ethnographic research online*. London: SAGE Publications.

Law, J., & Singleton, V. (2000). Performing technology's stories: On social constructivism, performance, and performativity. *Technology and Culture, 41*, 765–775. https://doi.org/10.1353/tech.2000.0167.

Levy, D. L., & Johnson, C. W. (2011). What does the Q mean? Including queer voices in qualitative research. *Qualitative Social Work, 11*, 130–140. https://doi.org/10.1177/1473325011400485.

Light, B., Burgess, J., & Duguay, S. (2016). The walkthrough method: An approach to the study of apps. *New Media & Society*, 1–20. https://doi.org/10.1177/1461444816675438.

Linnes, C., Metcalf, B. R., & Shahijan, M. K. (2017). The future of apps: A smart investment for business. In S. Rezaei (Ed.), *Apps management and e-commerce transactions in real-time* (pp. 293–313). Hershey, PA: IGI Global.

Lupton, D. (2015). Quantified sex: A critical analysis of sexual and reproductive self-tracking using apps. *Culture, Health & Sexuality, 17*(4), 440–453.

Maher, F., & Tetreault, M. K. (2001). *The feminist classroom*. Lanham, MD: Rowman & Littlefield.

Manago, A. M. (2013). Negotiating a sexy masculinity on social networking sites. *Feminism & Psychology, 23*, 478–497. https://doi.org/10.1177/0959353513487549.

Manovich, L. (2006). The poetics of augmented space. *Visual Communication, 5*, 219–240. https://doi.org/10.1177/1470357206065527.

Massey, D. (1994). *Space, place, and gender*. Minneapolis, MN: University of Minnesota Press.

Matney, L. (2015, September 16). Oscar Meyer releases Sizzl, a dating app for bacon lovers. *TechCrunch*. Retrieved from https://techcrunch.com

Merleau-Ponty, M. (2002). *Phenomenology of perception*. (C. Smith, Trans.). London: Routledge.

Mishna, F., McLuckie, A., & Saini, M. (2009). Real-world dangers in an online reality: A qualitative study examining online relationships and cyber abuse. *Social Work Research, 33*, 107–118. https://doi.org/10.1093/swr/33.2.107.

Mowlabocus, S. (2010). *Gaydar culture: Gay men, technology and embodiment*. London: Routledge.

Nayar, P. K. (2010). *An introduction to new media and cybercultures*. Malden, MA: Wiley-Blackwell.

nobullying.com. (2016). The real effects of cyber bullying. *NOBullying.com*. Retrieved from https://nobullying.com

O'Reilly, K. (2012). *Ethnographic methods* (2nd ed.). New York: Routledge.

Omernick, E., & Sood, S. O. (2013). *The impact of anonymity in online communities*. In Proceedings of the ASE/IEEE International Conference on Social Computing. Retrieved from http://labfs.eecs.northwestern.edu

Paasonen, S. (2011). Revisiting cyberfeminism. *Communications, 36*, 335–352. https://doi.org/10.1515/COMM.2011.017.

Parks, L. (2015). 'Stuff you can kick': Toward a theory of media infrastructures. In P. Svensson & D. Goldberg (Eds.), *Between humanities and the digital* (pp. 355–373). Cambridge, MA: MIT Press.

Pavlidis, A., & Fullagar, S. (2013). Narrating the multiplicity of 'derby grrrl': Exploring intersectionality and the dynamics of affect in roller derby. *Leisure Sciences, 35*(5), 422–437.

Perry Street Software, Inc. (n.d.). SCRUFF. *SCRUFF*. Retrieved from https://www.scruff.com

Pink, S., Horst, H., Postill, J., Hjorth, L., Lewis, T., & Tacchi, J. (2016). *Digital ethnography: Principles and practice*. London: SAGE Publications.

Race, K. (2015). Speculative pragmatism and intimate arrangements: Online hook-up devices in gay life. *Culture, Health & Sexuality, 17*, 496–511. https://doi.org/10.1080/13691058.2014.930181.

Rheingold, H. (1993). *The virtual community: Finding connection in a computerized world*. Boston, MA: Addison Wesley.

Rheingold, H. (2000). *The virtual community: Homesteading on the electronic frontier*. Cambridge, MA: MIT Press.

Riebel, J., Jaeger, R. S., & Fischer, U. C. (2009). Cyberbullying in Germany: An exploration of prevalence, overlapping with real life bullying and coping strategies. *Psychology Science Quarterly, 51*, 298–314. Retrieved from https://doaj.org.

Rodat, S. (2014). Cyberqueer: Major topics and issues in current research. *Revista Româna de Sociologie, 25*, 429–442. Retrieved from http://revista.acadsudest.ro/pdf-uri/nr.5-6-2014/03-SimonaR.pdf.

Rooke, A. (2009). Queer in the field: On emotions, temporality, and performativity in ethnography. *Journal of Lesbian Studies, 13*, 149–160. https://doi.org/10.1080/10894160802695338.

Roth, Y. (2014). Locating the "Scruff guy": Theorizing body and spaces in gay geosocial media. *International Journal of Communication, 8*, 2113–2133. Retrieved from http://ijoc.org.

Shade, L. R. (2013). Gender and digital policy: From global information infrastructure to internet governance. In C. Carter, L. Steiner, & L. McLaughlin (Eds.), *The Routledge companion to media & gender* (pp. 222–232). New York: Routledge.

Shontell, A. (2015, January 27). What it's like to found a $750 million startup, go through a sexual-harassment lawsuit, and start all over by age 25. *Business Insider*. Retrieved from http://www.businessinsider.com

Stampler, L. (2014, February 06). Inside Tinder: Meet the guys who turned dating into an addiction. *Time*. Retrieved from http://time.com

Star, S. L. (1999). The ethnography of infrastructure. *American Behavioral Scientist, 43*, 377–391. https://doi.org/10.1177/00027649921955326.

Sweatt Inc. (2017). Sweatt – A dating app for the fitness community. *iTunes Preview*. Retrieved from https://itunes.apple.com

Tepper, F. (2017, January 3). Here's who fared best on dating apps in 2016. *TechCrunch*. Retrieved from https://techcrunch.com

Tikkanen, R., & Ross, M. (2004). Looking for sexual compatibility: Experiences among Swedish men in visiting internet gay chat rooms. *CyberPsychology and Behavior, 3*, 605–616. https://doi.org/10.1089/109493100420205.

Tinder Blog. (2016, November 15). Introducing more genders on Tinder. *Tinder Blog.* Retrieved from http://blog.gotinder.com

Tinder Inc. (2017). Tinder. *iTunes Preview.* Retrieved from https://itunes.apple.com

Turkle, S. (1996). Virtuality and its discontents searching for community in cyberspace. In J. Turow & A. L. Kavanaugh (Eds.), *The wired homestead: An MIT press sourcebook on the internet and the family* (pp. 385–402). Cambridge, MA: MIT Press.

Tyson, G., Perta, V. C., Haddadi, H., & Seto, M. C. (2016). A first look at user activity on Tinder. *2016 IEEE/ACM International Conference on Advances in Social Networks Analysis and Mining (ASONAM)* (pp. 461–466). San Francisco, USA. https://doi.org/10.1109/ASONAM.2016.7752275

Valocchi, S. (2005). Not yet queer enough: The lessons of queer theory for the sociology of gender and sexuality. *Gender and Society, 19*, 750–770. Stable URL: http://www.jstor.org/stable/27640849.

Wakeford, N. (2000). Cyberqueer. In D. Bell & B. M. Kennedy (Eds.), *The cybercultures reader* (pp. 403–415). London: Routledge.

Walker, J. R. (2014). *How we use selfies, blogs and wearable devices to see and shape ourselves.* New York: Palgrave Macmillan.

Ward, J. (2017). What are you doing on Tinder? Impression management on a matchmaking mobile app. *Information, Communication & Society, 20*, 1644–1659. https://doi.org/10.1080/1369118X.2016.1252412.

ward, k. j. (1999). The cyber-ethnographic (re)construction of two feminist online communities. *Sociological Research Online, 4.* Retrieved from http://www.socresonline.org.uk/4/1/ward.html

Whitley, R. (2017, January 5). What is the link between Tinder and mental health?. *Huffpost: The Blog.* Retrieved from http://www.huffingtonpost.ca

Whitson, J. R. (2014). Foucault's fitbit: Governance and gamification. In S. P. Walz & S. Deterding (Eds.), *Gameful world: Approaches, issues, applications* (pp. 339–358). Cambridge, MA: MIT Press.

Woo, J. (2015). Grindr: Part of a complete breakfast. *QED: A Journal in GLBTQ Worldmaking, 2*, 61–72 Retrieved from https://muse.jhu.edu/article/575376.

Section III

Dilemmas at the Intersection of Gender, Gender Identity, and Digitality

Writing Recovery from Depression Through a Creative Research Assemblage: Mindshackles, Digital Mental Health, and a Feminist Politics of Self-Care

Simone Fullagar and Iesha Small

Introduction

Mindshackles volunteers are gay, straight and people who don't want to be labelled. We are entrepreneurs, unemployed and nine to fivers. One thing unites us, we have all had significant problems with our mental health during at least one point of our lives, or we care for somebody else who has, and we have made it through the other side. Some of us continue to experience ongoing mental health problems but each time we find a way to get out of bed and live another day. The majority of Mindshackles volunteers are people with a deep passion for something or someone and that aids our recovery. We want to tell our stories as part of our own journey to self-acceptance and ongoing recovery and to help others (and their loved

S. Fullagar (✉)
Department for Health, University of Bath, Bath, UK
e-mail: S.P.Fullagar@bath.ac.uk

I. Small
Mindshackles, Hertfordshire, UK

D. C. Parry et al. (eds.), *Digital Dilemmas*,
https://doi.org/10.1007/978-3-319-95300-7_6

ones) understand that they are not alone. Many of us have used our participation in the project to start conversations with our own families and friends about mental health. (Mindshackles, Volunteers[1]).

Trisha: 'When I come off the dancefloor I think, "'That was a good night, oooh I danced my socks off!" *laughs* I've cleared my mind, whatever problems I had before it doesn't seem to really bother me, once I've come off. I have to say, my mind's blank, I don't think of anything. A lot of the music's from Brazil, Columbia, Italian, Portuguese, it's a different language but music is universal. You don't have to be able to understand exactly what they are saying to be able to dance to the music. I'm just on that dance floor and that's that. I'm just listening to the music thinking, "Oooh that's a lovely record," *laughs* "Oooh I like that record. Let's find somebody to dance with"'. (Trisha: Rhythm of joy, Mindshackles)

Trisha's story on the Mindshackles website provides us with a unique point of departure for exploring how both leisure and digital practices can creatively transform public understanding about mental (ill) health and the possibilities of recovery. Our chapter is written through an academic-arts collaboration, or 'creative research assemblage' (Fox & Alldred, 2016; Fox, 2015), to explore the dilemmas surrounding cultural representations of women's experiences of recovery from depression. We focus our discussion on the Mindshackles[2] website that was developed by Iesha, to offer 'personal stories about reclaiming life from mental ill health'. As a documentary photographer (and teacher, parent, youth advocate), Iesha created the site in 2013 as a means of using digital technology to share the experiences and voices of different people to publicly counter the stigmatisation surrounding mental health issues. The Mindshackles site and its associated Twitter handle offer an alternative, creative approach that seeks to capture and evoke everyday moments significant in the ongoing experience of recovery for different women (and also some men). It was Mindshackles' focus on everyday leisure practices in people's recovery that began our conversations and connected our creative, personal, political, and academic interests. In our dialogue, we

[1] http://www.mindshackles.co.uk/volunteers/

[2] http://www.mindshackles.co.uk/

identified connections that emerged in our own distinct research and creative practices around different notions of recovery. Later in the chapter, we take up these threads of conversation as a means to collaboratively write through some of the digital dilemmas in producing creative-activist-academic knowledge. We focus largely on one personal story and photograph—Trisha: rhythm of joy—from the Mindshackles site as an evocative example for our discussion.

In writing this chapter, we drew inspiration from the traditions of creative analytic practice (Sjollema & Yuen, 2017; Berbary, 2015; Parry & Johnson, 2007; Richardson, 2000), arts-based methods (Boydell et al., 2016), post-humanism (Fox, 2012, 2015; Duff & Sumartojo, 2017), and post-qualitative inquiry (St. Pierre, 2014) to show how creative-activist-academic collaborations can generate different ways of 'doing' both digital and gendered mental health. Simone approached the Mindshackles project with a feminist interest in the possibilities of creatively articulating a politics of self-care that invites different ways of engaging with personal stories as political and affective sites of social change (on the politics of self-care, see Fullagar, 2008b). Critical insights from feminist theories of embodiment, affect theory, and digital assemblages provide a way of exploring the micropolitics of leisure and well-being and troubling normalised biomedical perspectives on mental illness/health as an individualised issue. Iesha was interested in alternative representations of mental health, where mental ill-health status was known and accepted but not actually the focus of the digital representations. The project gave the volunteers an opportunity to present a version of themselves beyond their mental health status that focused on experiences that provided them joy.

Creativity, Leisure, and Recovery: Digital Mental Health Practices

We draw upon Fox (2012, 2015) and Duff and Sumartojo's (2017) notion of a creativity-assemblage to conceptualise Mindshackles as a digital project of cultural activism. We employ different representational practices to unsettle the binaries of real/representation, fact/fiction, digital/analogue, labour/leisure, and mind/body. In this way, we position the writing-reading of digital sites as practices of 'cultural making' (Swist, Hodge, & Collin, 2016) that generate creative and critical forms of entanglement; as we write or read, we are also written through creativity as an embodied flow of affective meaning. Writing is not simply a rational, objective practice of producing knowledge that presumes to 'represent' a world that pre-exists it. Moving beyond a representational logic, writing-reading are understood as material practices through which a range of affects act upon us, as we write to affect others (pleasure, joy, sadness, anger, shame, etc.). In contrast to notions of creativity that privilege cognition, individual genius, or only specialised artistic practice, Fox (2015) argues more broadly that creativity is a profoundly affective aspect of everyday relations and embodied capacities that involve both human and non-human elements.

As a site for digital mental health promotion, Mindshackles produces an approach to recovery that emphasises the experience of creating-becoming that is oriented around diverse pleasures and leisure practices (as distinct from 'expert' biomedical definitions of symptoms, diagnoses, or treatment protocols). 'Readers/users' are engaged through affective and sensory relations that materialise through text and images. We can *feel* drawn to individual stories, compelled or repelled by certain images that move us (pleasurably, shamefully, empathically) as we connect, disconnect, react, or shun the everyday emotional lives of others that are grouped collectively (but not bound by diagnostic illness categories) around 'recovery' as a process of becoming. Digital re-presentations are thus read through the body, evoking memory, senses, and diverse affects that can produce new capacities, relations, and hence forms of agency. As Fox (2012, p. 499) states, 'Affects are "becomings" (Deleuze & Guattari, 1988: 256) that represent a change of state of an entity and its capacities: this change may be physical, psychological, emotional, or social'.

The experience of contemporary subjectivity and common mental health issues is profoundly shaped by diverse assemblages that produce meaning across physical and digital space-time. The sense-making process of understanding distress is often mediated by digital practices, such as, searching Google in waiting rooms, Instagram images on the bus, writing-reading blogs on chemical imbalances, or lifestyle balance and engaging with various platforms for sharing stories of recovery. As Fox (2012, p. 500) argues these ways of coming to know one's own emotional state in terms of 'depression' are produced through, 'the affective flows associated with biomedicine territorialise those involved in a health-care consultation, transforming a sick person into a patient, the professional into a healer and signs and symptoms into a disease …'. Many digital mental health interactions are heavily shaped by biomedical forms of expertise and recovery from symptoms rather than opening up capacities for creativity and different affective responses (pleasure, anger, joy, belonging, love, etc). This is not to deny the affective power of 'diagnoses' to produce relief for some, a sense of legitimacy for others, and access to services that are highly regulated (and in some cases profitable) by the State and market forces. However, the affective relations of diagnostic cultures are most often bound up with 'compliance' with professional expertise, rather than creative capacities to reconfigure boundaries of knowing and being.

Rather than position the humanist subject at the centre of creative processes, assemblage thinking understands creativity as *relational*, emerging through human and non-human encounters and affects. Duff and Sumartojo (2017, p. 419) theorise the creative assemblage as productive of capacities—'a more or less temporary mixture of heterogeneous material, affective and semiotic forces, within which particular capacities for creativity emerge, alongside the creative practices these capacities express'. In this way, we can think about how the affective relations of creativity are mediated through 'inextricable intertwinings of humans and their data' in broader digital assemblages (mobile and wearable devices, social media sharing, algorithms and data harvesting) (Lupton 2017, p. 3). It is this creative potential of digital practices to re-present and reconfigure the materiality of meaning about depression and recovery that we seek out as a means of generating a range of affective capacities in public culture.

Feminist explorations of women's mental health have also identified how creativity embodied through different leisure practices contribute to the conditions of possibility as one recovers from depression (Lafrance, 2011; Parry, 2013; Fullagar, forthcoming, 2008a, 2008b). Drawing upon different theorisations of power (e.g., constraints, ideology, discursive, and affective relations), these feminist approaches have examined the gendered conditions of possibility that enable women to move beyond the debilitating effects of depression (on the relationship between masculinity, digital mental health, and play see Chap. 7 by Swist and Collin in this collection). In Simone's analysis of digital mental health sites, gender was often ignored and women's experiences essentialised in representations of depression (Fullagar, 2008a). In relation to experiences of recovery, leisure figured as an everyday site through which women negotiated their sense of entitlement, creativity, and practices of self-care beyond a heteronormative masculinity that would assume the 'giveness or naturalness' of the right to free time, space, and freedom. She wrote:

> For many women recovery was linked to a sense of creativity, which they articulated as finding a voice and space for themselves. This creative sense of self manifested in pursuits such as journal writing, poetry, storytelling, writing letters to newspapers or friends, art classes or art at home, appreciating the beauty of nature, and performing in community theatre or the local circus group. (Fullagar, 2008b, p. 46)

While women's creativity was regulated and constrained, leisure practices also worked as 'counter-depressants' embodying particular transformative affects, and effects, in relation to destabilising gender norms (Fullagar, 2008b, p. 37). Feminist research understands the relation between creativity and recovery to be not just personal but also produced through the sociocultural, economic, and political contexts of advanced liberal, capitalist, and patriarchal societies as these forces act through our emotional lives, capacities, and opportunities for leisure.

Moving the interpretivist focus of this earlier work into the more feminist-oriented and posthumanist direction of this chapter, we return to assemblage thinking to offer a way of understanding how digital entanglements bring into relation human *and* non-human elements, objects and medical, work, leisure, home, and self-care practices (see also Fullagar, forthcoming; Berbary, 2015; Kumm & Johnson, 2017). As feminists have long argued, women's work and leisure lives, bodies, and emotions are entangled in biopolitical formations, patriarchal practices, and global flows (Lafrance, 2011; Ussher, 2011; Fullagar, 2008a, 2008b; Teghtsoonian, 2009; Stoppard 2000). These entanglements include a diverse assortment of human and non-human, individual, corporate, and state agencies. For example, the marketing practices of Big Pharma interact with the prescribing and diagnostic practices of doctors and individualised self-help discourses in popular and social media. Mental health promotion and treatment practices largely ignore, and hence discount, gender relations and other social conditions that undermine emotional, financial, and personal well-being.

If gender appears in discourses of mental health and illness, it is often reified as a biological or identity category across a rapidly expanding range of 'digital solutions' that seek to address gendered mental health problems such as depression and anxiety (more women are diagnosed than men) (McManus, Bebbington, Jenkins, & Brugha, 2016). In the UK, to alleviate growing pressure and cost in the national health system, digital technologies are positioned as a key response to the demand for psychological therapies and medication (anti-depressants are not advertised and must be prescribed by general practitioners and/or psychiatrists (McManus et al., 2016). We are witnessing the growth of various digital practices and platforms that aim to educate and improve self-care and social support. For example, mental health promotion websites and digital apps promote the 'five ways to well-being', circulate anti-stigma messages, encourage self-diagnosis through quizzes, and urge self-management of mood and behaviour via gamified therapies (Mood Gym) (see Fullagar, Rich, & Francombe-Webb, 2017; Rich & Miah, 2017).

While they may involve play-like forms of engagement (see Swist and Collin's chapter [Chap. 7] in this collection), there is a distinct lack of critical content or context when it comes to making visible the micropolitics of personal distress, especially as they are connected with inequalities related to gender, class, sexuality, ethnicity, and so on. The creative imagination of digital mental health promotion and pedagogy is highly normalised and shaped by biomedical notions of personhood where illness is a problem residing within the 'self'. In response, we argue that an understanding how creative leisure and digital representations are assembled across various practices and spheres of life can work to make the *gendered* relations of affect more visible as forces that regulate subjectivity *and* open up other possibilities of becoming (see Duff, 2014; Braidotti 2013; Keller 2015; Fullagar, 2017; McLeod 2017). As one digital practice of cultural activism, Mindshackles creates a public space where everyday 'lay' accounts circulate personal stories as different kinds of knowledge beyond the normalised focus of 'expert' accounts that focus on things like brain dysfunction, medication, cognitive behavioural therapy, and individualised prescriptions for healthy living.

In the following section, we present one particular narrative and photograph that is featured on the Mindshackles website as it articulates recovery through a visceral sense of affective relations and 'aliveness' (Fullagar & O'Brien, 2012). Trisha, who identifies as a Black British woman of Afro-Caribbean descent, is in her 50s. For us, the account evokes an experience of recovery that is sustained through pleasurable rhythms of dance, music, and friendship, entangled with issues about stigma and the invisibility of depression, as well as the stress of work and divorce. We present the narrative in its entirety with a subsequent conversational dialogue through which we explore questions about creative-academic-activist processes of digitally re-presenting women's experiences.

Trisha: Rhythm of joy

Whatever problems I had before don't seem to bother me.
I'm just on the dancefloor and that's that.

Fig. 1 Woman with Fan. (Photo: Iesha Small)

When I'm on the dance floor, the mind might feel tired but the bones don't, so I find that it's a stress release for me. It's a form of expression as well and the dancing replaces going to the gym. Financially, it's not expensive so you can go on a regular basis and I've met so many different people from all walks of life. Some who have experienced divorce, going through the change of life, and the age range is between 30s and 70s. I met a guy in his 70s and he's been dancing for years. Unfortunately, he lost his wife some years back. They used to dance together and he continued dancing. So the dancing knows no barriers. It's important for me, I quite enjoy it really.

You don't have to have a partner to go with [because in classes] they tend to mix you around from one person to the other, so you will get to dance with someone, they make sure you go around in a circle when you do La Reda. It's good for the figure and it's good for the mind, so what's happening is you are getting benefits for the whole body and you're meeting people at the same time. People from all different cultures and walks of life. Well, I have a really good friend, Karen, she was there more than 10 years ago, dancing, and she was on her own. I met her and we became really close friends.

I've always been dancing. I used to go once a month when the children were growing up, or once every two months. It's a bit difficult when you're working full time and [have] growing children but when the they started to get older... it wasn't just that... when I started to have difficulties in my first marriage I started to get back into it. I realised the benefits certainly helped me through my divorce. You can get dressed up as well and it's a feel-good factor. I started to go and I thought, 'Hang on a minute, this is something I enjoy and I don't need to have anybody to go with.' So that's when I started going every week. I think probably about 15 years ago. I don't drink or smoke [so] I save my money for dancing. *Laughter*.

At one point I was going of three of four times a week but now I'm a bit tired and I'm doing more studies again. I changed my profession some years ago and, after 30 years of being in the office, I now work with people with disabilities, so now I've gone to long hours and shift work. I definitely go about once a week.

At the moment I'm learning kizomba, not zumba, which is like African tango it's a lovely dance, very sensual, very beautiful. It reminds me a little bit of soca [a music and dance style from the Caribbean]. If you watch the dancing, there's an art to it. If a guy's really good he can make you look absolutely fantastic, professional. At the moment, everywhere I go now, they don't just do the salsa, they do the kizomba. It's very popular, especially with the men, because it's a slow dance and they are completely in the lead. With salsa the lady has a 5 minute window where she can shine but with kizomba you are totally reliant on the guy so he's in charge and I think a lot of the men like that! *laughter*.

Hubby goes sometimes as well but I tend to go with my girlfriends. I've met so many people and we just text each other. In the week I tend to go on my own because we have different commitments, it's difficult to get everybody together at the same time. I usually come home, get dressed, get showered and then go out dancing.

People found it very difficult to believe that I could get quite low because I'm such a happy person all the time. I would say be mindful of people around us. Sometimes when you see people putting a brave face on there's a lot going on, those are the people you have to watch because they never cry out until it's too late. Nobody is immune to depression, it can come at any time in your life and also any age. I'm at a good place in my life at the moment but, quite frankly, I'm one of the lucky ones. I have children, I have a husband, I've been married before, I've got a roof over my head. I thank God every day.

A Conversation About Digital Cultural Making

Simone: I really like how you have composed this piece as there is such a sense of movement and embodied pleasure. It evokes that sense of vitality or aliveness that Trisha embodies. You echo what Ahmed (2004) wrote about how, 'Pleasures open bodies to worlds through an opening up of the body to others…spaces are claimed through enjoyment' (p. 164). So, how did this come to be a preoccupation in your desire to create different ways of understanding recovery?

Iesha: Leisure and pleasure were actually central to the Mindshackles project when I conceived it. Art and a regular photography practice really helped me to overcome a very difficult time in my life. I wondered what hobbies or enjoyable practices other people used to help them through times of depression.

So photography was a way of seeing those intangible aspects of our recovery experiences that are important to feeling alive.

Simone: You capture the complexity of individual stories through particular shared moments that don't feel 'confessional'. And the photographs reverberate with your quite poetic rendering of your participants' words. What process do you go through to create stories and evoke a sense of aliveness?

Iesha: I was inspired to create the multiple narrative site for Mindshackles by a documentary series called 'Small Town Inertia' that was created by a photographer, Jim Mortram, whom I met initially via social media. The process has evolved over time as I have become more skilled as a photographer and storyteller through collaborating with my volunteer participants.

Simone: Was this about learning to listen, as well as see differently?

Iesha: Well at the very beginning of Mindshackles (or Into the Light as it was then) I saw myself as a photographer and it was visually driven. Now I consider it narrative based and use a combination of whatever media best works to tell my volunteer's story. For my first interviews I asked volunteers what depression (and other key words) meant to them. They did brain storms or mindmaps for me in my notebook which I intended to use on the website.

Then, just by chance, I decided to record a brief conversation that I had with one of my early volunteers, Gwen, about her mindmap. It was just on my iphone because that's what I had with me. When I was writing a few days later, I listened to our impromptu interview and found Gwen's own words really powerful. Rather than paraphrase, I wanted those actual words to write through me. That was how the style for Mindshackles was born – all posts are edited versions of participants' actual words from a conversational style interview, with nothing obvious from me apart from occasional [square brackets] for clarity or to anonymise something.

Simone: So how did you engage people in the process of telling their stories?

Iesha: The first interviews explored fairly loose questions and I'd just turn up to a venue they had chosen (the interview and photograph locations are always the volunteer's choice) only knowing what their leisure pursuit was and that they had suffered from depression (or similar) at some point. I'd then record the evolving conversation but later, I arranged 'pre interviews' where we'd have a freeform (unrecorded) discussion over the

phone before I came to visit. I would then offer my thoughts on an interesting angle to explore while volunteers also suggested ideas for photographs, or a particular location.
It became much more co-constructed. They felt more at ease with me and how they would be represented. We would spend anywhere from 1–3 hours and it was often at their own homes. After the interview I take photographs, as I've found people are much more relaxed then and it makes for a more pleasant experience for them and well as better photographs. Listening and responding was more important to me than sticking to a script.
For Trisha's post I went with her to her dance night at a Kizomba club in South West London, and took photographs while she danced and socialised. I also learnt some dance moves and got involved myself.

Simone: Having danced your way into this sense of the 'aliveness', how then do you write it up?

Iesha: I transcribe the interview recording then I edit it by hand from a paper print out to capture the essence of the volunteer. I rearrange sections for a more coherent narrative flow (on paper conversations aren't always linear or easy to follow). I may cut out repetition, or tangential lines of thought and edit out stories about other people. I've cut parts that refer to family members, for example, as I don't feel I have permission to tell those stories. All volunteers have consented and signed media release forms. I don't add anything to the narrative that wasn't said at the time.
After the narrative is complete, I select the most complimentary photographs that I feel will portray the person in a way they will feel happy with. I also select strong sections of the interview to include as audio in the posts as I want readers to hear the volunteers actually speak. I often have my long-time collaborator MC Small Mercies construct a custom piece of music that is inspired by their photographs and voice.
I send a link to the volunteer once the post is complete and they are able to comment on it. I remove anything they don't

want, but I can only remember this happening twice. One volunteer asked for a particular picture she thought was triggering to be removed. Another volunteer once asked me to anonymise a place.

Simone: If we accept that each step (interviews, telling and re-telling stories and taking/selecting photographs) produces a particular version of the person's experience, how do you find people deal with the issue of stigma and sharing their story publicly?

Iesha: I try my best to introduce elements of co-construction and participant control at various points. We only proceed to the next stage if they are happy with the process. We talk about possible approaches to the photography and interview topic together. I've found that when people are happy to say yes to Mindshackles it is often a time in their personal journey when they are ready to be more open about their mental health history or present.

Several of my volunteers have used their Mindshakles posts as an opportunity to 'come out' to their personal networks about their mental health via sharing on Facebook or equivalent. Much to my surprise, all of my volunteers so far have chosen to use their real names.

Simone: Going back to Trisha, it is not often we read about the recovery stories of older, Black women where there is a focus on the public pleasures of dance – embodied movement, socialising, music, creativity, etc. There is also a lot that remains unspoken in public discourses about mental health concerning the intersectional experiences of racism, sexism, classism, heterosexism, nationalism etc. that shape depression and recovery.

So, given that we are both women and queer, but from quite different cultural backgrounds, I'm interested in how your thinking and practice is evolving with respect to ways of articulating the personal-political context of recovery beyond representations of women as overly 'heroic' individuals or only 'victims' of oppression?

Iesha: Sadly, recovery stories and media or artistic representation about Black people and especially Black women are told by people who are observing their experience, but will never live it in its fullness. I am a woman and I am Black. I also happen to be queer. Neither of these were at the forefront of my mind when I first started Mindshackles. Over time I just contacted people who I had access to in my personal, professional and extended network. As a Black, queer woman these networks are probably more diverse than the average white male photographer or documentarian.

I also feel that, as a Black woman, the totality of the Black female experience is not exotic, alien or unusual to me. I don't need to project an idea of Black womanhood pre-conceived in ignorance. Sure, I see people being strong and heroic, but I also see them laughing, sometimes crying. I see them cooking, I see them living their day to day lives and having fun. I see women who have the structures of society against them, but I don't automatically see them as victims. Mindshackles is about re-presenting people beyond their mental health label. And I suppose that in doing that I'm re-presenting people beyond their gender, racial or sexuality stereotypes without explicitly setting out to do so.

Simone: This queer perspective resonates through our creative collaboration to unsettle the fixity of mental health and other identities. I'm drawn to how Mindshackles site creates a digital space for individuals to connect in multiple ways through the personal stories, images and possibilities for recovering-becoming. As you say these posts are also performative in particular ways as 'coming out' stories. They provide a digital archive of everyday practices (dancing, cooking, sport, art) that is important for sustaining a liveable life, as Judith Bulter says (2014). The site evokes a sense of aliveness that cannot be predefined or normalised, but emerges against stigma and shaming practices that 'stick' to mental health issues (and marginalised identities) that Sara Ahmed writes about (2004, 2017).

Complexity of Personal Narratives for Digital Publics

The question of how mental health issues are culturally imagined, felt, and represented becomes increasingly important for challenging the individualisation of responsibility for prevention and recovery. In relation to the digital assemblage of recovery stories, Mindshackles invites a different kind of *affective* engagement that differs from the pedagogical intention of many mental health sites to improve literacy (Fullagar et al., 2017). Yet, the sharing of personal stories via digital media is not simply a 'better' alternative for learning about recovery. As Grey (2017) has argued, many personal representations of people with lived experiences of mental ill health in public campaigns participate in a process of 'benevolent othering' that negatively stereotypes and obscures the social context. In this sense, *all digital stories* are performative (and have political affects), in that they render experiences and the context that shapes them visible or invisible in particular ways. For example, personal stories situated within biomedically oriented professional websites (such as, Jon's story on recovery, Rethink Mental Illness[3]) offer quite different 'readings' of recovery than personal stories shared through crowdsourced sites that offer a wide range of 'unedited' experiences (such as, A Day in the Life[4]). Jon's story of 'patient experiences' articulates a clinical view of normative recovery in terms of compliance with treatment protocols (therapy, medication, and self-care). In contrast, the Day in the Life site opens up diverse recovery practices that trouble the dominance of biomedical explanations (the negative affect of treatment is also visible) (see also, Rose, 2017).

As Swist et al. (2016) have argued, *cultural making* through digital practices can contribute to diversifying and challenging individual, organisational, policy, and pedagogic conversations. Simply trying to increase mental health literacy and help seeking to comply with medical and therapeutic discourses fails to understand the entanglement of the political and personal in the production of 'public feelings' through categories of depression, anxiety, and so on (Cvetkovich, 2012). Mindshackles

[3] https://www.rethink.org/living-with-mental-illness/recovery/recovery/recovery-aids
[4] https://dayinthelifemh.org.uk/

offers a creative rendering of individual experiences as documented stories and images to evoke different ways of engaging with mental health issues through leisure practices (involving sensory bodies, objects, spaces, etc. through cooking, sport, dancing, etc.). As a creative digital platform, it opens up questions about experiences of emotional distress and well-being beyond the dominant logic of our diagnostic (and gender neutralising) culture (Fullagar & O'Brien, 2014; Healy, 1998). The site simultaneously produces multiple stories and a collective re-presentation of recovery that is not overtly connected to an affirmation or rejection of identity politics surrounding mental health and illness (patients, service users, survivors, or mad movements), nor those of feminist, Black, queer, crip, or other identity politics (on the tensions of experiential authority see, Voronka, 2016).

This is not to say that Mindshackles is apolitical rather the points of connection are more diffuse, arising through affects, identifications, and practices that can open up multiple possibilities for change. One of the challenges arising from our conversations is how to retain the openness of identification when public accounts of recovery from mental health are often articulated as 'coming out' stories that have a range of affects and effects on identity formation (Ridge & Ziebland, 2012). There is an ongoing dilemma here about how we make visible the digital traces that forge connections across the politics of mental health, feminist, Black, queer, and related spaces.

While the narratives are personalised accounts, they also speak to the micropolitics of women's emotional lives that regulate how experiences can be voiced that may otherwise remain unheard. The value of joy and pleasure in the everyday practices of self-care in women's recovery is a unique feature of the stories and images on Mindshackles. In relation to Trisha's story, the pleasures of dance are positioned as significant in her practices of self-care. In this way, she articulates a sense of entitlement to leisure, her own friendship networks, and an embodied time-space that resists gendered, racialised, and heternormative notions of womanhood as defined primarily through care for others/self-sacrifice. Yet, notions of self-care are far from simply being 'activities' rather through the enactment of leisure practices women negotiate the contradictions of gendered embodiment. Trisha's account of dance echoes Sara Ahmed's (2017,

p. 248) reflections in *Living a Feminist Life*, where she says; 'A dancing feminist body, a dancing lesbian body, dancing black and brown bodies; the affirming of how we inhabit bodies through how we are with others ... Dance can be how we embrace the fragility of being thrown'.

Kisner has recently argued (2017) that the hashtag #selfcare rose to popularity in America during 2016 through representations of individualised practices (from face masks to creating 'me' time) of empowered (white, middle-class, heteronormative) femininity that intertwined digital media with expanding markets. Self-care has also been reclaimed by Black Feminists at different historical moments to politicise everyday strategies of making visible oppressive conditions and alternatives. For example, the oft-cited statement by Black lesbian feminist Audre Lorde from her book *A Burst of Light* (1988): 'Caring for myself is not self-indulgence, it is self-preservation, and that is an act of political warfare' (cited in Ahmed, 2014).

Ahmed (2014) exposes the social privilege that is assumed in notions of self-care and instead takes up Lorde's (1988) insistence that care for the self is political and a matter of survival for those who have not been afforded value because of race, gender, sexuality, and class. In her powerful essay Self-care as Warfare,[5] Ahmed (2014) says,

> in queer, feminist and anti-racist work self-care is about the creation of community, fragile communities[6], assembled out of the experiences of being shattered. We reassemble ourselves through the ordinary, everyday and often painstaking work of looking after ourselves; looking after each other. This is why when we have to insist, I matter, we matter, we are transforming what matters.

Mindshackles' exploration opens up different ways of engaging with the politics of self-care that brings into view embodied moments, voices, and images of everyday experiences that are produced through human and non-human assemblages that can sustain or undo well-being.

---

[5] https://feministkilljoys.com/2014/08/25/selfcare-as-warfare/

[6] https://feministkilljoys.com/2014/06/14/fragility/

Concluding Remarks

Exploring the digital practices and cultural making of Mindshackles has been a focal point for writing through this creative-academic assemblage. Our collaborative approach has sought to identify the challenges of creating public stories and images of recovery from depression to hold open spaces through which to reimagine women's lives. Theorising creativity as an assemblage provides a useful way of situating stories of recovery that make visible leisure practices within the growing area of digitalised mental health promotion and intervention. Through Trisha's account, we see the embodiment of dance as a spatial, (Black) historical and cultural practice that figures as a significant affective 'infrastructure of care' sustaining emotional life (Butler, 2014). Against the pervasiveness of medicalised, individualised, and pathologised histories that are entangled in the whiteness of mental health and recovery services, Mindshackles offers a site of digital 'cultural making' (Swist et al., 2016) where the intensities of 'feeling alive' are forged through text, image, and sound; memories, objects, spaces, bodies, and technologies entangle to create other possibilities for living. These citizen-led public spaces importantly diversify the digital mental health landscape by re-presenting experiences beyond biochemical deficits or neoliberal prescriptions for 'happiness', and thus move beyond the limitations of a medicalised imagination.

References

Ahmed, S. (2004). *The cultural politics of emotion*. Edinburgh, Scotland: Edinburgh University Press.

Ahmed, S. (2014). Self-care as warfare. Retrieved from https://feministkilljoys.com/2014/08/25/selfcare-as-warfare/. Accessed 28 July 2017.

Ahmed, S. (2017). *Living a feminist life*. Durham, NC: Duke University Press.

Berbary, L. A. (2015). Creative analytic practices: Attachments, uses and constructions within humanist qualitative leisure research. *International Leisure Review*, (2), 27–55. https://doi.org/10.6298/ILR.2015.4.11.

Boydell, K. M., Hodgins, M., Gladstone, B. M., Stasiulis, E., Belliveau, G., Cheu, H., et al. (2016). Arts-based health research and academic legitimacy:

Transcending hegemonic conventions. *Qualitative Research*. https://doi.org/10.1177/1468794116630040.

Braidotti, R. (2013). *The posthuman*. Cambridge: Polity Press.

Butler, J. (2014). Rethinking Vulnerability and Resistance. In Plenary Conference at the XV Simposio de la Asociación Internacional de Filósofas (IAPh), Universidad de Alcalá (Madrid), 24th June (pp. 1–19). Retrieved from http://www.institutofranklin.net/sites/default/files/files/Rethinking Vulnerability and Resistance Judith Butler.pdf.

Cvetkovich, A. (2012). *Depression: A public feeling*. Durham, NC: Duke University Press.

Duff, C. (2014). *Assemblages of health: Deleuze's empiricism and the ethology of life*. Rotterdam, The Netherlands: Springer.

Duff, C., & Sumartojo, S. (2017). Assemblages of creativity: Material practices in the creative economy. *Organization, 24*(3), 418–432.

Fox, N. (2015). Creativity, anti-humanism and the "new sociology of art". *Journal of Sociology, 51*(3), 522–536.

Fox, N., & Alldred, P. (2016). *Sociology and the new materialism*. London: Sage.

Fox, N. J. (2012). Creativity and health: An anti-humanist reflection. *Health (London, England: 1997), 17*(5), 495–511. https://doi.org/10.1177/1363459312464074

Fullagar, S. (2008a). Sites of somatic subjectivity: E-scaped mental health promotion and the biopolitics of depression. *Social Theory & Health, 6*(4), 323–341.

Fullagar, S. (2008b). Leisure practices as counter-depressants. *Leisure Sciences, 30*(1), 1–18.

Fullagar, S. (2017). Post-qualitative inquiry and the new materialist turn: Implications for sport, health and physical culture research. *Qualitative Research in Sport, Exercise and Health, 9*(2), 247–257.

Fullagar, S. (forthcoming). Diffracting mind-body relations: Feminist materialism and the entanglement of physical culture in women's recovery from depression. In J. Newman, H. Thorpe, & D. Andrews (Eds.), *Moving body: Sporting ecologies, assemblages, and new materialisms* (pp. 1–37). New Brunswick, CA: Rutgers University Press.

Fullagar, S., & O'Brien, W. (2012). Immobility, battles, and the journey of feeling alive: Women's metaphors of self-transformation through depression and recovery. *Qualitative Health Research, 22*(8), 1063–1072.

Fullagar, S., & O'Brien, W. (2014). Social recovery and the move beyond deficit models of depression: A feminist analysis of mid-life women's self-care practices. *Social Science and Medicine, 117*, 116–124.

Fullagar, S., Rich, E., & Francombe-Webb, J. (2017). New kinds of (ab)normal?: Public pedagogies, affect and youth mental health in the digital age. *Social Sciences, 6*(3), 99. https://doi.org/10.3390/socsci6030099.

Grey, F. (2017). Benevolent othering: Speaking positively about mental health service users., *Philosophy. Psychiatry, & Psychology, 23*(3), 241–251.

Healy, D. (1998). *The anti-depressant era*. Cambridge: Harvard University Press.

Keller, J. (2015). *Girls' feminist blogging in a postfeminist age*. London: Routledge.

Kisner, J. (2017). The politics of conspicuous displays of self-care. *The New Yorker*. Retrieved from http://www.newyorker.com/culture/culture-desk/the-politics-of-selfcare

Kumm, B., & Johnson, C. (2017). Subversive imagination: Smoothing space for leisure, identity, and politics. In K. Spracklen, B. Lashua, E. Sharpe, & S. Swain (Eds.), *The Palgrave handbook of leisure theory* (pp. 891–910). London: Palgrave.

Lafrance, M. N. (2011). Reproducing, resisting and transcending discourses of femininity: A discourse analysis of women's accounts of leisure. *Qualitative Research in Sport, Exercise and Health, 3*(1), 80–98.

Lorde, A. (1988). *A burst of light: Essays*. Ithaca, NY: Firebrand Books.

Lupton, D. (2017). Feeling your data: Touch and making sense of personal digital data. *New Media & Society, 19*(10), 1599–1614.

McLeod, K. (2017). *Wellbeing machine: How health emerges from the assemblages of everyday life*. Durham, NC: Carolina Academic Press.

McManus, S., Bebbington, P., Jenkins, R., & Brugha, T. (Eds.). (2016). *Mental health and wellbeing in England: Adult psychiatric morbidity survey 2014*. Leeds, UK: NHS Digital.

Parry, D. C. (2013). Women's mental health and the power of leisure. In V. Freysinger, S. M. Shaw, K. A. Henderson, & D. Bialeschki (Eds.), *Leisure, women and gender* (pp. 215–228). Urbana, IL: Venture Publishing Inc.

Parry, D. C., & Johnson, C. W. (2007). Contextualizing leisure research to encompass complexity in lived leisure experience: The need for creative analytic practice. *Leisure Sciences, 29*(2), 119–130.

Rich, E., & Miah, A. (2017). Mobile, wearable and ingestible health technologies: Towards a critical research agenda. *Health Sociology Review, 26*(1), 84–97.

Richardson, L. (2000). New writing practices in qualitative research. *Sociology of Sport Journal, 17*(1), 5–20.

Ridge, D., & Ziebland, S. (2012). Understanding depression through a "coming out" framework. *Sociology of Health & Illness, 34*(5), 730–745.

Rose, D. (2017). Service user/survivor-led research in mental health: Epistemological possibilities. *Disability & Society, 32*(6), 1–17. https://doi.org/10.1080/09687599.2017.1320270.

Sjollema, S., & Yuen, F. (2017). Evocative words and ethical crafting: Poetic representation in leisure research. *Leisure Sciences, 39*(2), 109–125.

St. Pierre, E. A. (2014). A brief and personal history of post qualitative research: Toward "post inquiry.". *Journal of Curriculum Theorizing, 30*(2), 2–19.

Stoppard, J. (2000). *Understanding depression: Feminist social constructionist approaches*. London: Routledge.

Swist, T., Hodge, B., & Collin, P. (2016). "Cultural making": How complexity and power relations are modulated in transdisciplinary research. *Continuum, 30*(4), 489–501.

Teghtsoonian, K. (2009). Depression and mental health in neoliberal times: A critical analysis of policy and discourse. *Social Science and Medicine, 69*(1), 28–35.

Ussher, J. (2011). *The madness of women: Myth and experience*. London: Routledge.

Voronka, J. (2016). The politics of 'people with lived experience': Experiential authority and the risks of strategic essentialism. *Philosophy, Psychiatry, & Psychology, 23*(3), 189–201.

Playing with Zombie Problems: Exploring the Gender-Digital-Play Assemblage in Online Mental Health Campaigns

Teresa Swist and Philippa Collin

Introduction

In countries like the USA, UK, and Australia, online campaigns aim to leverage the interactivity and anonymity of the Internet to address perceived barriers to men's help-seeking, such as lack of awareness, stigma, and fear (O'Brien, Hunt, & Hart, 2005, Ellis et al., 2012). However, there has been little critique of the kinds of gender positions made available in these campaigns or the role that digital cultures play in assembling gendered accounts of mental health. For example, in 2013, the Australian not-for-profit organisation beyondblue licensed and adapted the Man Therapy campaign (https://mantherapy.org/). Originally developed in the USA through a partnership between the Colorado Office of Suicide Prevention, the Carson J Spencer Foundation, and Cactus Marketing and Communications, the campaign aims to engage with 'working-age' men, deliver mental health information, and raise awareness of options

T. Swist (✉) • P. Collin
Institute for Culture and Society, Western Sydney University, Sydney, NSW, Australia
e-mail: T.Swist@westernsydney.edu.au; P.Collin@westernsydney.edu.au

D. C. Parry et al. (eds.), *Digital Dilemmas*,
https://doi.org/10.1007/978-3-319-95300-7_7

for help and support. Using 'dark humour', accessible language, and a safe, anonymous, online environment, the campaign seeks to bridge the gap between men in distress and the services that can help them. Similarly, the UK Campaign Against Living Miserably (CALM) (https://www.thecalmzone.net) was established to provide men with support and to challenge norms of masculinity which are seen as the primary barriers to men's help-seeking. Like Man Therapy, CALM is a government-initiated public health campaign which has grown through strong grassroots support and building a large volunteer base. Community-led campaigns have also emerged, such as Soften the Fck Up (http://softenthefckup.spurprojects.org/)—created by young men in Australia: speaking directly to their peers and challenging common language and discourse that guys should 'man up' or 'toughen up' when faced with a challenge. Using video and other visual messaging around key steps to take action, the campaign targets the perceived cultural norm that men don't talk about their feelings and which is seen as the key barriers to help-seeking for problems and reaching out to others to prevent suicide. The growing array of campaigns in this space draws attention to the need for opening up more critical and nuanced conversations around such representations. Such an approach can help query the many assumptions and gendered stereotypes which infiltrate our everyday lives.

In different ways, these campaigns illustrate two concerns of this chapter. The first is that, while genuine in their efforts to challenge problematic social and cultural constructions of masculinity, such campaigns perpetuate stereotypes of men's help-seeking by relying on generalisations about men and masculinity. They do this by smoothing over differences among men, as well as across social and cultural contexts and situations. Furthermore, such campaigns do not question gendered constructions of mental health per se but, rather, reinforce them. For example, "[t]he goal of Man Therapy is to show working age men that talking about their problems, getting help and fixing themselves is masculine" (Spencer-Thomas, Hindman, & Conrad, 2012, p. 5). Without disputing the importance of the mental health and well-being of men, we argue that these online campaigns reinscribe particular ways of performing gender and mental health through the digital and may have limited impact on efforts to address the drivers of poor mental health or suicide in the long term.

Our second concern is in the way online campaigns reproduce particular understandings of youthful digital culture which then become implicated in these gendered constructions of help-seeking. It is increasingly common for creators of online campaigns to draw on generalisations about youth digital practices in campaign design (e.g., 'boys love Youtube'; girls like talk-based activities). However, this misses the opportunity to understand how the messier entanglement of young people's play, pastimes, and pedagogy in the digital age informs the ways gender is performed, generally, and specifically in relation to mental health. We, therefore, explore the indivisibility of identity, technology, and leisure in the context of online campaigns aimed at fostering help-seeking, with a particular focus on the "gendering of the body" (Butler, 1988). Digital culture offers new challenges and opportunities for identity work. The increasingly mobile and personal digital devices used to search for information, communicate with others, explore and share content via social media platforms, and track and review movements and bodies produce data—what Lupton (2016) has called precisely 'lively data'. Lupton (2016) argues that, now more than ever, we must examine how "these data are generated and managed, the impact they have on people's lives and concepts of selfhood and embodiment" (p. 711). Moreover, this focus upon the sociotechnical vitality of our corporeal acts—including learning—is useful for understanding how digital practices are "disrupting traditional binaries between work/leisure, production/consumption, material/digital and human/non-human" (Silk, Millington, Rich, & Bush, 2016, p. 713) with implications for public health initiatives such as online campaigns. This is particularly important as play and learning move increasingly from 'traditional', 'inherited', or 'formal' modes towards informal and mediated practices and pedagogy (LEGO Learning Institute, 2003; Fullagar, Rich, & Francombe-Webb, 2017). To move beyond instrumental ideas and applications of youth digital practices via strategies such as 'gamification' (Johnson et al., 2016), we will explore how the notion of 'play' offers a productive way to show how pastimes, gender, and pedagogy can emerge and unfold via the digital in relation to mental health.

The chapter is an interdisciplinary exploration, drawing upon gender theory (Butler, 1988), Science and Technology Studies (STS) literature

(Akrich & Latour, 1992), theories of play (Eberle, 2014), and qualitative research conducted in the co-design of an Australian online campaign aimed to promote help-seeking, particularly by young men (see Spears et al., 2016; Collin & Swist, 2016). As members of the interdisciplinary research and design team, we conducted workshops, online discussions, and paired interviews with 133 young people (103 males and 30 females) aged 12–18 to inform an online campaign. We were also participants in the co-creation of the campaign through interpreting and advocating young people's perspectives, debating with team members from different disciplines and industries. In this way, we were both inside and outside the research in a form of 'cultural making' (Swist, Hodge, & Collin, 2016)—as researchers and active participants in a complex process. The resultant campaign—*Something Haunting You?*—was zombie-themed and web-based: using interactive videos and comics to encourage young people to engage with the idea that they can tackle everyday problems such as exam stress, the pressure to pass a driving test, or problematic drinking (see: https://www.zuni.com.au/yawcrc/somethinghauntingyou/).

To frame our exploration, we draw upon the notion of 'assemblage' (Deleuze & Guattari, 1987) to help disrupt binary or dualistic thinking in relation to identity, technology, and leisure. Assemblage theory recognises the interwoven, dynamic arrangements which are part of our emergent practices, or becoming, thereby opening up an experimental ethos and line of inquiry (Buchanan, 2014). From this perspective, the first section explores how gender and help-seeking can be reframed and the role campaigns can play. We explore how young people's gender, their pastimes, and informal pedagogies are entangled and unfolding as the "body becomes its gender through a series of acts which are renewed, revised, and consolidated through time" (Butler, 1988, p. 523). Then, working with ideas from the STS literature, such as 'in-scription' and 'de-scription' (Akrich & Latour, 1992), we trace how the 'performativity' (Butler, 1988) of gender takes place through digital technologies and cultures. In the third section, we suggest that digital culture is a new 'playground' in which young people's gender is cited in both restrictive and transformative ways. Drawing from Eberle's (2014) elements of play, we consider how online campaigns might enable more multidirectional and productive insights into how gender is performed as the ludic—or play—

always exceeds the spatial and temporal boundaries of prescribed gender norms and pastimes. In accord with an assemblage theory approach, we conclude with a discussion of the ways online campaigns might avoid unidirectional and reductive approaches to gender norms and behaviour change.

Reframing Gender and Young Men's Help-Seeking

> I think it's a lot more complex and drawn out than 'I need help'. (14 year-old-male, Western Sydney; paired interview)

Campaigns that target young men's help-seeking face a 'catch-22'. By focusing on stereotypes of how young men are (tough, afraid to ask for help, overly independent) and asserting how they should be (open about their feelings, receptive to support), campaigns reproduce a form of 'hegemonic masculinity' (Farrimond, 2011). This is the privileging of dominant characteristics generally accepted in patriarchal societies:

> This 'code' is a set of ideals and practices, such as being competitive, aggressive, emotionally contained, self-reliant and heterosexual ... Being 'naturally' 'strong', not prone to disease or illness, unconcerned with pain or minor health problems and self-reliance is typically masculine. (Farrimond, 2011, p. 210)

This dilemma is played out in the campaigns mentioned above which are directed at, and sometimes led by, young men precisely because in their efforts to challenge norms of masculinity, these campaigns also rehearse them. Judith Butler (1993) has argued that gender is not fixed; rather, it is a "reiteration of norms" (p. 10) which are enacted—or performed—always through negotiation and always with the possibility of acquiescence and resistance. This idea of 'performativity' (Butler, 1988) captures the idea that "gender is in no way a stable identity or locus of agency from which various acts proceed; rather, it is an identity tenuously constituted in time – an identity instituted through a stylized repetition of acts" (p. 519).

Campaigns, thus, perform gender dynamics in complex ways, reproducing while attempting to contest the kinds of binaries identified by Farrimond, such as 'Neanderthal Man' or the 'Action Man' (Farrimond, 2011, p. 16). Usefully, in studying help-seeking, health, and illness of higher socio-economic status men, Farrimond found that the 'interpretive repertoires' through which masculine identities were negotiated varied according to who was present, the type of illness, and the identity demands of the situation (Farrimond, 2011, p. 2). As argued by Connell and Messerschmidt (2005), masculine identities also "compromise formations between contradictory desires or emotions, or the results of uncertain calculations about the costs and benefits of different gender strategies" (p. 852). However, campaigns typically overly reduce this complexity. The question this poses for public health officials, researchers, and digital creatives is how can campaigns recognise and reflect the breadth of 'interpretive repertoires' as the basis for engagement with young men around the idea of help-seeking. Their creative challenge is how to depart from the 'hegemonic script'—the gendered construction of mental health and help-seeking itself—in order to engage broadly with the 'dynamics of masculinities' (Connell & Messerschmidt, 2005).

To create *Something Haunting You?*, we used a participatory design approach (Hagen et al., 2012) to explore how young people experienced everyday and common challenges. Rather than focusing on the deficits assumed to prevent help-seeking—especially among males—the aim was to uncover the settings, temporalities, knowledge, and networks through which young people navigate life problems. In workshops, online discussions, and paired interviews, young men identified a wide range of dynamics associated with help-seeking. In contrast with oversimplified explanations, young men described different issues (situated or generalised), past experiences of help-seeking, quantity (a single problem or cluster), the setting (where the challenge manifest materially as well as their broader life context), and timing of problems as well as knowledge of help options and the relevance and quality of resources available as influential in different combinations. They pointed to a wide variety of possible needs, settings, and choices and, as the quote at the top of this section indicates, many felt that help-seeking was a complicated and highly fluid thing.

When discussing these dimensions, young men identified a range of barriers to help-seeking, including recognising the problem and linking it to getting help; trying to fit in with perceived social norms and peer groups; community pressures and traditions; and prevailing misconceptions about mental health (Spears et al., 2016). At times, the discussions raised perceived differences between boys and girls. For example, a 15-year-old from Western Sydney who participated in a co-design workshop shared her perception that society stereotypes males as 'macho', or needing to protect a certain type of reputation "society stereotypes them", and "if they do have a problem they don't want to seek help because they don't want it to affect their reputation". Such discussions emphasised the power of the 'reiteration of norms' as young people draw on their everyday understanding of help-seeking. To address this, while young men were the primary audience, the focus of the messaging of *Something Haunting You?* was deliberately more subtle, more suggestive—dealing with 'zombie problems' rather than problems of 'gender'. Like other successful, strength-based initiatives, such as Reachout.com, the campaign attempted to foreground diversity and normalise problems and seeking help for all young people in a way that was appealing to young men but not overtly naming them as the target audience.

A key feature of the resultant campaign was the zombie theme. In workshops, young people identified 'the problem of problems' as a key issue campaigns could address—as opposed to a deficit in a person (or gender norm). Young people liked the idea of giving everyday problems a physical manifestation that could be 'tackled'. The zombie trope was adopted in large part because of its popularity and resonance with young people who saw it as 'cool', darkly humorous, and versatile. Young people also 'got' the idea that zombies, like problems, can follow you around. Indeed, zombies have been used in other public health initiatives targeting infection control, mental health, and ethics of disease (Nasirudin, Halabi, Dao, Chen, & Brown, 2013, p. 813). In *Something Haunting You?*, the zombie could also be understood as a reference to the 'problem' of young men's help-seeking itself. However, rather than rehearsing gender stereotypes that prevent young men from expressing their feelings or asking for help, the campaign used this cultural trope to connect with young men's imagination and inquisitiveness. The zombie is the 'in-scription' by which the campaign could appeal to potential beneficiaries via anticipation of what might follow—without reciting gender.

In-scriptions and De-scriptions of Digital Practices

> I think you should be aware that young people have diverse patterns of help-seeking. Some are more proactive, others are less likely to seek help due to fear of being stigmatized. I think it's good to be aware of that and see how you can reach these different "segments" of young people to reach as many of us as possible. (23-year-old female: Youth Brains Trust online discussion, May 2014)

Some online campaigns have targeted problematic behaviours common among young men using elements of the approach described above. For example, Dumb Ways to Die (DWTD) was a Victorian Government online public service announcement to promote rail safety. Using a catchy tune and a gory cartoon, the online campaign was a global advertising and marketing triumph with more than 150 million views on YouTube spawning a website, branded soft toys, and pencil cases, and online games.[1] Similarly, the NZ Legend campaign targeted drunk driving (particularly among young men). The campaign used youth culture references, culturally relevant humour, and video/YouTube execution to encourage men to stop a mate from driving while drunk. Like DWTD, Legend has also been lauded as a massive success—six years on from the original release, it has had a number of additional executions and the YouTube video has been watched nearly two million times. While these campaigns have effectively engaged with their target audiences, they have done so via a single issue and call to action (be safe near train lines; stop a mate from drink driving), and they treat the digital as an instrument: as a media channel for delivering the message, a type of instrumental pedagogy. However, as digital devices, practices, and cultures are imbricated in everyday life, media practices of 'prosumption' (Bruns, 2016) reach across

[1] YouTube views recorded 28/07/17

all aspects of the self and the social (Lupton, 2016; Silk, Millington, Rich, & Bush, 2016). This means we increasingly experience complex phenomena (such as peer expectations) through the digital, where online and offline settings always intermingle.

Akrich and Latour (1992) utilise the "semiotics of human and non-human assemblies" to highlight how diverse people and expertise 'write' particular norms and 'user representations' into a technology and how these develop over time. While norms are powerful, their 'signs' can be translated in different ways by the user; this involves 'de-inscription', or what Akrich calls 'de-scription': "they either underwrite it or try to extract themselves out of it or adjust the behaviour or setting through some negotiations" (Akrich, 1992, p. 261). From this perspective, gender norms are 'in-scribed' and 'de-scribed'—reproduced and transformed—through digital devices and digital cultures. Anthropologist Tim Ingold (2011) extends this thinking beyond simple additions (in-scriptions) or subtractions (de-scriptions). He argues that beings actually move through life in a more open-ended 'meshwork' and "discovery of trails", in contrast to the routes associated with specific locations and predetermined routes (Ingold, 2011, p. 47). The former recognises the complex, unfolding dimensions of lived experience, whereas the latter erases these aspects by assuming norms and imposing prescribed paths. We propose that this concept of wayfaring offers an alternative to the behaviour-change models that currently underpin many online campaigns. Wayfaring recognises the complex forms of being, sensory and affective knowing, and pathways of learning and transformation through and of the digital. This is in contrast to assumptions of a linear, transmission route of knowing which seek to separate the personal from the social and technical.

In the research for *Something Haunting You?*, young people described a complex interrelationship between online and offline places, communication, and resources for seeking help. As with many social interactions, they described informal practices embedded in their digital everyday as well as online tools that helped them reflect, communicate, and identify possible actions to address everyday challenges. For example, searching for content on particular issues via YouTube or sending a Snapchat or an SMS to a friend sharing how they're feeling were common ways these young people responded to problems. These common examples illustrate how the digital inscribes how young people experience problems and help-seeking. Beyond a "channel for delivering a message", it can act as a scaffold across which young people relate, share information, or contact people or organisations which can assist in addressing an issue. The mix of formal and informal and more or less 'mediated' places young people seek help included youth centres and services, online help forums, sporting and other interest clubs, Facebook, Twitter, Google, Yahoo answers, Bing, the police, group therapy, advocacy services, beyondblue, Kids Helpline, Crisis Helpline, Lifeline, eheadspace, and instant messaging. For many, schools played a very prominent role in their lives as sources of information and advice and shaped how they approached many problems.

Participants described a variety of peers and older people from whom they seek help. Intergenerational relations and communication formed an important part of the cultural context of their help-seeking. Friends were a primary source of help owing to a perception that they are supportive, accessible, and trustworthy. One 15-year-old female participant from the paired interviews described how: "[friends] give you support emotionally in many ways … they can share their worries with you"—emphasising that context and relationships can be significant along with access to information, support, and services. However, participants also identified a range of other supportive people including family, friends, counsellors, trusted adults, mutual friends, grandparents, and psychologists. Choices regarding who to seek help from depended upon levels of trust, accessibility, confidentiality, perceived ability to offer expertise, and the particular issue of concern. A 14-year-old male from the paired interviews noted the value of storytelling and hearing about other people's experiences: "Even [online] forums, – looking up other people's experiences of similar events. Seeing what other people have done and how they get through it, getting advice from people". This reflected evidence that (counter to other research and popular discourse) young men are often at ease seeking and providing help online (Ellis et al., 2012). Rather than work against this complexity, *Something Haunting You?* aimed to work with it to enable young people's 'wayfaring'. The resultant online campaign used a multi-modal online delivery (video, social media, text, graphical content) to encourage young people to explore and try out different ways of relating to problems and identify what sort of 'help-source' would suit them. Each comic and video scenario invited the viewer to choose "What will you do next? … Do something, or Give in to the problem zombie?" to encourage young people to experiment and play with their own ideas and feelings. The many entry points (via YouTube, placed advertising, and 'advertorial' in youth culture websites) and use of relatable content such as comics all sought to capitalise on the ways in which young people feel and relate to people, places, and issues in mediated ways (Chau, 2010; Schack 2014, p. 17). Similarly, the campaign recommended a vast range of resources and responses ranging from individual (self-help apps) to social (connecting with other online communities or campaigns).

In contrast with the strategy of 'gamification' to enhance message delivery and nudge behaviour change through a linear relationship between the campaign and the 'outcome', *Something Haunting You?* inscribed a form of wayfaring. This offered avenues of exploration and a more diverse array of choices and opportunities to begin to address particular issues. For example, young people advised that 'problems' are not experienced outside the broader ebb and flow of well-being. They experienced issues in relation to broader physical, psychological, and social contexts rather than as isolated issues or incidents. This suggests more thoughtful, longer-term tactics are required, rather than simply quick-fix solutions. For example, some young people described individualised strategies, such as learning techniques for overcoming anxiety and stress: "They can learn relaxation, meditation techniques" (15-year-old female, Western Sydney, paired interview). This illustrated the need to not just focus upon the linearity of 'fixing' something (which may then quickly arise again) but to also explore how diverse strategies can support sustained practices that foster the well-being of young people.

Similarly, though the video and graphic content of the campaign featured male protagonists, the campaign used gender-neutral language and sought to resonate with young men through the tone, style, and content. *Something Haunting You?* was a deliberate effort to acknowledge a broad range of 'interpretive repertoires' and 'inscribe' diversity in the digital delivery through the range of words, images, and possible actions (watch, share). At the same time, it sought to offer a number of choices and opportunities: 'de-scription' through the use of alternative storylines; options to 'do something' and 'do nothing'; as well as share particular pieces of content (or not) via social platforms.

Online Campaigns as Play

> If I was going through any of these issues, I would basically go to my friends first because I trust them and I see them nearly every day. (14-year-old male, Western Sydney; paired interview, April 2014)

Young people 'trust' and 'see' their friends nearly every day, not just in the schoolyard, but in the new digital playgrounds of Facebook, Snapchat, and Instagram. These 'platform playgrounds' constitute new, interconnected places in which young people play, participate, and learn, both formally and informally, with peers, family members, adults, and in view of other audiences. They involve new "architectures of participation in digital play" that emerge from a heterogeneous range of networks which require specific consideration in research (Harvey, 2011, p. 316). A focus on play—and building on the previous section of young people's wayfaring in the digital age—seeks to open up richer avenues for online campaign development: recognising the diversity of 'wayfaring' (Ingold, 2011) trails. We propose that recognising the intermingling of these trails, alongside more regulated, gendered routes, can open up new avenues for resistance and change. Platform playgrounds, we argue, are the digitised environments, range of people, and multiple places across which young people's lives unfold in everyday learning, working, and leisure. In the context of online campaigns, the idea of platform playgrounds helps us to reframe issues, cares, and concerns from young people's perspectives. That is, away from relying on prescribed routes of gender formation, narrow ideas of digital leisure, and adult-led assumptions around help-seeking—toward exploring the 'wayfaring' (Ingold, 2011) of young people's lived experiences and the intermingling of gender, the digital, and play. Rather than linear education models, online campaigns are the new formal and informal spaces of learning and ludic activities. This accords with the new type of 'education remix' (Vasudevan, 2010) emerging via the "reconfiguration of texts, technologies, and resources" (p. 64). Pedagogy and play cannot be easily extricated from how gender performativity and help-seeking cultures unfold: gender is learnt via a socio-historical accumulation of both repetitive and transformative practices, all of which can be imposed, resisted, and explored.

Eberle (2014) argues that play is "an ancient, voluntary, 'emergent' process driven by pleasure that yet strengthens our muscles, instructs our social skills, tempers and deepens our positive emotions, and enables a state of balance that leaves us poised to play some more" (p. 231). Play is significant for human development and well-being in relation to cognitive, social, emotional, and physical functioning (Whitebread, 2012, p. 37). Drawing on Eberle's (2014) elements of play and the gaming 'potential' (Fleming et al., 2017) for mental health, we examine the role of online campaigns for appealing to young men through anticipation and surprise; the role of engaging beneficiaries via pleasure and understanding; and effecting learning and change by developing strength and poise.

Amid the myriad of entertainment and information on offer, young people felt the recognisable and popular cultural trope of the zombie was a powerful and humorous drawcard. Recognising how humour can be deployed in a variety of ways—from increasing affiliation and cohesion to excluding others (Huuki, Manninen, & Sunnari, 2010)—*Something Haunting You?* sought to leverage the positive, sharing aspects of humour. Moreover, the zombie has had a comeback in popular culture attributed to the ways in which themes of transition and ambiguity "resonate with contemporary experience" (Hubner, Leaning, & Manning, 2014, p. 13). Practices of play, as Eberle (2014) suggests, begin with an inclination to play: "[t]his state of readiness, of anticipation, whether mild or intense, already feels rewarding as it makes way for play" (p. 223). The ludic aspects of the zombie trope in the campaign offered play elements of 'anticipation' and 'surprise' by showing the possibilities and appeal of help-seeking from a humorous perspective. It also supported the de-scription of young men's help-seeking practices within the campaign by being open-ended—inviting participants to engage with some or all of the content according to their own experiences and motivations and with the reward of a 'surprise' ending to the video and graphic treatments of particular issues. Furthermore, the usage of the zombie trope provides a connection to young men's knowledge of the icon, but provides an element of surprise in how it is used to point towards opening up the different ways they can seek help.

Campaign development focused on how to sustain the engagement of young people once their initial attention was gained. The campaign videos and comics provided affordances for young men to reframe issues and decision-making through the play elements of 'pleasure' and 'understanding'. 'Pleasure' is an element of play "because pleasure offers its own reward and because play entails pleasure, play perpetuates itself. We would not play if play were not, at least in some measure, fun" (Eberle, 2014, p. 224). Important for well-being, experiencing a sense of empathy and knowledge, tolerance, mutuality, and sensitivity also contributes positively to the experience of pleasure (Eberle, 2014, p. 225). The comics and videos described in the previous section, we argue, can be viewed as a way of fostering pleasure (through connecting with the leisure of everyday media practices), as well as understanding (by way of providing information and resources for informal help-seeking). In accordance with this, it has been recognised that Information and Communication Technology (ICT)-based mental health initiatives which "provide opportunities to seek information and support autonomously" alongside video content and social networking technology, "may also provide a powerful tool to promote social connectedness of young men that can support help-seeking" (Ellis et al., 2012). This play-informed mode of inquiry could be utilised to productively explore other performances of masculinity, such as Australian sport culture.

Young people also guided the way the campaign sought to facilitate, or scaffold, learning, and change. Identification of the array of places, people, and tools which support informal help-seeking informed how technology provides a prompt and scaffold to think about help-seeking, share information with others, or contact people or organisations which can assist in addressing an issue. This informed the design and content of the Survival Guide, a campaign feature drawing together a range of online and offline resources, apps, and advice—in a way opening up trails for 'wayfaring' (Ingold, 2011) or navigation of issues and negotiate needs in relation to their unique, lived experiences. These pathway affordances invited young men to explore and learn about informal help-seeking, promoting the play elements of 'strength' and 'poise'. Eberle (2014) describes how we profit from play "in intellectual, emotional, and social ways. The dividends pay out as expressions of poise such as dignity, ease, contentment, fulfillment, spontaneity, and balance" (p. 227). To help us understand how the campaign could foster poise, a review of online mental health and well-being tools was undertaken by young people. The group highlighted three desirable ways to scaffold confidence in seeking help: reflection (through articulating an emotion and actions to feel better), communication (through supporting expression of feelings, self-efficacy and identifying a plan), and options (by way of showing the possibilities of what to do, as well as the array of contacts and available support). More than simple cognitive knowledge, Eberle argues that in this way play "trains our physical skills, sharpens our mental abilities, and deepens our insights into our social capabilities" (Eberle, 2014, p. 225). In the campaign, this translates as affirmation of experience and empowerment through knowledge and the range of possible responses. The Survival Guide afforded opportunities for developing this strength, inviting the user to transform their help-seeking practices and to 'know their zombie'. For example, clicking on 'exam nerves' showed options to address this challenge: get help (links to 'Surviving Year 12' via beyondblue), communicate with a friend (links to 'Tips for Communicating' via ReachOut.com), speak out (links to 'Who can support you?' via beyondblue), and sleep and exercise (links to the Recharge sleep app via ReachOut.com). The elements of play—anticipation, surprise, pleasure, understanding, poise, and strength (Eberle, 2014)—examined in relation to the *Something Haunting You?* showed how dynamics of play could be interpreted for this online campaign. These elements also align, we propose, with advantages of applied games raised by Fleming et al. (2017): their appealing potential (increasing reach), engaging potential (drawn in by competition or storytelling), and effectiveness potential (opportunities for behaviour change and learning).

Conclusion: The Gender-Digital-Play Assemblage

Research finds that many young men are willing to express their feelings and search for information and advice for mental health, particularly online (Ellis et al., 2013). Yet the prevailing view is that they do not—and that this deficit must be remediated. Online campaigns still often target young men and construct mainstream masculinity as the problem that young men themselves must challenge directly, as individualised and unwell subjects. However, the reiteration of problematic norms of masculinity and targeting of young men, particularly through gendered readings of the role of digital in young people's lives, reinforce, rather than contest the gendered construction of help-seeking. Because gendered assumptions and constructions of help-seeking are often inscribed from a top-down, adult-led, and linear perspective in online campaigns, our interest has been in understanding how these can be disrupted to better reflect the complex, lived experiences of young people. In this chapter, we have sought to open up the space of gender performativity, recognising and working with the ways in which help-seeking is inscribed through the digital, by moving towards wayfaring which, as creative practice, calls for a playful orientation.

This chapter does not purport to pass judgement on the success or impact of *Something Haunting You?*. Rather, we use the campaign as an example of an alternative approach to narrower 'behaviour-change' models that focus on particular constructions of gender as the underlying problem for men's mental health. Nor do we suggest that a focus on wayfaring or play can produce gender neutrality. Certainly, 'representations' of gender can be found *Something Haunting You?* but what we argue is that the campaign attempts to avoid reinscribing gender by prescribing how it 'is' and how it 'should be'. We have attempted to argue that producers of online campaigns might recognise how gender performativity circulates as part of youth digital culture and leisure—as well as being mindful of how agency and personhood are co-constituted. Rather than position gender as the focus of campaigns, we advocate for a more nuanced approach to how health and education campaigns are co-designed with young men in the digital age. This involves exploring more closely the complex interplay between masculinities, technology, and leisure—what we term the gender-digital-play assemblage—so as to inform future campaigns and research pathways.

Acknowledgements: The authors would like to acknowledge the Young and Well Cooperative Research Centre funding which supported this project, the Safe and Well Online research team, and all of the young people who participated.

References

Akrich, M. (1992). The de-scription of technical objects. In W. Bijker & J. Law (Eds.), *Shaping technology/building society*. Cambridge, UK: MIT Press.

Akrich, M., & Latour, B. (1992). A summary of a convenient vocabulary for the semiotics of human and non-human assemblies. In W. Bijker & J. Law (Eds.), *Shaping technology/building society*. Cambridge, UK: MIT Press.

Buchanan, I. M. (2014). Assemblage theory and schizoanalysis. *Panoptikum, 13*(20), 115–125.

Butler, J. (1988). Performative acts and gender constitution: An essay in phenomenology and feminist theory. *Theatre Journal, 40*(4), 519–531.

Butler, J. (1993). *Bodies that matter*. London/New York: Routledge.

Bruns, A. (2016). Prosumption, produsage. In B. Jensen, C. Klaus, T. Robert, J. D. Pooley, & E. W. Rothenbuhler (Eds.), *The international encyclopedia of communication theory and philosophy*. London: John Wiley & Sons, Inc.

Chau, C. (2010). Youtube as a participatory culture. *New directions for student leadership, 128*, 65–74.

Collin, P., & Swist, T. (2016). From products to publics? The potential of participatory design for research on youth, safety and well-being. *Journal of Youth Studies, 19*(3), 305–318.

Connell, R. W., & Messerschmidt, J. W. (2005). Hegemonic masculinity: Rethinking the concept. *Gender & Society, 19*(6), 829–959. https://doi.org/10.1177/0891243205278639.

Deleuze, G. & Guattari, F. A (1987). *A thousand plateaus: Capitalism and schizophrenia* (Brian Massumi, Trans.). Minneapolis, London: The University of Minnesota Press.

Eberle, S. G. (2014). The elements of play: Towards a philosophy and a definition of play. *Journal of Play, 6*(20), 214–233. Retrieved from http://www.journalofplay.org/sites/www.journalofplay.org/files/pdf-articles/6-2-article-elements-of-play.pdf.

Ellis, L., Collin, P., Davenport, T., Hurley, P., Burns, J., & Hickie, I. (2012). Young men, mental health and technology: Implications for service design and delivery in the digital age. *Journal of Medical Internet Research, 14*(6), e160.

Ellis, L., Collin, P., Hurley, P., Davenport, T., Burns, J., & Hickie, I. (2013). Young men's attitudes and behaviour in relation to mental health and technology: Implications for the development of online mental health services. *BMC Psychiatry, 13*, 119.

Farrimond, H. (2011). Beyond the caveman: Rethinking masculinity in relation to men's help-seeking. *Health: An Interdisciplinary Journal for the Social Study of Health, Illness and Medicine, 16*(2), 208–225.

Fleming, T. M., Bavin, L., Stasiak, K., Hermansson-Webb, E., Merry, S. N., Cheek, C., Lucassen, M., Lau, H. M., Pollmuller, B., & Hetrick, S. (2017). Serious Games and Gamification for Mental Health: Current Status and Promising Directions. *Frontiers in Psychiatry, 7*, 215.

Fullagar, S., Rich, E., & Francombe-Webb, J. (2017). New kinds of (ab)normal?: Public pedagogies, affect, and youth mental health in the digital age. *Social Sciences, 6*(99). https://doi.org/10.3390/socsci6030099.

Hagen, P., Collin, P., Metcalf, A., Nicholas, M., Rahilly, K., & Swainston, N. (2012). *Participatory design of evidence-based online youth mental health promotion, prevention and early intervention and treatment*. Abbotsford, BC: Young and Well CRC.

Harvey, A. (2011). Architectures of Participation in Digital Play. *Information, Communication & Society, 14*(3), 303–319.

Hubner, L., Leaning, M., & Manning, P. (2014). Introduction. In L. Hubner, M. Leaning, & P. Manning (Eds.), *The zombie renaissance in popular culture* (pp. 3–14). Basingstoke, UK: Palgrave Macmillan.

Huuki, T., Manninen, S., & Sunnari, V. (2010). Humour as a resource and strategy for boys to gain status in the field of informal school. *Gender and Education, 22*(4), 369–383.

Ingold, T. (2011). *Being alive: Essays on movement, knowledge and description*. Abingdon, UK: Routledge.

Johnson, D., Deterding, S., Kuhn, K.-A., Staneva, A., Stoyanov, S., & Hides, L. (2016). Gamification for health and wellbeing: A systematic review of the literature. *Internet Interventions, 6*, 89–106.

LEGO Learning Institute. (2003). *The changing face of children's play culture: Children's play, learning and communication in a technology driven world*. Retrieved from http://www.carsten-jessen.dk/Play_Culture.pdf

Lupton, D. (2016). Foreward: Lively devices, lively data and lively leisure studies. *Leisure Studies, 35*(6), 709–711.

Nasiruddin, M., Halabi, M., Dao, A., Chen, K., & Brown, B. (2013). Zombies – A pop culture resource for public health awareness. *Emerging Infectious Diseases, 19*(5), 809–813.

O'Brien, R., Hunt, K., & Hart, G. (2005). 'It's caveman stuff, but that is to a certain extent how guys still operate': Men's accounts of masculinity and help-seeking. *Social Science and Medicine, 61*, 503–516.

Schack, M. H. (2014). *Perspectives on comics and their literary merit*. Retrieved from http://www.makingithappen.us/wp-content/uploads/2015/02/Perspectives-on-Comics-and-their-Literary-Merit.pdf

Silk, M., Millington, B., Rich, E., & Bush, A. (2016). (Re-)thinking digital leisure. *Leisure Studies, 35*(6), 712–723.

Spears, B. A., Taddeo, C. M., Barnes, A., Collin, P., Swist, T., Webb-Williams, J., Brock, C., Kavanagh, P., Drennan, J., Razzell, M., & Borbone, V. (2016). *Something haunting you? Reframing and promoting help-seeking for young men: The co-creation and evaluation of a social marketing campaign*. Melbourne, VIC: Young and Well Cooperative Research Centre.

Spencer-Thomas, S., Hindman, J., & Conrad, J. (2012). *Man therapy: An innovative approach to suicide prevention for working aged men*. Retrieved from https://mantherapy.org/pdf/ManTherapy.pdf

Swist, T., Hodge, B., & Collin, P. (2016). 'Cultural making': How complexity and power relations are modulated in transdisciplinary research. *Continuum, 30*(4), 489–501.

Vasudevan, L. (2010). Education remix: New media, literacies, and the emerging digital geographies. *Digital Culture & Education, 2*(1), 62–82.

Whitebread, D. (with M. Basilio, M. Kuvalja and M. Verma). (2012) *The importance of play: A report on the value of children's play with a series of policy recommendations*. Retrieved from http://www.importanceofplay.eu/IMG/pdf/dr_david_whitebread_-_the_importance_of_play.pdf

The Impact of Digital Culture on Women in Sport

Katie Lebel, Ann Pegoraro, and Alanna Harman

"You are so f***ing bad. I hope you die slowly, but f***ing painfully." This was but one of the many hurtful Twitter messages awaiting American tennis professional, Nicole Gibbs, following a straight-sets loss in the 2016 Moscow Open—to an opponent with a higher ranking (Rossingh, 2017). Gibbs posted a screenshot of her Twitter account in an effort to draw attention to the issue of cyber bullying, which she labeled an "epidemic" in women's sport. While women athletes have long been plagued

K. Lebel, PhD (✉)
Ted Rogers School of Management, Ryerson University,
Toronto, ON, Canada
e-mail: klebel@ryerson.ca

A. Pegoraro, PhD
School of Human Kinetics, Laurentian University, Sudbury, ON, Canada
e-mail: apegoraro@laurentian.ca

A. Harman, PhD
Kinesiology & Physical Education, Wilfrid Laurier University,
Waterloo, ON, Canada
e-mail: aharman@wlu.ca

D. C. Parry et al. (eds.), *Digital Dilemmas*,
https://doi.org/10.1007/978-3-319-95300-7_8

by inequitable, often inferior media coverage in comparison to men (Cooky, Messner, & Musto, 2015), the rise of digital culture has brought with it a slew of new challenges, including new outlets for harassment, as in the example above. Portrayals of women in sport by traditional media outlets have historically emphasized femininity and heterosexuality over athletic competence (e.g., Fink & Kensicki, 2002; Knight & Giuliano, 2003; Krane et al., 2010). As digital media opportunities have increased, many hoped women's representation in sport might showcase more of their athletic abilities and strength; but results of this remain mixed. While the digital media landscape has in some cases provided an outlet for strong female sport brands, it has also reflected deeply engrained female stereotypes, and at times, revealed an ugly, vicious, and patriarchal digital culture (e.g., Clavio & Eagleman, 2011; Hum, Chamberlin, Hambright, Bevan 2011; Kane, LaVoi, & Fink, 2013; Lebel & Danylchuk, 2014).

This chapter details the results from several research projects related to women in sport and their interaction with social media platforms. The purpose is to provide a comprehensive look at the issues faced by sportswomen on social media. We begin by providing a brief background on the media inequities faced by sportswomen. This is followed by an investigation of the self-presentation strategies employed by women athletes to present themselves on Instagram. A thematic analysis of audience comments is offered to illustrate the types of engagement various digital presentations motivate among audiences. A sub-case analysis is then presented to explore the phenomenon of fan-generated content relative to women athletes. Finally, we look at the experience of women sport journalists in the digital space. In total, this chapter seeks to provide a deeper understanding of the impact of digital culture on women in sport, while generating insight into the negotiation of gender in digital media.

Background on Media Inequities for Sportswomen

Women have made significant inroads in the field of sport with more opportunities to participate than ever before (Women's Sport Foundation, 2011). In contrast to these gains, the media coverage of women's sports still remains disproportionately low. Current research suggests women's sport receives just 2% of total sport media coverage (Cooky et al., 2015), despite women making up 40% of all sport participants in North America (Kane, 2013). When women athletes do receive coverage by traditional media outlets, their portrayal is often quite gendered. As noted by Mean and Kassing (2008), "gender remains the primary categorization of women athletes, re-producing female athletes as women who play sport rather than as athletes first and foremost" (p. 127). Women athletes are often mentioned as mothers by the media with visuals and stories focusing on their femininity as opposed to their athletic abilities and achievements. While Cooky et al. (2015) suggested that sexualized coverage of women athletes is dissipating, they also noted that media outlets often cover women's sports in a manner that conforms to conventional gender norms (e.g., increased media coverage of "gender appropriate" sports like tennis).

Researchers have produced a significant body of research that has examined differences in traditional media coverage for men and women athletes concluding that women athletes are often depicted in feminine ways, including frequent mentions of their families or personal lives, while men athletes are often portrayed as more powerful and dominant (e.g., Knight & Giuliano, 2002, 2003). Much of this research has focused on how mass media visually portrays women athletes in both broadcast media and photographs (e.g., Angelini, MacArthur, & Billings, 2012; Billings & Angelini, 2007; Fink & Kensicki, 2002; Hardin, Lynn, & Walsdorf, 2005; Jones 2006).

Kane and Maxwell (2011) highlighted the far-reaching influence of the "sports media commercial complex" in framing how society perceives women's sport. Researchers have demonstrated that the portrayal of women athletes can have substantial social and economic outcomes in terms of both the general acceptance of women athletes in society and their marketability as elite athletes (Kim, Walkosz, & Iverson, 2006). While research relative to the representation of women athletes in traditional media outlets has provided a dim outlook toward the progress of women's equality in sport by these measures—the surging popularity of social media tools have offered women athletes a new juncture of opportunity to present themselves to the world.

The portrayal of women athletes in new media remains a burgeoning area of research. In one of the first studies conducted on the online world, Jones (2013) investigated photographic coverage of the 2008 Olympic Games on digital sites finding that men athletes were 1.6 times more likely to be the subject of photographs on these sites. Scholars have also turned their attention to investigating the topic of gender portrayal and gender performance within the realm of social media. Clavio and Eagleman (2011) focused on the ten most popular sports blogs in the United States for their study on photographic coverage of athletes. The authors found that men received significantly more photographic coverage than did women and discovered that photos of women athletes were "far more likely to be sexually suggestive in nature" (p. 295). In their analysis of self-presentation among women and men tennis players on Twitter, Lebel and Danylchuk (2012) found that both men and women utilized backstage (i.e., candid) performances more often than frontstage (i.e., calculated) performances. Overall, they discovered that men utilized the role of super fan (e.g., informal discussion of sport) most often, while women utilized the brand manager role (e.g., formal, brand conscious acknowledgments) more often than men, indicating a persistence of hegemonic values.

More recently, scholars have focused their attention on the self-presentation tactics of athletes on the visual social media platform, Instagram. In their study, Geurin-Eagleman and Burch (2015) found that women athletes were more likely to share personal photos from private settings, while men athletes posted a variety of photos, which stimulated more engagement among their followers. Smith and Sanderson (2015) also analyzed the Instagram feeds of both men and women professional athletes finding that women athletes utilized more active photos than men athletes in their sample. This finding ran counter to past research which indicated that women are more likely to be shown in a passive role (i.e., on the sidelines) thereby demonstrating that perhaps women athletes are using social media platforms to counteract traditional media narratives (e.g., Hardin, Chance, Dodd, & Hardin, 2002).

Bruce (2016) found that the utilization of social media has led to the emergence of two new rules for sportswomen referring to these rules as *our voices* and *pretty and powerful*. With regard to *our voices*, social media has allowed women athletes to gain control of communicating their "sporting truths" (p. 369) to the masses. In terms of *pretty and powerful*, Bruce claims that social media platforms allow for discourse to appear that stresses the notion that femininity is empowering, which is in "stark contrast to sexualization" (p. 369) that has permeated traditional media coverage of women athletes for several decades. The emergence of these new rules related to communication via social media makes it particularly interesting to examine how individual athletes use social media to portray themselves as well as how social media users respond to these portrayals.

Athletes in the Digital Landscape

One of the key drivers behind the success of social media in sport has been the novelty of extending athletes the control to shape their own public image (Pegoraro, 2010). Fundamentally, this has positioned social media as a stage for self-presentation (Lebel & Danylchuk, 2012). While scholars have produced an extensive body of evidence demonstrating how traditional media have consistently portrayed women athletes in a biased manner that trivializes their place in sport, social media has afforded athletes the opportunity to build brands capable of turning the table on traditional power structures. It has served as a catalyst to create relationships not possible through traditional media outlets and inspired a revolution in sport consumption strategies.

Though the relative novelty of social media's influence on sport remains difficult to quantify, *Forbes* suggested that professional soccer star Ronaldo, currently the most followed athlete on social media, generated US$ 500 million in value for Nike through his social media properties in 2016 (Badenhausen, 2017). The social media insight platform, *Hookit*, tracks the social media activity of athletes based upon metrics of influence, engagement, and interactions (likes, comments, shares, re-tweets, and views of videos). As of June 2017, *Hookit* calculated that the top ten most followed athletes in the world had a combined 1,150,400,000 total followers on Facebook, Twitter, and Instagram, speaking volumes to the potential reach of social platforms. Table 1 illustrates the social footprint of the most-followed athletes in the world. Engagement was calculated

Table 1 Athlete rankings on social media

Athlete	Total followers	New followers	Total posts	Engagement (%)	Total interactions
Cristiano Ronaldo	281.6M	5.0M	119	0.8	272.1M
Neymar da Silva	166.7M	2.0M	82	0.7	92.6M
Conor McGregor	24.4M	1.5M	126	2.2	66.6M
Paul Pogba	26.3M	868.9K	104	2.3	63.5M
Sergio Ramos	52.4M	1.3M	126	0.9	61.2M
Marcelo Vieira	44.9M	1.5M	134	0.8	47.8M
Lebron James	91.8M	1.7M	38	1.3	46.4M
Ronaldinho Gaucho	74.0M	985.3K	196	0.3	42.6M
Floyd Mayweather	36.2M	424.9K	241	0.4	38.8M
Antoine Griezmann	22.4M	775.6K	78	2.1	36.6M

Ranked by total interactions, June 1–June 30, 2017

by dividing the total number of interactions by the total number of fans following a particular athlete. Interactions were defined as a combined measurement of the total number of likes, comments, and re-tweets each athlete post received. It should be noted that female athletes are noticeably absent among this top-ten ranking. Mixed Martial Arts athlete, Ronda Rousey, was the highest positioned sportswoman. She was listed as 29th on the list of most-followed athletes in the world with a following of 24.5 million (Hookit, 2017).

Krane et al. (2010) pointed to the paradox that female athletes often experience as they negotiate their powerful bodies against social conventions. However, Krane and her team found that when given a choice on how they wished to be perceived, a majority of the college-aged female athletes they investigated elected to emphasize their power, strength, and athleticism. The decision of these women athletes to select physical competence as a means of self-presentation contradicts years of research that has suggested an inclination of sportswomen to balance traditional gender identities with athletic selves (e.g., Griffin, 1992). In line with this research, Shreffler, Hancock, and Schmidt (2016) conducted a review of

206 female athlete avatars on Twitter and similar to Krane et al. (2010), their results indicated that female athletes were more likely to present themselves as athletically competent individuals as opposed to depicting themselves as sexualized beings. On the heels of this research, Wirtz, Sparks and Zimbres (2017) conducted an investigation of the effect of sexual appeal on a person's perception of advertisements. The research included a review of 78 advertising studies across three decades and found that study participants were very unlikely to remember a brand based upon sexual appeal. To the contrary, participants were more likely to propagate a negative brand opinion for advertisements that employed sexual objectification. Despite these findings, the worth of a digital brand seems to be inextricably linked to popularity. For many of the most followed sportswomen on social media, they have found they are able to gain more followers, and therefore more marketing opportunities, by focusing on their beauty and sex, as opposed to their athleticism.

Digital Self-Presentation Strategies of Women Athletes

In order to explore gender representations in the digital space, the self-presentation strategies of four female athletes were examined on the social media platform, Instagram. A two-stage analysis was devised wherein the first phase a random sample of 100 posts were qualitatively analyzed for each athlete, building upon the framework outlined by Kane, LaVoi, and Fink (2013) that distinguishes photographic representations based upon a series of five categorizations: "athletic competence" (on-court, in-action images with emphasis on athleticism), "mixed messages" (off-court, posed images with athletic marker, but emphasis on femininity vs. athleticism), "enhanced femininity" (off-court, posed image with no athletic marker, enhanced femininity), "sexy/classy lady" (off-court, posed image with no athletic marker, in fashionable attire), and "soft pornography" (off-court, posed image that emphasizes sexual objectification). In addition, a "wholesome" category was created, defined as an off-court photo that focused on family or a girl next-door image (n=400).

Table 2 Athlete digital self-presentation

Athlete	Athletic competence (%)	Mixed message (%)	Enhanced femininity (%)	Sexy/ Classy lady (%)	Soft porn (%)	Wholesome (%)
Alana Blanchard	20	7	12	8	43	10
Ronday Rousey	48	4	2	4	0	42
Lindsey Vonn	36	4	0	30	5	25
Serena Williams	15	26	18	21	10	10

The sample of athletes analyzed was purposeful and included four of the top followed female athletes active on the Instagram platform in the 2015 calendar year: Serena Williams (tennis), Alana Blanchard (surfing), Lindsey Vonn (skiing), and Ronda Rousey (mixed martial arts). Table 2 illustrates categorized results depicting how each athlete elected to portray herself. While fan engagement is notably dependent upon the type of audience each athlete attracts through their presentation of self, it is significant to note that photos depicting athletic competence generated the most likes among this sample of athletes. Sexually suggestive photos, particularly those in the "soft pornography" category, continued to engender significant attention, however, and typically garnered the greatest number of comments among followers.

The second stage of the analysis more closely investigated the fan engagement motivated by athlete photos. Fan comments were thematically analyzed to determine the impact of fan engagement on the athlete's overall brand. Initial results indicated that sexualized self-presentation tactics were reinforced by fans through increased fan engagement (e.g., likes, comments). However, the review of comments revealed differing forms of fan engagement. Sexualized images, for example, tended to evoke comments focused on the "beauty" of the athlete, while images depicting athletic competence were linked to inspiration and respect for the athlete. This suggests that increased fan engagement may not necessarily equate positive brand exposure. While sexualized images may receive the greatest number of likes and comments, objectification is unlikely to enhance the credibility of the female athlete's "athletic brand." Conversely, self-presentation strategies that feature images of athletic competence may be of significant benefit to women athletes looking to authenticate their brands based upon their athletic prowess. Given the rise of visual culture, these findings illustrate important implications for the personal branding strategies of women athletes in the construction of their digital brands. Perhaps most notably, it appears to be in the best interest of women athletes to embrace their strength on social media and celebrate their athletic capabilities, as this seems to engender the most positive engagement among their fans.

Sport Fans in the Digital Landscape

With the growth of the Internet, sport fans have experienced an increased opportunity to interact with other fans, teams, and athletes (Pegoraro, 2013). These various avenues (e.g., message boards, social media platforms) allow fans to choose different environments to connect and engage in fandom related activities. Traditionally, sport fans have been non-influential in the production of sport-related content, acting as consumers of content that are uninvolved in how the content is shaped and presented (Sanderson & Kassing, 2011). As noted by Clavio (2008), the unique characteristics of online message boards that allow for users to participate both as the creators and the consumers of content should be seen as a new area for scholars to investigate.

The content produced by sport fans is referred to as user-generated content (UGC) and is defined as "media content created or produced by the general public rather than by paid professionals and primarily distributed on the Internet" (Daugherty, Eastin, & Bright, 2008, p. 16). UGC exists in a variety of forms, including content uploaded to social media platforms (e.g., Facebook), online forums (e.g., myfootballforum.com), blogs (e.g., SB Nation), micro-blogs (e.g., Twitter), photographs and videos uploaded to file-sharing sites (e.g., YouTube), and information uploaded to wikis (e.g., Wikipedia) (Glickman & Fingerhut, 2011).

Today, sport media production is increasingly driven less by formal publishers and more by sports fans or the general public.

With respect to female sports fans in the digital media, the question is what does this content look like? In their study on women's sport blogs, Antunovic and Hardin found that women tend to conceptualize sport differently than male fans (Antunovic & Hardin, 2015). Male sport blogs tend to be dominated by discussions centered on power and performance in sport (Messner, 2013). While women fans were found to also discuss power and performance, Antunovic and Hardin found that they framed sport in empowering and inclusive ways that facilitated women's physical and emotional development as an avenue for relationship building (Antunovic & Hardin, 2015, p. 669).

Researchers have also investigated Twitter, a microblog, to see if women sports fans use this social media platform in similar ways to sports blogs. Heinecken (2015) studied the postings and followers of @ SoccerGirlProbs—an anonymous account that used humor to portray the everyday struggles of girls who play soccer. Through this work, the author was able to conclude that Twitter provides "a forum for female sport fans to construct their identities in relation to other users and demonstrate their membership in a distinct affinity group marked by a shared reality" (Toffoletti, 2017).

Social media platforms are also discussed as ways to draw attention to women athletes and women's sport predominately through the development of hashtags on specific platforms—Twitter and Instagram. Hashtags allow users to associate their content with a broader conversation. With regard to women in sport, this practice can be particularly powerful in drawing attention to gender issues; it also provides women athletes with an opportunity to share and discuss their personal experiences with sport. One of the fastest growing sites has been Instagram, a visual-based social media platform where users can upload pictures, videos, and engage with the visuals shared by other users. Duggan et al. (2015) indicated that roughly half (53%) of internet-using young adults aged 18–29 use Instagram and 26% of all adults online use the platform. In addition, half of all Instagram users (49%) use the site daily (Duggan et al., 2015).

When investigating the visual representation of women athletes, researchers have found that they are often portrayed through visuals that emphasize their femininity and heterosexuality more than their athletic competence (e.g., Jones, 2006; Daniels & Wartena, 2011; Weber & Barker-Ruchti, 2012). These portrayals often reaffirm traditional notions of femininity and heterosexuality (LaVoi & Kane, 2011). Kane and Maxwell (2011) indicated that the focus on sexuality of women athletes perpetuates the notion that sexualizing these athletes is the only way to generate fan interest, primarily from their male fans, and ultimately sexualizes the women athletes as the only way to sell women's sports. Essentially, traditional media reinforces that while women can be fully engaged in competitive sports, they can only do so in ways that are deemed not to threaten conventional gender norms (Boyle, 2006).

While numerous scholars have analyzed the role traditional media plays in reinforcing gender stereotypes, few researchers have examined the portrayal of women athletes by individual users via social media platforms. Previous research on women athletes and social media has investigated blogs (e.g., Clavio & Eagleman, 2011), Twitter (e.g., Lebel & Danylchuk, 2012), and Instagram (Geurin-Eagleman & Burch, 2015; Smith & Sanderson, 2015) all from the point of view of the athlete.

In one of the few studies to investigate how users have engaged with Instagram to demonstrate their fandom, Pegoraro, Comeau, and Frederick (2017) investigated two hashtags associated with the 2015 FIFA Women's World Cup of Soccer—#FIFAWWC the official hashtag for the event and #SheBelieves created by US Soccer in support of the American women's team. Photos shared on both hashtags throughout the month-long tournament were collected and analyzed to determine how fans were using these hashtags to frame the participating athletes. The results of this study revealed that users primarily portrayed women athletes as athletically competent with almost 90% of posts on either hashtag portraying athletes in either athletic action or preparing for athletic action (Pegoraro et al., 2017). While this was one of the first studies to focus on how fans use social media to frame women athletes, the findings demonstrate that social media can provide users with an avenue to challenge gender stereotypes in women's sports as generated by traditional media. It also illustrates that fans are willing and capable of creating their own frames around women athletes (Pegoraro et al., 2017).

Researchers have been able to discern that fans of women's sport use social media in different ways to practice their fandom. Toffoletti (2017) explains the "feminist potential of social media lies in its ability to increase the profile of women fans and women's sport, allowing women to search the relatively unfiltered medium of social media to advocate for women's sport" (p. 119). Researchers have only begun to broaden our understanding on how women fans of women's sport use digital media. Opportunity for continued research exploring the potential use of social media to facilitate women's practices of sport fandom is needed. Indeed, the platforms themselves continually evolve and so must our research.

Sport Journalists in the Digital Space

Media has long been regarded as a socializing agent (Gerbner, 1998), and the lens through which the media presents "reality" can have a confirming affect for those who belong to powerful majority groups (van Dijk, 1995), and a detrimental effect on those who are portrayed in unbecoming ways (Cohen & Young, 1981). Hetsroni and Lowenstein (2014) suggested that "the process through which the content are chosen is intentionally selective, prioritizing certain societal segments" (p. 377), thus reflecting only certain members of society. Non-representation or under-representation of certain groups, including women, has been described as *symbolic annihilation* (Tuchman, 1978). The stark underrepresentation of women in the media was first highlighted in the 1968 Kerner Commission's Report and continues to be an unresolved issue (Women's Media Center, 2015).

The presence of women in the sport media realm is truly in its infancy, as it took until 1975 before a "female [Phyllis George] had a prominent role in network sports broadcasting" (Mead, 2010), and it wasn't until 1978 when a federal judge ruled that banning female reporters from locker rooms was a violation of the 14th Amendment (Ludtke v. Kuhn, 1978). While legal barriers limiting female reporters access to players to conduct interviews have been eliminated, and the number of female reporters have increased, women still only represent 10–20% of the sports media (Lapchick, 2014). The underrepresentation in this particular context is further compounded by the few opportunities that are available to female sport journalists. Female sport journalists are usually relegated to sideline reporting with limited timeframes for interviews or opportunities to demonstrate intricate knowledge of sport. In the National Football League's (NFL's) history, only four females have had the opportunity to provide color commentary, and only one during the regular season (Deitsch, 2016). It also wasn't until the 2014 Sochi Olympic Games that a woman, Meredith Vieira, anchored National Broadcasting Company's (NBC's) primetime coverage of the Olympic Games solo, and this only resulted because of a health issue experienced by the pre-booked male journalist, Bob Costas.

While there is an increase in the number of female sports journalists, their mere presence is not enough to support the pursuit of equality in which women are perceived and treated as equals among their male counterparts. Popular lists that document the "Hottest Female Sports Reporters" continue to be abundant in a culture that continues to emphasize the appearance of female sport reporters and often presents appearance in a manner that is just as important, if not more important, than their journalistic skill. The ill treatment of female sport journalists is further heightened in this digital age. As cable networks expand their broadcasting to the digital realm, there are expectations that journalists also engage in the digital arena (Gibbs & Haynes, 2013). This new platform, which unlike traditional broadcasts allows for two-way communication between the consumer and journalist, has highlighted the attitudes of some sport consumers toward women in sport media. One only has to read comments on social media to appreciate the disparity of how male and female sport journalists are perceived and treated.

Julie DiCaro, a radio anchor and columnist for CBSChicago.com and *Sports Illustrated's* The Cauldron, used her legal knowledge from her 15-year career in criminal and family court to report on sexual assault allegations against National Hockey League (NHL) athlete, Patrick Kane. During this time, DiCaro found herself the target of severe online harassment, receiving as many as 30 harassing tweets a day (Ryan, 2016). DiCaro and fellow Chicago sport journalist Sarah Spain appeared in a public service announcement (PSA) entitled #MoreThanMean, a parody of Jimmy Kimmel's "Mean Tweets", to highlight the harassment experienced by women in sports media. The tweets were so offensive in nature that they required a graphic language warning; many also alluded to criminal acts against the women journalists. Despite this vulgar language, the PSA has to date been viewed over four million times on YouTube.

Jessica Mendoza, an Olympic gold and silver medal winning softball player for Team USA, became the first female analyst for a nationally televised Major League Baseball (MLB) postseason game in October 2015 (Boren, 2016). Her foray into the MLB, however, was not well received by spectators or peers. In particular, Mike Bell, a sport talk radio host on Atlanta's CBS Sports affiliate, trolled Mendoza on Twitter. Many of his tweets focused on Mendoza's appearance and her ability to call plays since she had never played in the MLB. "You tell us Tits McGhee when you're up there hitting the softball you see a lot of 95 mile an hour cutters?" and "Really? A women's softball slugger as guest analyst on MLB Wildcard Game? Once again ESPN too frigging cute for their own good," Bell's Twitter rant included over ten tweets of a similar nature (Glasspiegel, 2015).

These experiences are not unique. Many female sport journalists have noted that much of the engagement they receive from viewers is highly critical of their appearance and falls into the domain of harassment (Harbison, 2016). In this day and age, the opinions expressed on social media have caused sponsors to cease relationships and even forced the hand of major corporations to terminate public personas (e.g., Bill O'Reilly). However, we have also witnessed corporations excel as a result of their conservative views, for example, Chick-fil-A saw an increase in sales, despite public backlash at the company's president's stance against same-sex marriage (Kim, 2012). While sport networks cannot fire their consumers for their public statements in the digital domain, they might be listening and perpetuating homogeneous, hegemonic reproductions within the sport media industry as a means to appease them, thus symbolically annihilating females from successful careers in the sport media. Imagine, however, the possibilities for future generations if they were given greater opportunity to both consume women's sport and see it presented by knowledgeable female sport personalities. The increased presence of strong women role models, who are viewed as credible sources of sport information and respected accordingly for the quality of their work, has the potential to change societal expectations and cultivate gender equality in sport.

Conclusion

The changing tide of digital culture has had a profound effect on the negotiation of gender and athletic identities in sport. Indeed, the revolutionary nature of social media extends beyond the reach of traditional media outlets to more diverse audiences, giving wind to a greater number of voices. Under the strong leadership of elite sportswomen lies the potential to capitalize on the novelty of social media to achieve positive societal acceptance for women athletes, lucrative marketing opportunities for women's sport, and gender equitable career prospects in sport. The re-negotiation of our concepts of femininity combined with the freedom inherent of social media self-presentation could prove a valuable key to unlocking the time-honored tradition of hegemony in sport. While it is true there exists a dark side to social media, a sustained vigilance to monitor and dissuade this negativity, combined with a concerted effort to promote athletic success and women's equality in sport have the potential to go a long way toward ensuring this cultural shift bends in a positive direction.

References

Angelini, J. R., MacArthur, P. J., & Billings, A. C. (2012). What's the gendered story? Vancouver's prime time Olympic glory on NBC. *Journal of Broadcasting & Electronic Media, 56*(2), 261–279.

Antunovic, D., & Hardin, M. (2015). Women and the blogosphere: Exploring feminist approaches to sport. *International Review for the Sociology of Sport, 50*(*60*), 661–677.

Badenhausen, K. (2017, February 23). *Ronaldo beats Messi by 800% when it comes to return on social media for their brands.* Retrieved from https://www.forbes.com/sites/kurtbadenhausen/2017/02/23/ronaldo-beats-messi-by-800-when-it-comes-to-return-on-social-media-for-their-brands/?utm_source=TWITTER&utm_medium=social&utm_content=823145558&utm_campaign=sprinklrForbesMainTwitter#18fda9f7401b

Billings, A. C., & Angelini, J. R. (2007). Packaging the games for viewer consumption: Gender, ethnicity, and nationality in NBC's coverage of the 2004 Summer Olympics. *Communication Quarterly, 55*(1), 95–111.

Boren, C. (2016, May 9). *Fox sports radio tweets ESPN's Jessica Mendoza would be fired 'if she was a man'.* Retrieved June 13, 2017 from https://www.washington-post.com/news/early-lead/wp/2016/05/09/fox-sports-radio-tweets-espns-jessica-mendoza-would-be-fired-if-she-was-a-man/?utm_term=.19bff846a3a8

Boyle, R. (2006). Gendered sport? Gendered journalism? In R. Boyle (Ed.), *Sport journalism: Context and issues* (pp. 144–159). Thousand Oaks, CA: Sage.

Bruce, T. (2016). New rules for new times: Sportswomen and media representation in the third wave. *Sex Roles, 74*, 361–376.

Clavio, G. (2008). Demographics and usage profiles of users of college sport message boards. *International Journal of Sport Communication, 1*(4), 434–443.

Clavio, G., & Eagleman, A. N. (2011). Gender and sexually suggestive images in sports blogs. *Journal of Sport Management, 7*, 295–304.

Cohen, S., & Young, J. (1981). *The manufacture of news. Deviance, social problems, and the mass media*. Beverly Hills, CA: Sage.

Cooky, C., Messner, M., & Musto, M. (2015). "It's dude time!" A quarter century of excluding women's sports in televised news and highlight shows. *Communication and Sport, 3*(3), 261–287.

Daugherty, T., Eastin, M. S., & Bright, L. (2008). Exploring consumer motivations for creating user generated content. *Journal of Interactive Advertising, 8(2)*, 16–25.

Daniels, E., & Wartena, A. (2011). Athlete or sex symbol: What boys think of media representations of female athletes. *Sex Roles, 65*(7–8), 566–579.

Deitsch, R. (2016, August 24). *Uphill battle for women in NFL play-by-play role may soon reach a turning point*. Retrieved June 13, 2017 from https://www.si.com/nfl/2016/08/24/nfl-women-announcers-beth-mowins-kate-scott

Duggan, M., Ellison N. B., Lampe C., Lenhart A., & Madden M. (2015). Social media update 2014. *Pew Research Center.* http://www.pewinternet.org/2015/01/09/social-media-update-2014/. Accessed 12 June 2016.

Fink, J. S., & Kensicki, L. J. (2002). An imperceptible difference: Visual and textual constructions of femininity in sports illustrated and sports ilustrated for women. *Mass Communication and Society, 5*(3), 317–339.

Gerbner, G. (1998). Cultivation analysis: An overview. *Mass Communication and Society, 1*, 175–194. https://doi.org/10.1207/s15327825mcs0103&4_4.

Geurin-Eagleman, A. N., & Burch, L. M. (2015). Communicating via photographs: A gendered analysis of Olympic athletes' visual self-presentation on Instagram. *Sport Management Review*. https://doi.org/10.1016/j.smr.2015.03.002.

Gibbs, C., & Haynes, R. (2013). A phenomenological investigation into how Twitter has changes the nature of sport media relations. *International Journal of Sport Communication, 6*, 394–408.

Glasspiegel, R. (2015, October 7). *Here's the Twitter rant about ESPN's Jessica Mendoza that got an Atlanta radio host suspended.* Retrieved June 14, 2017 from http://thebiglead.com/2015/10/07/mike-bell-jessica-mendoza-twitter-suspended/

Glickman, L., & Fingerhut, J. (2011). User-generated content: Recent developments in Canada and the U.S. *Internet and E-Commerce Law in Canada, 12*(6), 49–76.

Griffin, P. (1992). Changing the game: Homophobia, sexism, and lesbians in sport. *Quest, 44*, 251–265.

Harbison, M. (2016, May 19). *Female media pros often face gender backlash, online harassment.* Retrieved June 14, 2017 from http://mediaschool.indiana.edu/news/female-media-pros-often-face-gender-backlash-online-harassment/

Hardin, M., Lynn, S., & Walsdorf, K. (2005). Challenge and conformity on contested terrain: Images of women in four women's sport/fitness magazines. *Sex Roles, 53*(1/2), 105–117.

Hardin, M., Chance, J., Dodd, J. E., & Hardin, B. (2002). Olympic photo coverage fair to female athletes. *Newspaper Research Journal, 23*(2,3), 64–78.

Heinecken, D. (2015). So tight in the thighs, so loose in the waist: Embodying the female athlete online. *Feminist Media Studies, 15*(6), 1035–1052.

Hetsroni, A., & Lowernstein, H. (2014). Is she an expert or just a woman? Gender differences in the presentation of experts in TV talk shows. *Sex Roles, 70*, 376–386.

Hookit. (2017, June). *Hookit index top 100.* Retrieved from: http://www.hookit.com/ranks/. Accessed June 2017.

Hum, N., Chamberlin, P., Hambright, B., & Bevan, J. (2011). A picture is worth a thousand words: A content analysis of Facebook profile photographs. *Computers in Human Behavior, 27*(5), 1828–1833.

Jones, D. (2006). The representation of female athletes in online images of successive Olympic Games. *Pacific Journalism Review, 12*(1), 108–129.

Jones, D. (2013). Online coverage of the 2008 Olympic games on the ABC, BBC, CBC and TVNZ. *Pacific Journalism Review, 19*(1), 244–263.

Kane, M. (2013). The better sportswomen get, the more the media ignore them. *Communication & Sport, 1*(3), 231–236.

Kane, M., & Maxwell, H. (2011). Expanding the boundaries of sport media research: Using critical theory to explore consumer responses to representations of women's sports. *Journal of Sport Management, 25*, 202–216.

Kane, M. J., LaVoi, L. M., & Fink, J. S. (2013). Exploring elite female athletes' interpretations of sport media images: A window into the construction of social identity and 'Selling Sex' in women's sports. *Communication and Sport, 1*(3), 269–298.

Kerner, O. (1968). *Report of the national advisory commission on civil disorder.* New York: Bantam Books.

Kim, S. (2012, October 25). *Chick-fill-A benefited from summer's gay marriage flap with more customer visits.* Retrieved June 14, 2017 from http://abcnews.go.com/Business/chick-fil-benefited-summers-gay-marriage-debate/story?id=17562204

Kim, E., Walkosz, B. J., & Iverson, J. (2006). *USA Today's* coverage of the top women golfers, 1998–2001. *The Howard Journal of Communications, 17*, 307–321.

Knight, J. L., & Giuliano, T. A. (2002). He's a Laker, she's a looker: The consequences of gender-stereotypical portrayals of male and female athletes by the print media. *Sex Roles, 45*(3/4), 217–229.

Knight, J. L., & Giuliano, T. A. (2003). Blood, sweat, and jeers: The impact of the media's heterosexist portrayals on perceptions of male and female athletes. *Journal of Sport Behavior, 26*(3), 272–284.

Krane, V., Ross, S., Miller, M., Rowse, J., Ganoie, K., Andrzejczyk, J., & Lucas, C. (2010). Power and focus: Self-representation of female college athletes. *Qualitative Research in Sport and Exercise, 2*, 175–195.

Lapchick, R. E. (2014). *The 2014 associated press sports editors racial and gender report card.* Retrieved May 9, 2017 from http://nebula.wsimg.com/038bb0ccc9436494ebee1430174c13a0?AccessKeyId=DAC3A56D8FB782449D2A&disposition=0&alloworigin=1

LaVoi, N. M., & Kane, M. J. (2011). Sociological aspects of sport and physical activity. In P. Pedersen, L. Thibault, & J. Quarterman (Eds.), *Contemporary sport management.* Champaign, IL: Human Kinetics.

Lebel, K., & Danylchuk, K. (2012). How tweet it is: A gendered analysis of professional tennis players' self-presentation on Twitter. *International Journal of Sport Communication, 5*, 461–480.

Lebel, K., & Danylchuk, K. (2014). Facing off on Twitter: A generation Y interpretation of professional athlete profile pictures. *International Journal of Sport Communication, 7*(3), 317–336.

Ludtke v. Kuhn. 461 F. Supp. 86 (S.D. NY. 1978).

Mead, D. (2010, August 21). *Twelve women who pioneered the era of female sports broadcasters*. Retrieved June 12, 2017 from http://bleacherreport.com/articles/440556-twelve-women-who-pioneered-the-era-of-female-sports-broadcasters

Mean, L. J., & Kassing, J. W. (2008). 'I would just like to be known as an athlete': Managing hegemony, femininity, and heterosexuality in female sport. *Western Journal of Communication, 72*, 126–144.

Messner, M. (2013). Reflections on communication and sport: On men and masculinities. *Communication and Sport, 1*, 113–124.

Pegoraro, A. (2010). Look who's talking-athletes on Twitter: A case study. *International Journal of Sort Communication, 3*(4), 501–514.

Pegoraro, A. (2013). Sport fandom in the digital world. In P. Pedersen (Ed.), *The Routledge handbook of sport communication* (pp. 248–258). New York, NY: Routledge.

Pegoraro, A., Comeau, G., & Frederick, E. (2017). #SheBelieves: Fans' use of social media to frame the US women's soccer team during #FIFAWWC. *Sport and Society*. Retrieved from https://doi.org/10.1080/17430437.2017.1310198

Rossingh, D. (2017). *Australian open: 'Hope you die slowly'—Tennis stars trolled*. Retrieved from http://edition.cnn.com/2017/01/18/tennis/australian-open-tennis-trolls-social-media-hate-epidemic/index.html

Ryan, S. (2016, June 20). *WSCR's Julie DiCaro a lightening rod on local sports media scene*. Retrieved June 13, 2017 from http://www.chicagotribune.com/sports/ct-julie-dicaro-wscr-spt-0621-20160620-story.html

Sanderson, J., & Kassing, J. W. (2011). Tweets and blogs: Transformative, adversarial and integrative developments in sport media. In A. Billings (Ed.), *Sports media: Transformation, integration, consumption* (pp. 114–127). New York: Routledge.

Shreffler, M., Hancock, M., & Schmidt, S. (2016). Self-presentation of female athletes: A content analysis of athlete avatars. *International Journal of Sport Communication, 9*, 460–475.

Smith, L. R., & Sanderson, J. (2015). I'm going to Instagram it! An analysis of athlete self-presentation on Instagram. *Journal of Broadcasting and Electronic Media, 59*(2), 342–358.

Toffoletti, K. (2017). *Women sport fans – Identification, participation, representation*. New York: Routledge.

Tuchman, G. (1978). *Making news: A study in the construction of reality*. New York: Free Press.

van Dijk, T. A. (1995). Discourse semantics and ideology. *Discourse and Society, 6*, 243–289. https://doi.org/10.1177/0957926595006002006.

Weber, J., & Barker-Ruchti, N. (2012). Bending, flirting, floating, flying: A critical analysis of female figures in 1970s gymnastics photographs. *Sociology of Sport Journal, 29*(1), 22–41.

Wirtz, J., Sparks, J., & Zimbres, T. (2017). The effect of exposure to sexual appeals in advertisements on memory, attitude, and purchase intention: A meta-analytic review. *International Journal of Advertising*. https://doi.org/10.1080/02650487.2017.1334996.

Women's Media Center. (2015). *WMC status of women in U.S. media 2015*. Retrieved June 12, 2017 from http://wmc.3cdn.net/83bf6082a319460eb1_hsrm680x2.pdf

Women's Sport Foundation. (2011). *Women's sports & fitness facts & statistics*. East Meadow, NY: Women's Sports Foundation.

This Girl Can? The Limitations of Digital Do-It-Yourself Empowerment in Women's Active Embodiment Campaigns

Annaleise Depper, Simone Fullagar, and Jessica Francombe-Webb

Introduction

This Girl Can is a new digital campaign mobilized to inspire English women and girls to be more active. Initially launched by Sport England in 2015, and again in 2017, This Girl Can responds to concerns about health and higher levels of physical inactivity related to the 'gender gap' that exists between women and girls' participation compared to men and boys (Sport England, 2015). This novel approach to health promotion mobilizes 'real' bodies and a range of leisure practices, rather than just competitive sport, to motivate and inspire women to become active and be more culturally visible. Launched at a time of 'austerity' in the UK with increasing cuts to the welfare state, This Girl Can marks a wider societal shift towards the responsiblization of individuals. Based on a

A. Depper (✉) • S. Fullagar • J. Francombe-Webb
Department for Health, University of Bath, Bath, UK
e-mail: A.F.Depper@bath.ac.uk; S.P.Fullagar@bath.ac.uk;
J.M.Francombe-Webb@bath.ac.uk

D. C. Parry et al. (eds.), *Digital Dilemmas*,
https://doi.org/10.1007/978-3-319-95300-7_9

neoliberal rhetoric of 'free choice', the campaign invites women to tone, sculpt and 'work on' their bodies through active leisure.

Encouraging women to overcome the affective forces of shame and fear of judgement to engage in sport has been a key message of This Girl Can. Individuals are urged to engage in this active journey through interconnected virtual and visceral spaces; the multiple digital and social media platforms enable women to share their stories. The campaign utilizes various 'empowering' messages that speak directly to the fears women have about body image and appearance in physical activity. Mantras such as 'I jiggle therefore I am', 'Damn right I look hot', 'Sweating like a pig, feeling like a fox', 'Hot and not bothered', and 'A kick right in the stereotypes' articulate the campaign's intent to question gender stereotypes in adverts that have been shared across social media. In the context of increasing pressures affecting young women's body confidence (Girl Guiding UK, 2016), This Girl Can aims to counter body shaming that women are subjected to and marks a significant contrast to previous social marketing campaigns that have utilized athletic bodies to promote women's sport.

Reaching over 95 million views of the campaign's original 90-second video on Facebook and YouTube alone, This Girl Can has been an online viral 'success' (Sport England, 2017). The campaign video clip challenges "negative feelings about body size, shape or competency" (Fullagar & Pavlidis, 2018, p. 452), as we watch women's bodies moving, running, dancing, swimming, and boxing in time to Missy Elliott's 'Get Ur Freak On'. With the more recent re-release of This Girl Can, Sport England has launched a new video clip and women remain an active part of this campaign. Women are encouraged create their own personalized mantra image through the official app, and share their own stories in sport, along with the #thisgirlcan across social media platforms (This Girl Can, 2017). These stories highlight the intense affective response amongst women to the 'real' bodies featured in the adverts. With innovative digital marketing strategies, everyday women have become the face of the campaign to promote the This Girl Can brand across virtual and visceral spaces, to inspire and 'liberate' women through sport.

Despite the sentiments of the campaign that seek to counter body shaming amongst women, This Girl Can has generated mixed reactions that bring to the fore critical questions about digital advertising campaigns related to sport and physical culture in an era that has been described by some as post-feminist. Within British culture, the post-feminist era that was encapsulated in the late 1990s by 'girl power' (as individualized 'freedom', empowerment and heterosexual femininity) has signified the end to, and indeed relevance of, feminism. In this chapter, we challenge the post-feminist sentiments of Sport England's This Girl Can campaign, which stem from the narrow range of subject positions that are rendered meaningful by an overemphasis on individualized empowerment. We further complicate the do-it-yourself notion of femininity in the campaign by exploring how issues of inequality are intensified by a market based leisure economy. Take, for instance, the way that gender and middle lifestyles are assumed as a feminine 'norm' through corporate partnerships between This Girl Can and the retailer Marks and Spencer. As a retailer that sells high-end home, clothing, and food products, Marks & Spencer is largely associated, within the UK, with middle-class consumptive spaces. The online/offline consumerism works to entangle women's leisure with the branded campaign activewear merchandise produced by Marks and Spencer.

This chapter offers a material-discursive approach to develop a more nuanced account of the powerful affects, and effects, of This Girl Can that *move* women's bodies in particular ways (Fullagar & Pavlidis, 2018; Wetherell, 2012). We highlight how the campaign positions women to become active bodies and question the extent to which the campaign has successfully 'empowered' women to conquer fears of judgement. Situated within feminist scholarship, we explore how the gendered conditions of possibility for (in)active embodiment are made visible through the digital practices of the campaign (text, images, and invitations to engage via social media). Contextualized alongside popular post-feminist forms of address, the supposed novelty of the campaign is its attempt to redress the invisibility of active feminized bodies (sweating, jiggling, moving) in the public domain (on billboards, tv adverts, social media) by inviting all women to identify with sport and active leisure as a source of individual agency and as a site where the inclusion of difference occurs. Yet, with respect to the norms of individual success and responsibility for active lifestyle practices that shape sport cultures, we ask how is women's difference digitally constituted in relation to masculine norms and with respect to differences between women themselves?

Within this chapter, we analyse how advanced liberal rationalities are gendered in the campaign's promotion of women's freedom to break free from the 'barriers' preventing engagement in sport. We question the extent to which the campaign can claim to have successfully empowered women to conquer fears of judgement and participate in sport regardless of their ability, shape, or size. This Girl Can is situated within the neo-liberal everyday, micro-governance of women's bodies that make women accountable for their 'choices', while the campaign disregards the materialities that women must negotiate in gendered leisure spaces. Our discussion is situated within post-feminist debates around 'freedom' and personal choice (McRobbie, 2008), as we explore the inclusive, and the complex, individualized and limiting aspects of the campaign. We argue that This Girl Can continues to unproblematically position women as responsible for making the 'right' choices to be active, rather than supporting more inclusive cultures and structures for active living.

Women's Leisure and a Post-Feminist Sensibility: Thinking Through Intersectionality

We are interested in making visible the discursive positioning of women and the normative representations of women's bodies throughout the campaign and more broadly within what has been described as post-feminist, advanced liberal societies (Gill, 2007a). Post-feminism is a contested term, fraught with conflicting meaning and assumptions about its deployment and utility for feminist theorizing. For some, post-feminism is an apolitical project discursively constituted across everyday spaces and through popular media; for others, it is synonymous with third wave feminism and, increasingly outside of leisure studies, it is being conceptualized as a *sentiment* that warrants scholarly attention. Aligned to this final positionality, our engagement with post-feminism is informed by the work of Rosalind Gill (2007a) and Angela McRobbie (2004a, b, 2008) who suggest that "post feminism positively draws on and invokes feminism as that which can be taken into account to suggest that equality is achieved, in order to install a whole repertoire of new meanings which emphasise that it is no longer needed, it is a spent force" (McRobbie, 2004a, p. 4). Against this backdrop, our research (Francombe, 2010, 2014; Francombe-Webb, 2015; Francombe-Webb & Toffoletti, 2017) is attempting to clarify how and why engaging with the notion of post-feminism is important when looking to better understand women's experiences of sport and physical culture. While there are common threads in the globalized post-feminist discourse relating to empowerment, we are mindful of the cultural specificities through which they play out in British and North American contexts. In Britain, we have seen post-feminist address produced and reproduced throughout leisure, digital and media spaces, and directed at women through commodification and consumption (from music, magazines, fashion, and also sport). This research offers an alternative way of understanding post-feminism that treats it as a *critical object of enquiry* rather and an assumed state of being, or an analytic perspective (Toffoletti, 2016).

Gendered ways of thinking and feeling about the performance of feminine subjectivity are assembled across the material-discursive practices of academia, policy, and popular culture. Women are being increasingly celebrated for their discernible 'progress' and achievements in education, employment, sport, and the media. Recently, Stewart and Caudwell (2017) suggest that there has been an "increase in the visibility of female athletes in the sporting media", including self-authored representations across a range of digital platforms in contemporary Western culture. This progress implies liberation through choice, opportunity, and upward mobility. Such success is often attributed to many interrelated developments and the changing social conditions of free market capitalism, namely the way in which feminist movements have eliminated the gendered barriers around education and employment; the reform of legislation; and transformation of attitudes regarding the personal domain. For Toffoletti (2016), women are precariously placed within these economic conditions and global labour markets as they are expected to perform and reinvent themselves to adapt to constant change. They are also increasingly identified in terms of their bodily property (Gill, 2007a) and for the entrepreneurial 'choices' they make.

Moving beyond definitional accounts of post-feminism (Gill, 2007a, 2016) we critically explore post-feminist forms of address and ways of knowing, across digital and physical cultures, to open up space for activism. As one example, this work demonstrates that the material and discursive assemblage of post-feminist rationalities—particularly those related to individualization, self-work, and choice that are evident across social media platforms—need to be the object of feminist inquiry. This is due to entrenched patterns of class, race, religious, heteronormative, age-related, able-bodied inequities that are eschewed in the discursive imaginary of 'Top Girls', 'Future Girls', and 'Can Do Girls' (Harris & Dobson, 2015). Indeed, as we problematize later in this chapter, these embodied affects and feelings of 'empowerment' and control that are indicative of post-feminist digital cultures are not necessarily all positive in gendered leisure contexts (Probyn, 2005).

Within popular culture, notions of empowerment and choice are not deemed to be influenced by any structural conditions or affective forces (Gill & Scharff, 2011). Yet as Harris and Dobson (2015, p. 148) emphasize, "one's own preferences and decisions can never be disentangled from the social context within which they are arrived at". Feminist post-structuralism has emphasized the complexities of agency and highlighted the need for a more nuanced understanding of subjectivity as entangled with material-discursive relationalities (Braidotti, 2013; Harris & Dobson, 2015), whereby agency is not simply equated with individual autonomy and choice (Gill, 2007b). As Evans, Riley and Shankar (2010, p. 127) suggest, this means avoiding positioning "other women as problematic (either in terms of their choices or their agency to make choices)", while also attending to how regimes of power operate through affective practices (Wetherell, 2012) that equate success with good choices. Like many campaigns, This Girl Can participates in the governance of women's bodies 'at a distance' through market driven rationalities of choice that are assumed to have gender neutral effects (Fullagar, 2009).

Thinking through the interrelations between gendered leisure and sports policy, we trouble the heteronormative representation of 'girls' and the ways in which feminized subjects are positioned in this digital campaign. We draw upon feminist thinking about intersectional analyses of the multiple power relations, identities, and inequalities at play through This Girl Can (Watson & Ratna, 2011). Intersectional feminism involves thinking about gendered inequities in leisure and physical activity as "multi-layered and multiplicitous" (Watson & Scraton 2012, p. 45). An intersectional understanding can inform our understanding of how gender is mobilized in Sport England's focus on 'women and girls'. This Girl Can was launched at a time when sporting bodies and initiatives were called to prove their engagement with underrepresented and marginalized groups (Sport England, 2016a). A year after the launch of the campaign, Sport England (2016b) reported that "2.8 million 14–40 year old women say they have done some or more activity as a result of our campaign". The most recent Active People Survey figures show that "15.97 million people over the age of 16 are now playing sport weekly", an increase of 229,400 from 12 months prior (Sport England, 2016c).

While Sport England claims a positive impact on women's participation arising from This Girl Can, they present no analysis of the gender data to enable differences *between* women and patterns of inequality to be identified (gender, ethnicity, age, income, sexuality, and disability). The publicly available data identifies the greatest gender gap between young women and men and between older and younger women as participation rates decline with age. We are told that recent participation data shows an increase for 'people' from black and ethnic minority backgrounds, but not for 'people' from the lowest income groups where there is the greatest disparity. Hence, there is a lack of intersectional thinking about gender, and evidence, to support increased participation for women who experience greater inequalities (see also, Long, Hylton, Lewis & Ratna, 2011). Despite the campaign's desire not to use a 'one size fits all' approach, the lack of detailed analysis in their market segmentation strategy (Sport England, 2015) means This Girl Can may actually contribute to widening inequalities for women of colour and those on low incomes. This is a major shortcoming in such an important data resource for the sport and recreation workforce.

We extend our analytic focus on embodied leisure practices by engaging with cultural theories of affect that enable "more complex understandings of the entanglement of material, visceral, discursive dimensions of gendered subjectivities" (Fullagar & Pavlidis, 2018, p. 447). In this way, we examine the performative relations of the campaign as they shape how different women's digital and visceral bodies are enacted through affective practices and intensities. Active embodiment in This Girl Can can be understood in terms of affective practices (pleasurable, shameful) that are produced in relation to culturally imagined others (masculine gaze, normative comparison, health moralization). As women move, they are also *moved by* forces of affect within a broader 'affective economy' (Ahmed, 2004) that connects bodies in leisure contexts (gyms, sports fields, pools) with power relations that produce social inequities (class, ethnicity, gender, age, sexuality, disability, etc.). We theorize gendered leisure practices as more than individual agency instead emphasizing the inseparability of women's embodiment from the multiplicity of meanings assembled through the digital and physical cultures.

This shift in thinking about the relations that shape what women's bodies can 'do' and how they 'act' through digital campaigns focuses our attention on the assemblage of "human subjectivity through a complex range of forces that constitute human and non-human embodied life in particular ways (that matter)" (Fullagar, 2017, p. 250). Moving beyond perspectives that assume digital 'representations' are a reflection of the world that can be decoded, our analytic 'reading' is a relational dynamic through which digital text and images are entangled with our affective responses. As Wolfe (2017, p. 491) argues in her feminist media analysis, "The entangled audience productively creates their own boundaries of difference through a desire to belong and what it means to be the right sort of girl (Beverley Skeggs, 2004)". We identify the feminist intensities that trouble notions of empowerment—the tensions across images and text, moments that disturb and also those that invite pleasurable responses (Wolfe, 2017). Importantly, the wide-ranging public responses of women to this campaign point towards a variety of material readings that are evoked through engagement with digital media. What follows is a discussion of how these affective, material, and discursive forces are at play through This Girl Can, as they shape how women's bodies are positioned and what they can 'do' and 'act' through the campaign. Our discussion of This Girl Can is situated in relation to other cultural texts across gendered leisure and post-feminist, advanced liberal societies more broadly.

Discussion

Evoking the 'Real' Bodies of This Girl Can

Sport England's (2017) strategy for This Girl Can involved using 'real' bodies to inspire women to conquer fears of judgement that have traditionally held women back in sport. Such fears, are identified as; "being judged on their appearance, during and after exercise; on their ability, whether they were a beginner or 'too good'; or spending time exercising instead of prioritising their children or studying" (Sport England, 2016b, p. 4). As we have argued elsewhere (Fullagar & Pavilidis, 2018, p. 452), these promotional videos work to "materialize intense affects (pleasure in sweating, strength, pushing beyond limits, enjoying collective practices) through vision and sound". Sport England has also released still images of 'real' bodies in sport, accompanied by catchy mantras, as part of the online digital campaign. One of the 'hard-hitting' slogans, across an image of a woman on a rowing machine reads:

Hot and not bothered.

The campaign has resonated strongly with millions of women across the UK and beyond (Sport England, 2016b), producing significant affects, such as pleasure, passion, sense of belonging, and control.

Unlike previous social marketing campaigns around women's sport, the promotional videos for This Girl Can work to materialize ideas about the capacities of women with different abilities, social backgrounds and body sizes to conquer self-limiting fears, as opposed to young models or professional athletes. According to Sport England (2016b), these images and slogans represent the "real story of women who play sport", as the images are "the complete opposite of the idealised and stylised images of women we are now used to seeing". The campaign strives to challenge assumptions about femininity and identify pressures about body image that prevent women from engaging in sport and leisure, which, ironically, inform anti-obesity strategies (Francombe-Webb, Depper, & Rich, 2016). We were drawn into the compelling visualization (interconnecting with a funky soundscape) of women's diverse body shapes ranging from 'jiggly' to 'toned' that contested their invisibility in broader popular culture. Yet, the multiple images and text are subsumed by a performance of (largely white, middle class) heteronormative femininity; the female body is matter to be 'worked on', toned, and shaped through multiple possibilities of individualized pleasure, health, desirability, and so on.

Despite the intent of the campaign to counter body shaming, This Girl Can mobilizes assumptions about 'real' gender difference (individual and collective bodies) to activate women's desires. Echoing the genre of reality television, the 'real' bodies of This Girl Can reveal the impossibility of 'representing' all women's bodies. For example, there is a normative sameness articulated through feminine bodies that are predominantly white, able bodied, younger, cisgendered, and unmarked by tattoos, piercings, forms of scarring, motherhood, or culturally specific clothing. Those largely absent gendered bodies are consequently marginalized, remaining 'other' and outside the scope of 'real' women in the campaign. The recent re-release of This Girl Can campaign could be read as the marketing team responding to some early criticisms of the lack of representation of women from ethnic minorities, as they now incorporate the voice and poetry of African-American poet and civil rights activist, Maya Angelou. The text 'Girl Power' is emblazoned across the image of Bisi as a black woman pushing weights in the gym and it is positioned prominently on the '*meet the girls*' page, with her story of wanting to become healthier and build muscle. This new visualization of difference and diversity sits uncomfortably alongside the absence of research data or critical discourse about racial inequalities in the key report *Go Where the Women Are* (Sport England, 2015). Without any means of articulating intersectional inequalities, the images risk essentializing racial and gender differences as 'barriers' to participation (such as fear of participation), materialized through discourses of market segmentation that position women as responsible for their 'choices'. For example, two types of barriers are identified: (1) "Practical/logistical challenges (often presented as the justifiable excuse for lack of action)" and (2) "Personal/ emotional reasons (may be less explicitly stated but represent underlying real issue)" (Sport England, 2015, p. 22). Questions of how gender inequities play out to create fear and embodied shame in sport cultures remain largely invisible beyond behaviours and 'excuses'.

Another disturbing moment in our reading of the campaign arose from the problematic reference to women of all ages through the subject position of 'girls' and the extent to which other possible identifications are precluded or invited through the individualized mode of address—This '*Girl*' Can. Perhaps we should not have been surprised about this utilization given the connection between the commercial and economic rationalities of neo-liberalism "which has as its ideal subject the category of 'girl'" (McRobbie, 2008, p. 531). Yet, this point became a focus of discussion on social media with some older women commenting on how they were comfortable with referring to themselves as girls as it evoked forgotten girlhood pleasures. While other women reacted angrily with comments about the demeaning discourse that did not represent them as competent adults who were deserving of respect in sport as in other aspects of life. As we have previously argued, the collective identification of women as 'girls' can produce a "patronizing and infantilizing" mode of public address (Fullagar & Pavlidis, 2018, p. 452). Invoking the girl as a subject position also reiterates adult/child, good/bad dualisms that operate through regulatory gender discourses—shaming 'bad girls' who don't enjoy performing active embodiment. However, as Silas (2017) writes, "just as the sportswear manufacturers don't represent me, #thisgirlcan doesn't represent me as a woman in the campaign slogan". Silas points to the resistance of collective identities that have disempowering effects and are also bound up with corporate influence of merchandising and branding—perhaps This Woman Can just didn't have the same slick marketing appeal.

The essentializing approach to gender categorization is not a new phenomenon in government health and sport policy. For example, in a recent publication by Sport England (2016d, p. 3), young men and women have been further categorized into various psychologized market segments as 'youth personalities' to understand the "attitudes, behaviours and preferences of young people" in sport. As Francis (2006) emphasizes, this act of 'naming' categorical gender groups can serve to further maintain and exacerbate differences that inferiorize women. Heteronormative representations of 'girls' further limits the campaign's credibility to truly 'empower' women. In the recent re-release of This Girl Can in January 2017, the campaign's target audience, that was initially 14–40, was extended to 14–60 years. The digital campaign video attempts to shift focus through the inclusion of the poem, *Phenomenal Woman*, by Maya Angelou. The camera pans across diverse images of women moving, stopping at a key moment to focus in on one woman's 'booty dance'. In doing so the clip simultaneously hails us collectively as 'girls' who enjoy moving while also inviting us to share a universalized pleasure that emanates from an essence of womanhood to be celebrated in and through the moving body.

The dangers of "institutionalized diversity" have been articulated by Black Feminists who question the way women's bodies are positioned as different and needing to be included "within" white culture (Ahmed, 2012). While the campaign emphasizes what feminized bodies 'can do' through physical activity, the dominant framing of a whole campaign around this 'girl' obscures differences between women in terms of the effects of racism, homophobia and class inequities in terms of access to opportunities. Older women, those with disabilities and women from diverse ethnic backgrounds have the lowest sport participation rates across all age groups, yet the 'real' challenges of everyday microaggression, sexism, racism, ableism, and ageism remain invisible in the digital rendering of celebratory womanhood.

'Can-do' Girls

With the central aim of This Girl Can being to empower women to overcome personal feelings of shame, Sport England (2016e, p. 6) sought to "liberate women from the judgements that hold them back". For example, women of all sizes are portrayed confidently in campaign images and through mantras that enact a performance of active womanhood through affective capacities:

> I swim because I love my body. Not because I hate it

The mantras are seductive, appealing to women through individualized emotions and self-help discourses. In this way, the campaign images are infused with post-feminist appeals to individual empowerment. As a digital campaign that operates across multiple public sites (apps, TV, billboards at train stations), This Girl Can invites women to imagine and feel their way into becoming the sporting body that has perhaps eluded them to date. By identifying with This Girl Can, women are invited to embody the subject position of the do-it-yourself active womanhood. This 'can-do' girl is positioned as the 'ideal', empowered citizen within the campaign (Harris, 2004), whereby overcoming fears of judgement becomes a neo-liberal, 'do-it-yourself' project of the self (Heywood, 2007). Within this do-it-yourself assemblage, women are positioned as flexible subjects, at a time where notions of girlhood are being challenged, redefined and replaced with "a unique category of girls who are self-assured" (Harris, 2004, p. 17). For example, with the simple, hard-hitting mantra splayed across a woman working out in the gym:

Girl. Power.

In some respect, the campaign marks a significant shift away from gender stereotypes that are prevalent in female subject positioning, with clips focusing on women playing football, embracing their own body, running without make-up on, running with make-up on (i.e., smudged under the eyes after exercise), and sweating. Changing social conditions in advanced liberal societies have enabled this generation of can-do women "to see themselves, and to be seen, as enjoying new 'freedoms' and opportunities" (Harris, 2004, p. 8). However, as we have previously critiqued, the "hallmark of a have-it-all femininity that is equally available to all is a fictional storyline: it is representative of the few, not the many" (Francombe, 2014, p. 582). This Girl Can is then one example of a campaign enacted across post-feminist digital cultures, that further "*incites* judgement by inviting us to *view* girls and women no matter what they are doing, where they are doing it, or how they look doing it" (Dobson, 2015, p. 157) rather than focusing on some of the material conditions of possibility that shape what women do and where they do it. Diverse leisure spaces (gyms, bike paths, running tracks, zumba classes, football fields) are simply evoked as accessible, inviting sites of active embodiment, free from the effects of all kinds of discrimination, sexual harassment, or violence. Moreover, McMurria's (2008, p. 322) work, for instance, on social inequalities in the US context highlights the difficulties that working-class women face, as "neoliberal policies decrease state funds for social services such as health care, childcare, and housing", increasing the strain on families. The intersections of class are disregarded in This Girl Can, whereby having choice and autonomy for women *who can*, is marked as post-feminist subjectivity formation and ethical citizenship.

This do-it-yourself active womanhood is not accessible, nor may it be desirable to all. Gillis and Munford (2004, p. 165) draw out these tensions "implicit in the contemporary feminist project" as the individualism of girl power sits uneasy with patriarchal privilege and oppressed marginalized identities (see also, Harris & Dobson, 2015). It is, therefore, important to question the ways in which This Girl Can claims to 'empower' women in sport, as this notion is embedded in "complex, mobile social relations that shape how we feel, act and become gendered subjects" (Fullagar & Pavlidis, 2018, p. 448). This Girl Can is bound up with an economy of affect where autonomy *feels* like successful womanhood, entices women to *feel* that they are no longer inhibited by the social constraints that exist in gendered leisure. Yet, as Amy-Chinn (2006, p. 156) argues, heteronormative discourses position women as active, desiring subjects and the "discourse of liberation" serves to further underpin restrictive versions of 'normality' that ignore how gender power relations work through and on bodies.

Othering Girls Who *Can't Do*

This neo-liberal project of the self is embedded in complex power relations that enable a specific form of productive, aspirational feminine subjectivity (Fusco, 2006). Through participating in the campaign, women's bodies are thus regulated through technologies of the self as they perform an assumed unified active subjectivity and self-responsibility. For example, alongside an image of a women cycling up a hill is the strapline:

> Still slow. Still lapping everyone on the couch.

The female body is thus imbued with cultural values through which moral virtue is achieved. According to Wright (2014, p. 841), within advanced liberal societies, "body shape and weight have become symbolic of 'good' or 'bad' health and bodies have become a reflection of moral choice and a measure of identity". And while women must work to monitor and improve a specific kind of body, it can never be a complete project. What is problematic in This Girl Can are the bodies that are left "on the couch" or do not (re)present 'normality'—albeit a reconfigured 'normative' imaginary—are consequently labelled as lazy and pathologized as outsiders. We question what is left for This Girl (who) Can*not* (and may not identify with normalized desires) meet the normalizing expectations of the 'ideal' cultural body?

Moreover, there is a seductive message within the campaign that by overcoming fears of judgement and taking part in sport, women can eliminate the barriers associated with self-esteem and body confidence. However, what is missing from this discourse of personal liberation is a critique of the heteronormative versions of femininity and relations of shame in which women's bodies are positioned. Those who do not perform acceptable forms of 'feminine' subjectivity and liberate themselves to be physically active (through 'working on', toning and shaping the body) are positioned as objects of shame. These shaming practices create further anxiety and uncertainties for women, as the empowerment discourse overwhelms the focus of This Girl Can. The campaign positions women's emotions as the site of problems to be overcome (judgement as a barrier to overcome, rather than masculine cultural norms) and this formulation ignores the gendered violence and inferiorizing practices that shape a range of affective relations with the body (everyday sexism through to trauma arising from sexual assault and childhood assault) (van Ingen, 2016). We question the ways in which emotions are positioned as "psychological states that emerge (my feeling of joy, anger, sadness) from the interior self as authentic expressions of individuality (the personal realm)" (Fullagar & Pavlidis, 2018, p. 451).

Directing the 'Gaze' in This Girl Can

A final dimension of the campaign we would like to explore is the sexualization of women's bodies through This Girl Can. In 2015, the original campaign video was released by Sport England, and the women's bodies featured in this video centralized and sexualized women's flesh. As we commented at the time (Fullagar & Francombe-Webb, 2015), Sport England attempts to sell this "as somehow radical or revolutionary" because the active woman is positioned as *knowing*. Yet, this form of address is widely critiqued as the conjuncture is predicated on a trademark of female knowingness, where being 'up for it' (in sexual and other ways) escapes criticism as it is being represented in an ironic, parodic way (McRobbie, 2004c). Traditional theories of women's objectification and sexualization need to be reconfigured on the basis that women themselves are presented (such as This Girl Can). They 'choose' to present themselves (e.g., through wearing clothing with slogans such as Porn Queen, Hello Boys, social media tagging #feelinglikeafox) as self-consciously sexualized by the participatory dynamics in leisure and everyday life from which feminist critiques are seemingly redundant. Freedom is emphasized for women at the same time a form of silencing is produced (McRobbie, 2004c, p. 260).

Against this backdrop, we analyze the campaign's symbolism and new forms of self-conscious sexualization of women's flesh as it highlights the desire to 'work on' the body, to eradicate the excess flesh that doesn't belong and its positioning of 'girls' as reflexive in regard to all aspects of their lives including their physical activity practices. Through a critical post-feminist sensibility, this process of sexualization not only positions feminism as apolitical, it is embedded in power relations of "gendering, radicalization and classing" (Gill, 2009, p. 137). The focus remains on women's bodies that are active, (hetero)sexy, and middle class. These 'technologies of sexiness' are corporeal technologies that direct the gaze at the women's bodies, normalizing the cultural 'ideal' body that is 'worked on' (Evans & Riley, 2014; Ferris, 2003). In the campaign video for This Girl Can, the camera spans across women's bodies in slow motion, directing the gaze onto women's moving and 'jiggling' bodies. A close-up shot focuses on one women dancing, while the caption reads:

> Sweating like a pig, feeling like a fox.

In Dobson's (2015, p. 158) analysis of post-feminist digital spaces, she emphasizes that audiences are invited to gaze at the women (in This Girl Can) in a way that is "quite voyeuristic and fetishistic … [as] several shots depict young female bodies together on a dancefloor, with breasts and bottoms shaking vigorously". The discursive positioning of the 'knowing' woman who feels 'foxy' irrespective of sweating is the epitome of the post-feminist forms of address McRobbie (2004c) identified. The scrutiny of women's bodies is further intensified through the virtual spaces of This Girl Can, as women are encouraged to share their own images in sport and investment of their bodies, write and imagine their own active biographies and are compelled to both self-confess and profess their (in)active body-projects. Salter (2015, p. 2736) highlights the complexities of such "empowering" social media spaces where women are still left "highly visible and legitimate objects of public scrutiny and judgement". It is difficult to contemplate Sport England creating a campaign for empowering men in sport that celebrates the male body as This Girl Can does.

However, alongside the hallmarks of post-feminist digital cultures such as self-conscious sexualization (McRobbie, 2004c), there are elements of Sport England's campaign that are far from revolutionary in terms of the feminist critique required. In the campaign video for This Girl Can, women dance and perform to Missy Elliot's 'Get Ur Freak On' and we are reminded of Missy Elliot's music video for this song, embedded with sexual images whereby women dance suggestively for onlooking males. So, while This Girl Can is mobilized as a campaign to inspire women to overcome fears of judgement and feel ownership and empowerment of their own bodies, "at the same time, women are reminded that "others" are implicitly *authorized to view and judge female bodies*" (Dobson, 2015, p. 158).

It is thus important for future campaigns to *challenge* the "spectacular display of female bodies" (Dobson, 2015, p. 158) and cultural discourses around women's bodies as objects of the public gaze. This is pertinent at a time when young women, in particular, are experiencing the negative effects and *affects* of the objectification of women in popular culture (see Girl Guiding UK, 2016). Yet, we must also remain mindful of the subtle and insidious reconfiguration of feminine forms of address that populate digital spaces and campaigns. The failure to provide a feminist vocabulary to contest the discursive and material subjectification of women will only perpetuate inequity across the lifecourse (McRobbie, 2004c).

Concluding Thoughts: Towards More Inclusive Physical Cultures for Women

Throughout this chapter we have explored a number of digital dilemmas raised by the This Girl Can campaign. We have emphasized the contradictions of do-it-yourself active womanhood and 'empowerment' discourses that disregard how gender inequities are entangled with "bodies, discourses and technologies" (Fullagar & Pavlidis, 2018, p. 459). The new category of girlhood, that is ironically imbued in the title of the campaign, the 'can-do' girl, emerging in our post-feminist era fails to represent *all* women (Harris 2004). Although campaigns may attempt to make diverse bodies more visible, critical questions remain about how gender difference is materialized *about* and *between* women and girls in digital re-representations to contend with essentializing categories. It is thus imperative for sport and leisure policies to incorporate feminist research to avoid perpetuating gender stereotyping and individualizing responsibility for change. With respect to public representations of women, there have been promising changes in Britain with the *Advertising Standards Authority* introducing new regulatory standards to reduce gender stereotyping in advertisements. While we agree with This Girl Can about the importance of issues such as body shame and confidence, we differ with respect to the need to locate individual experiences within the collective context that produces inequities of all kinds (Francombe-Webb et al., 2016). National governing bodies and local authorities could work together more effectively *with women* to challenge gender inequities in the design and delivery of digital and physical practices.

Future physical activity campaigns for women should continue to highlight the diversity of what women *can* do, however, we need to move beyond the collective 'girls' who 'can', towards identifying the cultures of sexism, exclusion, and inferiorization that actively discourage the participation of girls and women. Indeed, this is not an easy task in the face of seductive post-feminist discourses that signify the end of feminism (Douglas, 2010). Feminist research into how women are engaging with (and are also regulated through) social media *across* multiple platforms is opening new directions to explore the micropolitics of digital assemblages as they are implicated in modes of learning to "do" gendered leisure (see Fullagar, Pavlidis & Francombe-Webb, 2018; Baer, 2016). Such questions may inform further research into the "intra-actions" of physical and digital cultures as new technologies and virtual spaces become significant sites that both reinscribe and challenge gender relations with respect to policy, provision, pedagogy, and participation.

References

Ahmed, S. (2004). *The cultural politics of emotion*. New York: Routledge.

Ahmed, S. (2012). *On being included: Racism and diversity in institutional life*. Durham, NC: Duke University Press.

Amy-Chinn, D. (2006). This is just for me(n): How the regulation of post-feminist lingerie advertising perpetuates woman as object. *Journal of Consumer Culture, 6*(2), 155–175.

Baer, H. (2016). Redoing feminism: Digital activism, body politics, and neoliberalism. *Feminist Media Studies, 16*(1), 17–34.

Braidotti, R. (2013). *The posthuman*. Cambridge, UK: Polity Press.

Dobson, A. S. (2015). *Postfeminist digital cultures: Femininity, social media, and self-representation*. New York: Palgrave Macmillan.

Douglas, S. J. (2010). *Epilogue: The f-word. Enlightened sexism: The seductive message that feminism's work is done*. New York: Times Books.

Evans, A., & Riley, S. (2014). *Technologies of sexiness: Sex, identity and consumer culture*. New York: Columbia University Press.

Evans, R., Riley, S., & Shankar, A. (2010). Technologies of sexiness: Theorizing women's engagement in the sexualization of culture. *Feminism & Psychology, 20*(1), 114–131.

Ferris, J. E. (2003). Parallel discourses and "appropriate" bodies: Media constructions of anorexia and obesity in the cases of Tracey Gold and Carnie Wilson. *Journal of Communication Inquiry, 27*(3), 256–273.

Francis, B. (2006). The nature of gender. In C. Skelton, B. Francis, & L. Smulyan (Eds.), *The Sage handbook of gender and education* (pp. 7–17). London: Sage.

Francombe, J. (2010). I cheer, you cheer, we cheer': Physical technologies and the normalized body. *Television & New Media, 11*(5), 350–366.

Francombe, J. (2014). Learning to leisure: Femininity and practices of the body. *Leisure Studies, 33*(6), 580–597.

Francombe-Webb, J. (2015). Body image & female identity: A multi-method approach to media analysis. In *Sage research methods cases*. London: Sage.
Francombe-Webb, J., & Toffoletti, K. (2017). Sporting females: Power, diversity and the body [forthcoming]. In B. Wheaton et al. (Eds.), *Handbook of feminism in sport, leisure and physical education*. Houndmills, UK: Palgrave.
Francombe-Webb, J., Depper, A., & Rich, E. (2016). Why young women need to be given a louder voice in the obesity debate. *The Conversation*. Retrieved July 7, 2017, from https://theconversation.com/why-young-women-need-to-be-given-a-louder-voice-in-the-obesity-debate-68861
Fullagar, S. (2009). Governing healthy family lifestyles through discourses of risk and responsibility. In J. Wright & V. Harwood (Eds.), *Biopolitics and the "obesity epidemic": Governing bodies* (pp. 108–126). New York: Routledge.
Fullagar, S. (2017). Post-qualitative inquiry and the new materialist turn: Implications for sport, health and physical culture research. *Qualitative Research in Sport, Exercise and Health, 9*(2), 247–257.
Fullagar, S., & Francombe-Webb, J. (2015). This girl can campaign is all about sex not sport. *The Guardian*. Retrieved December 17, 2015, from https://www.theguardian.com/commentisfree/2015/jan/16/this-girl-can-campaign-sex-sport-real-women-bodies-objectifying-female-flesh
Fullagar, S., & Pavlidis, A. (2018). Feminist theories of emotion and affect in sport. In B. Wheaton et al. (Eds.), *Handbook of feminism in sport, leisure and physical education* (pp. 447–462). London: Palgrave Macmillan.
Fullagar, S., Pavlidis, A., & Francombe-Webb, J. (2018). Feminist theories after the post-structuralist turn [forthcoming]. In D. Parry, C. Johnson, & F. A. Warner (Eds.), *Fourth wave feminism*. New York: Routledge.
Fusco, C. (2006). Inscribing healthification: Governance, risk, surveillance and the subjects and spaces of fitness and health. *Health & Place, 12*(1), 65–78.
Gill, R. (2007a). Postfeminist media culture: Elements of a sensibility. *European Journal of Cultural Studies, 10*(2), 147–166.
Gill, R. (2007b). Critical respect: The difficulties and dilemmas of agency and "choice" for feminism: A reply to Duits and van Zoonen. *European Journal of Women's Studies, 14*(1), 69–80.
Gill, R. (2009). Beyond the 'sexualization of culture' thesis: An intersectional analysis of 'sixpacks', 'midriffs' and 'hot lesbians' in advertising. *Sexualities, 12*(2), 137–160.
Gill, R. (2016). Post-postfeminism? New feminist visibilities in postfeminist times. *Feminist Media Studies, 16*(4), 610–630.
Gill, R., & Scharff, C. (2011). Introduction. In R. Gill & C. Scharff (Eds.), *New femininities: Postfeminism, neoliberalism, and subjectivity* (pp. 1–20). London: Palgrave Macmillan.

Gillis, S., & Munford, R. (2004). Genealogies and generations: The politics and praxis of third wave feminism. Women's. *History Review, 13*(2), 165–182.
Girl Guiding UK. (2016). *Girls' attitudes survey*. London: Girl Guiding UK.
Harris, A. (2004). *Future girl. Young women in the twenty-first century*. London: Routledge.
Harris, A., & Dobson, A. S. (2015). Theorizing agency in post-girlpower times. *Continuum, 29*(2), 145–156.
Heywood, L. (2007). Producing girls: Empire, sport, and the neoliberal body. In J. Hargreaves & P. Vertinsky (Eds.), *Physical culture, power and the body* (pp. 101–120). London: Routledge.
Long, J., Hylton, K., Lewis, H., Ratna, A., & Spracklen, K. (2011). Space for inclusion? The construction of sport and leisure spaces as places for migrant communities. In A. Ratna & B. Lashua (Eds.), *Community and inclusion in leisure research and sport development* (pp. 33–53). Eastbourne: Leisure Studies Association.
McMurria, J. (2008). Desperate citizens and good Samaritans. Neoliberalism and makeover reality TV. *Television and New Media, 9*, 305–332.
McRobbie, A. (2004a). Notes on postfeminism and popular culture: Bridget Jones and the new gender regime. In A. Harris (Ed.), *All about the girl: culture, power and identity* (pp. 3–14). London: Routledge.
McRobbie, A. (2004b). Notes on 'what not to wear' and post-feminist symbolic violence. *The Sociological Review, 52*(2), 97–109.
McRobbie, A. (2004c). Post-feminism and popular culture. *Feminist Media Studies, 4*(3), 255–264.
McRobbie, A. (2008). Young women and consumer culture. *Cultural Studies, 22*(5), 531–550.
Probyn, E. (2005). *Blush: Faces of shame*. Sydney, NSW: University of New South Wales Press.
Salter, M. (2015). Privates in the online public: Sex(ting) and reputation on social media. *New Media and Society, 18*(11), 2723–2739.
Silas, S. (2017). #thisgirlcan? I much prefer #thiswomandoes. *The Guardian*. Retrieved April 6, 2017, from https://www.theguardian.com/commentisfree/2017/mar/06/thisgirlcan-i-prefer-thiswomandoes-branding-infantilises
Skeggs, B. (2004). *Class, self, culture*. London: Routledge.
Sport England. (2015). *Go where women are: Insight on engaging women and girls in sport and exercise*. London: Sport England.
Sport England. (2016a). *Sport England 2015–16 annual report*. London: Sport England.

Sport England. (2016b). *This Girl Can delivers results one year on*. Retrieved July 7, 2017, from https://www.sportengland.org/news-and-features/news/2016/january/12/thisgirlcanbirthday/

Sport England. (2016c). *Record number of women get active*. Retrieved July 7, 2017, from https://www.sportengland.org/news-and-features/news/2016/december/8/record-numbers-of-women-getting-active/

Sport England. (2016d). *Youth insight under the skin*. London: Sport England.

Sport England. (2016e). *This Girl Can is our nationwide campaign to get women and girls moving, regardless of shape, size and ability*. Retrieved July 7, 2017, from https://www.sportengland.org/our-work/women/this-girl-can/

Sport England. (2017). *This Girl Can returns to our screens*. Retrieved April 3, 2017, from https://www.sportengland.org/news-and-features/news/2017/february/24/this-girl-can-returns-to-our-screens/

Stewart, C., & Caudwell, J. (2017). Vicious cycle: The "troublemakers" tackling sexism in elite sport. *The Conversation*. Retrieved 7 July, 2017, from http://theconversation.com/vicious-cycle-the-troublemakers-tackling-sexism-in-elite-sport-75687

This Girl Can. (2017). *Stories archive – This Girl Can*. Retrieved April 4, 2017, from http://www.thisgirlcan.co.uk/stories/

Toffoletti, K. (2016). Analyzing media representations of sportswomen—expanding the conceptual boundaries using a postfeminist sensibility. *Sociology of Sport Journal, 2*(33), 199–207.

van Ingen, C. (2016). Getting lost as a way of knowing: The art of boxing within shape your life. *Qualitative Research in Sport, Exercise and Health, 8*(5), 472–486.

Watson, B., & Ratna, A. (2011). Bollywood in the park: Thinking intersectionally about public leisure space. *Leisure/Loisir, 35*(1), 71–86.

Watson, B., & Scraton, S. J. (2012). Leisure studies and intersectionality. *Leisure Studies, 32*(1), 35–47.

Wetherell, M. (2012). *Affect and emotion. A new social science understanding*. London: Sage.

Wolfe, M. J. (2017). Puberty blues—then and now: Diffracting semblances of being girl in Australia. *Feminist Media Studies, 17*(3), 489–504.

Wright, J. (2014). Beyond body fascism: The place for health education. In K. Fitzpatrick & R. Tinning (Eds.), *Health education: Critical perspectives* (pp. 233–248). Oxon/New York: Routledge.

Making Gender and Motherhood Through Pedagogies of Digital Health and Fitness Consumption: 'Soon It Made Us More Active as a Family'

Emma Rich

Introduction

The relationship between gender and technology has long been the attention of feminist scholars and activists, in terms of both constituting gender (Wajcman, 2004, 2007) and, more recently, issues of self-representation (Dobson, 2015) and the potential of digital platforms in disseminating feminist ideas (Baer, 2016). As technology has become increasingly part of our everyday lives, questions have been raised about the impact this has on gender inequalities and the possibilities for challenging injustice. One notable area in which everyday leisure practices are being transformed by the digital is through the recent proliferation of digital technologies designed for health and fitness.

Around the world, digital technologies have revolutionised the practices and policies of healthcare, profoundly changing the ways that health knowledge is being created, accessed, used, and interpreted. Of particular prominence, are those applications which focus on promoting healthy lifestyles, as a mechanism of preventative medicine/health care. This

E. Rich (✉)
Department for Health, University of Bath, Bath, UK
e-mail: e.rich@bath.ac.uk

D. C. Parry et al. (eds.), *Digital Dilemmas*,
https://doi.org/10.1007/978-3-319-95300-7_10

advanced functionality within mobile devices has led to the rapid growth in wearable and mobile health (mHealth) technologies, which is now a priority area of investment by governments and health agencies, used by millions of individuals and presenting major questions about the potential of emerging technologies to influence health practices. These technologies provide significant opportunities for improving health and fitness, yet for these to be realised, existing research must be accompanied by studies of their social and cultural contexts, including gendered inequalities.

Digital health technologies include a broad range of devices and software, including social media platforms, telemedicine and telehealth (remote access health care), big data health tracking, gaming technologies, and wearable technologies. In particular, there is a rapid growth in what can be described as technologies that are pertinent to promoting healthy lifestyle behaviours, such as physical activity, body weight management, sleep and food consumption, and other bodily aspects such as menstruation, fertility, sexual activity, and pregnancy (Lupton, 2014b). Many of these mobile and wearable devices offer a range of tools for individuals to measure, monitor, and regulate their health and provide new ways of representing the body through quantified data. While there is much to celebrate about the transformative potential of these technologies, there is also a more critical discourse emerging in response to what Lupton (2014a, p. 706) describes as the 'prevailing solutionist and instrumental approaches to the application of digital technologies to medicine and public health.'

In this context, many of the digital health devices available for monitoring different aspects of our behaviours are categorised as 'wellness and lifestyle.' Although these technologies now represent a critical mass in the digital health landscape, they are not subject to the same forms of regulation (Powell, Landman, & Bates, 2014) as medical devices. These digital health technologies afford new opportunities to produce data about one's body and also orient users towards relations of the body that are about not only demonstrating the correct behaviours, morally coding particular ways of learning about one's own body. A growing market of technologies afford individuals new opportunities to measure, monitor, and regulate their bodies and aspects of their daily lives and behaviours including sleep, calorie intake, exercise/physical activity, mood, heart rate, sleep patterns, and sleep quality. These practices are increasingly recognised as part of phenomenon described as self-tracking and involves the measuring and charting of these everyday behaviours. Their popularity reflects the trend towards self-tracking as a way of managing one's lifestyle (Lupton, 2013) in line with the logic of a growing movement known as 'the quantified self' (Smarr, 2012; Swan, 2012). The quantified self is where one collects and charts data, shares it, and gathers real-time feedback and then uses that information to modify behaviour. Although much is being written about the influence of quantification on people's health practices and identities, much less has been written about how digital health practices are connected to the learning that takes place through *consuming* digital health. Furthermore, little is known about how different social groups are being constituted through these technologies.

In 2014, with my colleague Andy Miah, we outlined a theory of digital health technologies as a form of public pedagogy (Rich & Miah, 2014) p. 301):

> In advancing a public pedagogy approach to theorising digital health, it is necessary to recognise how technology is inextricable from the manner in which people learn about health. Furthermore, these apparatus dictate conditions of self-tracking, collection of data, and monitoring, which have a bearing on what and how people learn about their bodies and health.

The capacity for accumulating and sharing data is part of a broader shift of responsibility from medical expert to the individual, which is typically framed through neoliberal discourses of individual (patient) empowerment and democratisation (Fotopoulou & O'Riordan, 2017). As such, many of the technologies above are 'instructive' and play a pedagogic role in people's everyday lives. They offer an instructional pedagogy—messages about how to monitor and regulate the body in ways that are deeply infused with a 'coporeal ethic, a socially regulative moral code' (Evans & Rich, 2011, p. 365).

Building on this work, in this chapter, I examine how the health and fitness related digital technologies we are encouraged to consume come to shape gendered subjectivity. In doing so, I examine consumption in relation to digital health technologies specifically focused on 'healthy lifestyles,' highlighting the gendered nature of the discourses mobilised around their production and consumption practices. Throughout, I draw on the work of scholars who are developing understandings of consumption as a type of learning and education as one becomes a 'literate' consumer as part of this call for learning to care for oneself. In doing so, I build towards an understanding of the digital health market as having potentialities and capacities through which to teach appropriate forms of health behaviour. In other words, to understand how consumption of digital health technologies operates as pedagogy, asking what kinds of gendered consumers are being co-created. My analysis builds on conceptions of pedagogy that describe the individualisation of consumption, which presupposes a rationalist conception of learner but which also signals the way public pedagogy might give rise to potential for change.

Consumption as Pedagogy

Since earlier work which understood consumption as 'the process by which consumer goods and services are created, bought and used' (McCracken, 1990, p. xi), a range of theoretical perspectives on consumption have emerged within the field of sociology of consumption. While there is not space to explore these varied approaches (for an account of these, see Sandlin & McLaren, 2010b), it is notable that a number of authors have urged scholars with the field of education to examine consumption and take it seriously as a site of learning (e.g. Sandlin & McLaren, 2010a; Usher, Bryant, & Johnston, 1997) Furthermore, much of the work within public pedagogy, recognised sites of popular culture through which everyday practices of consumption take place, can be understood as sites of learning, for example, shopping, leisure activities, sport, film, the Internet, and social media. However, Sandlin and McLaren (2010b) observe that much of the literature that focuses on the 'market as educator' tends to focus on the hegemonic power of the market and sites of consumption within advanced liberal societies. In this next section, I outline the particular theoretical approach to understanding how digital health consumption operates as pedagogy, before specifically examining some of the implications for gender, power relations, and social justice across the life span.

Pedagogies of Digital Health Consumption

My focus here is not on particular modes of consumption, nor how they are a reflection of particular kinds of social economic or class dispositions. In this regard, rather than focusing on consumption as simply the selection and purchasing of products shaped by the market, consumption can be understood as part of everyday life practices (Paterson, 2006) as consumers place 'their conscious experiences of acts of consumption into larger processes of globalization' (p. 7). This would include the consumption practices which form part of our everyday leisure. Sandlin and McLaren (2010b) encourage 'educators to explore consumption as it is situated in particular everyday contexts' (p. 11). To do so, it is important to question the rationalist and individualistic language through which consumption is often understood. In their handbook of public pedagogy, Sandlin, Schultz, and Burdick (2010) observe that many authors 'focus on forms of learning existing beyond the dominant focus of language with most formal educational sites. These learnings elevate body, position, and affect to serve as direct modes of address, rather than tangential *learning styles* to be deployed as an accompaniment to the *real* education inherent in illocution' (p. 32).

Furthermore, digital health technologies are not simply consumed to meet pre-existing needs. Rather, informed by new materialist work, we can understand these practices as entangled and as such integral to the process of emerging meanings and practices. I examine the implications of this work in developing the concept of body pedagogies (Evans, et al. 2008) in ways that draw attention to the relationalities and materialities of learning through and with everyday consumption practices. These pedagogies produce meanings, but also desire and therefore provide a lens through which to understand what it means to be a consumer of these products. In other words, how public pedagogy (Rich & Miah,

2014) comes to influence consumers relationships with particular digital health technologies and the assemblages[1] through which they are marketed.

Intergenerational Data Practices: Digital Health, Morality, and Parenthood

A range of formal institutions and organisations (e.g. schools, health organisations) are involved in crafting subjects engaged with commercially based digital technologies and their associated data practices (Gard, 2014; Lupton, 2015). Williamson (2016) notes that digital data technologies play an increasingly prominent role in the collection, calculation, and circulation of information about children. As such, a more recent trend includes the growth in digital health technologies that increasingly and actively target younger children. This is perhaps unsurprising given the rise of commercialism within schools (Spring, 2003). Many of these technologies call upon parents to consume these digital products to track their child's activities. For example, in 2014 a fitness band designed for children aged as young as four was launched, a technology through which children and parents can monitor a child's physical activity (See Rich, 2017). More recently, a range of fitness trackers designed specifically for children have emerged in commercial marketplace.

Technologies such as these reflect attempts to transform children into consumers. In certain respects, none of this is new, but perhaps represents an extension of the way in which childhood is increasingly commodified and children learn appropriate ways of consuming through various media such as television and advertising (Giroux, 1999; Kenway & Bullen, 2001; Kincheloe, 2002). However, the pedagogies of consumption positions parents as particular kinds of subjects in consuming the right

[1] According to Fox (2017: 139), this shift from entities to relationalities suggests a focus towards 'towards the capacities to do, think and feel thereby produced in bodies and collectivities of bodies. Concomitantly, this shift from an agentic human to flows of "affect" in assemblages acknowledges that things, organisations, social formations, and concepts contribute to social production as much as—if not more than—human bodies/subjects.'

technologies to properly monitor their children. Many of these digital technologies are directed at parents of young children to enable them to monitor their physical activity. These are infused with instructional discourses about healthy parenting (e.g. obesity).

These campaigns connect with a set of concerns about obesity and childhood. Over the last decade there has been a rise in moral panic associated with increasing childhood obesity (Campos, Saguy, Ernsberger, Oliver, & Gesser, 2005; Gard & Wright, 2005; Monaghan, 2005) which has led to increased responsibilisations and pedagogisation of parents and families, but most notably mothers. Obesity discourse, in particular, has focused on the relationship between childhood, inactivity, and diets in relation to the ostensible 'crisis' of childhood obesity. As (Burrows, 2009, p. 131) observes, 'in the context of escalating concerns over childhood obesity, a startling array of parent-focused biopedagogies has arisen.' Digital technologies are part of a broad array of resources designed to encourage parents and children to gather and use information to monitor and regulate various aspects of health (e.g. weight) through everyday 'leisure' practices. The mobilisation of digital technology as 'solutionist' (Lupton, 2014a) extends not only to working on one's body for oneself but also in terms of their capacity for monitoring others.

Moreover, many of these technologies are designed to help navigate the 'choice architecture' users are confronted with in their everyday lives '('the physical, socio-cultural, and administrative environment') in which people live out their lives and make decisions' (Peeters & Schuilenburg, 2016). For example, in the UK, the Change4life 'be food smart' mobile phone has been developed to help parents monitor food consumption. The digital app enables parents to scan a product barcode to see how much sugar, fat, and salt it contains so they can make healthier choices.

Maher, Fraser, and Wright (2010, p. 309) observe that when consumption is situated in childhood obesity, 'mothers and children are trapped in tussles over excessive or problematic consumption practices.' As such there are specific moralities circulating which entangle with existing discourses about becoming a 'good mother' within the pedagogies of these technologies. In other words, these are mutually reinforcing discourses which subtly (or not) encourage mothers to monitor the activity of their young children as a way of meeting the imperatives of good parenting.

These digital technologies are offered through the marketplace to women as a means through which to achieve and perform Mothering and family practices. Being a good Mother entails being the sort of consumer who buys the appropriate digital products for this purpose. Organisations and companies thus facilitate the adoption of particular technologies not only as a form of ethical consumption, but of performing the subject of 'good' mother—one who not only cares about the health of their children but is active in collecting, assimilating, and reflecting on digital data and to respond to instructional and regulative discourse. The various products circulating in this assemblage are therefore entangled with moral discourse that produce gendered norms which are explored in the following section.

The Cultural Production of Digital Health Pedagogies and Gendered Imaginary: The Case of the Fitbit

The examples offered above clearly illustrate the way in which the commercial market has thus entered into a field that is premised on the management of risk as a morally appropriate form of parenting. In the next section, I examine how the pedagogies of consuming certain digital health technologies relies on the production of a particular kind of imaginary of gender and motherhood; towards a seemingly contradictory subject who is both responsible for others, but must adhere to the imperatives of self-optimisation. Specifically, these pedagogies enable individuals to develop a subjectivity through consumption and indeed subsequent data practices as subjects who utilise data to 'generate stories for and about the body/self' (Smith & Vonthethoff, 2016, p. 15).

The purchasing and use of digital health technologies can be considered as a lifestyle practice, which according to (Usher et al., 1997) are 'practices of consumption and moreover of a consumption which is potentially unending, since desire can never be satisfied, there is always the need for new experiences and new learning' (p. 18). Advancing this line of enquiry, I will draw on the example of the wearable fitness tracker,

Fitbit. These wearable and mobile technologies with their tracking sensors have become popular within consumer culture (Fotopoulou & O'Riordan, 2017). The Fitbit Alta HR is a wearable wrist band which can monitor heart rate and also track activity, sleep, exercise, display notifications, and reminders to move. I will provide a description of a recent television advert promoting the Fitbit Alta HR, before outlining how its pedagogic address reflects many of the broader pedagogies of consumption present within the contemporary digital health market:

> The advert begins with a Young Girl lying on a bed looking at her Mother. Her Mother appears to be in her late 20's early 30's and of a relatively slim build. She is wearing a loose shirt over a t-shirt and is looking at herself in a full length mirror; her eyes fixed on her waist. The young girl says:
> "one day my Mum decided to live healthier so she got a FitBit"
>
> The next scene shows the Mother out in green space walking on her own.
>
> "she started out by walking more" comments the girl. The video then moves towards an image of the Mother's fitbit on her wrist which has begun to record data on how many steps she has taken.
>
> The next image shows the Mother walking up a hill with her daughter and husband/partner walking behind her. The mother turns around to wave them towards her and encourage them up the hill.
>
> "soon, it made us more active as a family"
>
> In the next image, the young girl is on her bike, with her Mum running behind her.
>
> "It motivated her to move a little more"
>
> Next, the Mum is in lying in her bed whilst the daughter is holding a mobile phone and opens a sleep tracker to look at her Mum's sleep stages.
>
> "and told her how well she was sleeping"

The girl and the male adult (presumably father/husband) are sat at the kitchen table. In front of them is a bowl of crisps and a bowl of apples. The mum walks and reaches in between them and takes an apple from the bowl.

"she started to choose healthier food"

In the final scene, the Mum can be seen wearing fitness clothing, smiling and running with other women.

"Fitbit helped her feel good and get in better shape."

The Mum then picks up her daughter, with the husband in view and everyone smiles

"and if she can do it, you can too"

'Find your fit' then appears across the screen.

Adverts such as these provide spaces that 'open up the imaginary in lives of real people' (Hoechsmann, 2010, p. 23) and make clear that self-care through digital apps and wearable technology is to be learned through the pedagogies of these technologies (Fotopoulou & O'Riordan, 2017). Purchasing and using a Fitbit is therefore not simply the result of buying tracking technology, but is also a choice of when, where, and which particular fitness band. However, I also argue that subsequent digital health practices contribute to making up of gender subjectivity and more specifically motherhood and that this process of consumption is not simply a reflection of a particular fixed or pre-existing identity. As Coleman (2009) writes about becoming of female bodies through media images, subjectivities are not merely affected but rather produced through media images. In this advert, digital health technologies are positioned in such a way (Hoechsmann, 2010) to promise many 'solutions' to a range of problems that are constructed in gendered ways.

These pedagogies of digital health consumption speak to way in which 'the lived experience of learning is always affective'(Hickey-Moody, 2013, p. 126). Hoechsmann (2010) suggests that 'it is thus the desire to consume rather than the act of consumption that is significant' (p. 39). Take the above Fitbit advert, where each new experience brought about through the engagement with the technology provides a means through which new desires are potentially generated. The pedagogic address is one which indicates that the affective flow of these experiences has a generative potential to remake new experiences and subjectivities, from walking on one's own to encouraging healthy behaviours across the family.

The framing of motherhood and maternal responsibility evident in this assemblage is similar to the ways in which pedagogisation of families (Burrows, 2009) has positioned mothers as responsible for children's weight and obesity. However, I would argue that in new terrains of digital health, the discourse that socialises responsibility of mothers into this role extends beyond the idea of nurturing or as food providers (Lupton, 2001) towards a seemingly contradictory subject who is both responsible for others and must adhere to the imperatives of self-optimisation. Moral and instructional discourses task women with the neoliberal responsibility towards managing their own health, not only for themselves but for the good of others; as suggested in the advert, after a period of the Mother tracking her own activity, diet, and sleep 'soon, it made us more active as a family.'

As a theme running through this advert is the idea that managing the contemporary risk of ill-health becomes the focus of learning, both for the Mother but also as part of a relational family practice through girls can learn how to become more active. This learning involves developing knowledge of appropriate health technologies of the literacies to make sense of the data that is produced by these goods and knowledge of the appropriate consumption practices so as to perform self-improvement. The design and functioning of these digital technologies and their associated data practices draw on a 'foundational understanding of educational activity,' which 'targets the self, or more specifically the western notion of the self as developmental, autonomous, and rational isolate, as the object of pedagogical and curricular energies' (Burdick & Sandlin, 2013, p. 145). As (Fotopoulou & O'Riordan, 2017 p. 54) observe 'users are offered training in self-care through wearable technologies.' This pedagogical activity takes place 'through a series of micropractices that involve processes of mediation and sharing their own data via social networking.' Users learn not only the correct practices of self-care but the importance of performing this through public sharing of information about their everyday leisure activities.

Self-tracking devices such as the Fitbit are premised on this modernist notion of self-betterment; through the pedagogies of the advert centred on an ethic of care, women are to learn to vigilantly engage with the correct products and technologies to protect themselves from risks of various lifestyle diseases and to adhere to moral codes of Motherhood which make up healthy family practices and 'productive biocitizen' (Rail & Jette, 2015). The relationality between mother and daughter also implies a process of pedagogisation of the family along gendered lines. Consequently, health is constructed as dependent on making appropriate market choices, engaging in appropriate consumption practices which might then encourage others to 'take up' similar practices, as depicted in the image of the young girl riding her bike as her Mother runs and tracks the number of steps she takes. As symbolic of post-feminist 'can-do' girls (Harris, 2004), the young girl in this advert is learning to take cues from her mother about how to practice good health.

The positioning of technologies, such as Fitbit within contemporary health care reflects a preventative model and neoliberal turn towards the market. The purchasing and use of these commercial health and fitness trackers can therefore be considered as lifestyle practices, which according to (Usher et al., 1997, p. 18) are 'practices of consumption and moreover of a consumption which is potentially unending, given desire can never be satisfied, there is always the need for new experiences and new learning.' As others have indicated, learning to care for the body can be a 'boundary-less project' (Petherick, 2015, p. 363), which is open ended and ongoing, whereby there is always the need for new knowledge. The use of commercially produced and driven devices to optimise one's body and life draw on this logic.

The discourses of self-improvement and optimisation implore women and girls to consume the correct digital products to work on their bodies. The body is taken to be an ongoing project to be continually worked on through the consumption of the right products and services and engagement in particular health practices. To this end, these and other digital health products cast themselves as offering up solutions to a range of problems providing opportunities for creating a new thinner, healthier self; a happier healthy family; and the ethical mother who demonstrates not only appropriate health practices but also appropriate moralities around family life. They are marketed on the promise of offering the potential for new subjectivities and new affective states.

In part, users are expected to engage with these products as they are positioned as 'free and autonomous creatures who exercise choice in determining their behaviour' (Merriam & Brockett, 2007, p. 40). These behavioural techniques reflect the 'essential premise of liberalism [...] not to impose external control but to trigger internal self-control' (Peeters & Schuilenburg, 2016). The digitally engaged self learns the various techniques to manage and reduce the 'risks' related to the body (exercise, diet, sleep) in the pursuit of particular notions of personhood derived from the concept of the digitally engaged patient (Lupton, 2013). A number of authors describe how the body becomes knowable as an object of quantified knowledge, reflecting a 'techo-utopian' view of the body (Lupton, 2014a). Increasingly, digital health technologies such as these promise the means through which to achieve 'self-betterment' or 'self-optimisation' (Ruckenstein, 2014, p. 69).

In doing so, this neoliberal logic of the knowable body is part of a broader culture of risk management demarcating a shift towards 'posthuman optimisiation' (Millington, 2016). Modes of quantifying the body and capturing data have prompted debates about ontological assumptions made about how bodies are experienced and rendered knowable, and I argue, gendered. For instance, Ruckenstein (2014, p. 71) suggests that 'self-tracking tools abstract human bodies and minds into data flows that can be used and reflected upon' (ibid, 2014, p. 71). Thus, this becomes an ongoing project of the self, reflecting a gendered subjectivity which, in a post-feminist era, is to be continually worked on and always becoming. In the context of neoliberalism, 'hegemonic discourses of individual choice and empowerment, freedom, self-esteem, and personal responsibility have conspired to make feminism seem second nature and therefore also unnecessary for women, especially in the Western world, where structural inequalities are increasingly viewed as personal problems that can be resolved through individual achievement' (Baer, 2016, p. 20).

Yet, as noted in the chapter by Fullagar et al., affective relations (pleasure, shame, etc.) work to complicate individualised messages of empowerment in the post-feminist era. As McRobbie argues, in this era, 'elements of feminist have been taken into account, and have been absolutely incorporated into political and institutional life' (2009, p. 1).

A number of these digital health technologies operate through the commodification of particular affects oriented towards the desire to become fit, thin, and healthy. These pedagogies of consumption promise empowerment and self-betterment, positioning, self-tracking and digital health practices as providing solutions to that which needs fixing. In these affective assemblages, it is important to consider what it is these self-tracking devices 'do'. Employing a Deleuzian analysis in her study on relationship between school and online assemblages and bodies (Ringrose, 2011, p. 605) reveals how 'energy flows towards fulfilling conditions of lack to be desirably feminine.' Similarly, opportunities for self-tracking offered through new digital technologies such as the Fitbit are offered as 'solutions' to that which is lacking. For example, the opening scene of the Fitbit advert mobilises affect, specifically the desire for the ideal feminine body, thin, and stylized—juxtaposed by the image of the 'sad' mother staring into the woman (presumably disaffect with her body). In the advert, this is seen through the transformation not only in the mother's health practices, but through learning about appropriate consumption choices. In the opening scene she is wearing a loose shirt over a t-shirt, but by the end of the advertisement she is wearing fitness clothing, which comes to convey the performance and investment in working on oneself through market choices. By the end of the advert, self-transformation is deemed to have taken place, 'fixing' family life, self-fulfilment, and health. The growth in the digital tracking technologies in this way 'reterritorializes or "axiomatizes" desire, re-ordering flows through capitalist relations that exploit the connection between desire and lack (Ringrose, 2011, p. 601).'

Furthermore, these wearable products are positioned as solutions to optimise one's affective state (wellbeing/happiness) contributing to what Ahmed (2010) describes as the promise of happiness, that active consumption and engagement with these technologies will fill gaps in what we lack and optimise one's affective state. In the final scenes of the advert, the Mother, who is now wearing fitness clothing, is smiling (we assume happy) and running with other women (now connected with others). 'Fitbit helped her feel good and get in better shape' and the Mother then picks up her daughter, with the husband in view and everyone smiles. 'And if she can do it, you can too.' The message presumably that as a 'productive bio-citizen,' she is investing in conditions for 'health' through tracking and monitoring, or the active consumption and engagement of which is deemed to return these women to conditions of the idealised gendered subject.

Concluding Comments

The digital health technologies described in this chapter need to be understood in relation to changing notions of freedom, choice, and social wellbeing. They are therefore positioned within particular assemblages of governance, within which discourses of moral panic about obesity and discourses of risk are entangled with bodies, subjectivities, and consumption practices in ways which position digital health technologies with the capacity for remedy. I have offered some reflections on the ways in which viewers of the promotional adverts of technologies such as Fitbit are instructed how to think about their bodies, families, and 'solutions' to a range of problems along gendered lines. However, while promising empowerment and democratisation through individual self-care, these pedagogies fail to account for diversity among women, as well as different social, cultural, and political contexts, which come to limit opportunities to achieve good health. In this regard, social materialist approaches might provide theoretical lenses through which to understand how subjectivity, discourses, consumption practices, affect, the body, and digital devices are entangled with pedagogy. Digital health practices can be considered as occurring in relation to other lived bodies, materialities, practices, and discourses in the context of society which is conceptualised as a multiplicity of 'assembled relations' (Fox et al., 2016, p. 5). As per new materialist ontology, bodies are not contained and distinct but produced through their relationships with other bodies, things, and entities. In this regard, individuals do not simply possess the agency to choose to take up or change behaviours on the basis of having more information, as suggested in neoliberal discourses and the pedagogies of consumption described above. There is a need for more nuanced understandings of the material forces which are contributing to what are otherwise considered isolated and/or simple behaviours in the use of digital health technologies and how this contributes to gendered inequalities. Digital health technologies can in this sense can be understood as part of an open assemblage, continually unfolding as individuals variously engage with them and learn about their own health and bodies through socio material relations.

In their edited collection, Sandlin and McLaren (2010b) call for a critical pedagogy of consumption, bringing together a variety of education scholars to not only focus on consumerism but also resistance to it and neoliberal discourses. In this regard, consumption is not only a site of learning, but has potential for change. Users of these technologies are not passive consumers, but instead negotiate meanings and there are of course potential sites of resistance and multiple forms of appropriation of these technologies. With forecasts of continued growth in the digital health market, it will become increasingly important that we help future generations develop skills through which they can continue to critically interrogate the consumer culture within which these digital health techs are positioned. Such agendas may be suited to new forms of critical enquiry and public pedagogies involving citizens themselves as researchers or utilising creative analytical practices (see Trussell, Apgar, & Kovac in this collection, and Fullagar & Small in this collection) which create possibilities for a feminist politics of digital health.

References

Ahmed, S. (2010). *The promise of happiness*. Durham, NC/London: Duke University Press.

Baer, H. (2016). Redoing feminism: Digital activism, body politics, and neoliberalism. *Feminist Media Studies, 16*(1), 17–34.

Burdick, J., & Sandlin, J. (2013). Learning, becoming and the unknowable: Conceptualizations, mechanisms and the process in public pedagogy literature. *Curriculum Inquiry, 43*, 142–177.

Burrows, L. (2009). Pedagogizing families through obesity discourse. In J. Wright & V. Harwood (Eds.), *Biopolitics and the "obesity epidemic": Governing bodies* (pp. 127–140). London: Routledge.

Campos, P., Saguy, A., Ernsberger, P., Oliver, E., & Gesser, G. (2005). The epidemiology of overweight or obesity: Public health crisis or moral panic? *International Journal of Epidemiology, 35*(1), 55–60.

Coleman, R. (2009). The becoming of bodies: Girls, media effects and body image. *Feminist Media Studies, 8*(2), 163–179.

Dobson, A. R. S. (2015). *Postfeminist digital cultures: Femininity, social media, and self-representation*. New York: Palgrave Macmillan.

Evans, J., & Rich, E. (2011). Body policies and body pedagogies: Child matters in totally pedagogised schools. *Journal of Education Policy, 26*(3), 361–379.

Evans, J., Rich, E., Davies, B., & Allwood, R. (2008). *Education, disordered eating and obesity discourse: Fat fabrications*. Abingdon, UK: Routledge.

Fotopoulou, A., & Kate O'Riordan, K. (2017). Training to self-care: Fitness tracking, biopedagogy and the healthy consumer. *Health Sociology Review, 26*(1), 54–68.

Fox, et al. (2016). The micropolitics of obesity: Materialism, markets and food sovereignty. *Sociology*, 1–17. https://doi.org/10.1177/0038038516647668.

Gard, M. (2014). eHPE: A history of the future. *Sport, Education and Society, 19*(6), 827–845. https://doi.org/10.1080/13573322.2014.938036.

Gard, M., & Wright, J. (2005). *The obesity epidemic: Science, morality and ideology*. London: Routledge.

Giroux, H. A. (1999). *The mouse that roared: Disney and the end of innocence*. Lanham, MD: Rowman & Littlefield.

Harris, A. (2004). *Future girl: Young women in the twenty-first century*. London: Routledge.

Hickey-Moody, A. (2013). *Youth, arts and education: reassembling subjectivity through affect*. Abingdon, UK/New York: Routledge.

Hoechsmann, M. (2010). Rootlessness, reenchantment and educating desire: A brief history of the pedagogy of consumption. In *Critical pedagogies of consumption: Living and learning in the shadow of "shopocalypse"* (pp. 23–35). Oxon/New York: Routledge.

Kenway, J., & Bullen, E. (2001). *Consuming children: Education-entertainment-advertising*. Buckingham, UK: Open Univeristy Press.

Kincheloe, J. L. (2002). *The sign of the burger: McDonald's and the culture of power*. Philadelphia: Temple University Press.

Lupton, D. (2001). "Where's me dinner?": Food preparation arrangements in rural Australian families. *Journal of Sociology, 36*, 172–186.

Lupton, D. (2013). The digitally engaged patient: Self-monitoring and self-care in the digital health era. *Social Theory and Health, 11*, 256–270.

Lupton, D. (2014a). Beyond techno-Utopia: Critical approaches to digital health technologies. *Societies, 4*(4), 706–711. https://doi.org/10.3390/soc4040706.

Lupton, D. (2014b). Quantified sex: A critical analysis of sexual and reproductive self-tracking using apps. *Culture,Health and Sexuality, 17*(4), 440–453. https://doi.org/10.1080/13691058.2014.920528.

Lupton, D. (2015). Data assemblages, sentient schools and digitised health and physical education (response to Gard). *Sport Education and Society, 20*(1), 122–132. https://doi.org/10.1080/13573322.2014.962496.

Maher, J., Fraser, S., & Lindsay, J. (2010). Between provisioning and consuming? Children, mothers and 'childhood obesity. *Health Sociology Review, 19*(3), 304–316. https://doi.org/10.5172/hesr.2010.19.3.304.

McCracken, G. (1990). *Culture and consumption*. Bloomington, IN: Indiana University Press.

McRobbie, A. (2009). *The aftermath of feminism: Gender, culture and social change*. London: Sage.

Merriam, S. B., & Brockett, R. G. (2007). *The profession and practice of adult education: An introduction* (updated ed.). San Francisco, CA: Jossey-Bass.

Millington, B. (2016). 'Quantify the invisible': Notes toward a future of posture. *Critical Public Health, 26*(4), 405–417.

Monaghan, L. (2005). Discussion piece: A critical take on the obesity debate. *Social Theory and Health, 3*, 302–314.

Paterson, M. (2006). *Consumption and everyday life*. New York: Routledge.

Peeters, R., & Schuilenburg, M. (2016). The birth of mindpolitics: Understanding nudging in public health policy. *Social Theory and Health, 15*(2), 138–159. https://doi.org/10.1057/s41285-016-0024-z.

Petherick, L. (2015). Shaping the child as a healthy child: Health surveillance, schools, and biopedagogies. *Cultural Studies – Critical Methodologies*. https://doi.org/10.1177/1532708615611716.

Powell, A. C., Landman, A. B., & Bates, D. W. (2014). In search of a few good apps. *Journal of the Americal Medical Association, 311*(18), 1851–1852. https://doi.org/10.1001/jama.2014.2564.Conflict.

Rail, G., & Jette, S. (2015). Reflections on biopedagogies and/of public health: On Bio-others, rescue missions, and social justice. *Cultural Studies – Critical Methodologies, 15*(5), 327–336.

Rich, E. (2017). Childhood, surveillance and mHealth technologies. In E. Taylor & T. Rooney (Eds.), *Surveillance futures: Social and ethical implica-*

tions of new technologies for children and young people (pp. 132–146). oxon: Routledge.
Rich, E., & Miah, A. (2014). Understanding digital health as public pedagogy: A critical framework. *Societies, 4*, 296–315.
Ringrose, J. (2011). Beyond discourse? Using Deleuze and Guattari's schizoanalysis to explore affective assemblages, heterosexually striated space, and lines of flight online and at school. *Educational Philosophy and Theory, 43*(6), 598–618. https://doi.org/10.1111/j.1469-5812.2009.00601.x.
Ruckenstein, M. (2014). Visualized and interacted life: Personal analytics and engagements with data doubles. *Societies, 2*, 68–84.
Sandlin, J. A., & McLaren, P. (Eds.). (2010a). *Critical pedagogies of consumption: Living and learning in the shadow of the "shopocalypse"*. Oxon/New York: Routledge.
Sandlin, J. A., & McLaren, P. (2010b). Introduction: Exploring consumption's pedagogy. In J. A. Sandlin & P. McLaren (Eds.), *Critical pedagogies of consumption: Living and learning in the shadow of "shopocalypse"* (pp. 1–20). Oxon/New York: Routledge.
Sandlin, J. A., Schultz, B. D., & Burdick, J. (2010). *Handbook of public Pedagogy: Education and learning beyond schooling*. New York: Routledge.
Smarr, L. (2012). Quantifying your body: A how-to guide from a systems biology perspective. *Biotechnology Journal, 7*(8), 980–991.
Smith, G. J. D., & Vonthethoff, B. (2016). Health by numbers? Exploring the practice and experience of datafied health. *Health Sociology Review, 26*(July), 1–16. https://doi.org/10.1080/14461242.2016.1196600.
Spring, J. (2003). *Education the consumer-citizen*. Mahwah, NJ: Lawrence Erlbaum.
Swan, M. (2012). Health 2050: The realization of personalized medicine through crowdsourcing, the quantified self, and the participatory biocitizen. *Journal of Personalized Medicine., 2*(3), 93–118.
Usher, R., Bryant, I., & Johnston, R. (1997). *Adult education and the postmodern challenge*. London: Routledge.
Wajcman, J. (2004). *Technofeminism*. Cambridge, UK: Polity Press.
Wajcman, J. (2007). From women and technology to gendered technoscience. *Information, Communication & Society, 10*(3), 287–298.
Williamson, B. (2016). Coding the biodigital child: The biopolitics and pedagogic strategies of educational data science. *Culture and Society, 24*(3), 401–416. https://doi.org/10.1080/14681366.2016.1175499.

Digital Dilemmas Through Networked Assemblages: Reshaping the Gendered Contours of Our Future

Simone Fullagar, Diana C. Parry, and Corey W. Johnson

"And now THIS? You allow Twitter freedom to our president but you silence a woman speaking out about sexual harassment?" tweeted actress Jamie-Lee Curtis after the account suspension of feminist activist and performance artist Rose McGowen's account after speaking out about the behaviour of Harvey Weinstein (Bowles & Buckley, 2017). As a prominent boycott of the platform ensued, Twitter eventually unlocked McGowen's account and promised to be 'more transparent' in their terms of service. Political moments such as this one highlight the complex

S. Fullagar
Department for Health, University of Bath, Bath, UK
e-mail: S.P.Fullagar@bath.ac.uk

D. C. Parry (✉)
University of Waterloo, Waterloo, ON, Canada
e-mail: dcparry@uwaterloo.ca

C. W. Johnson
Department of Recreation & Leisure Studies, University of Waterloo, Waterloo, ON, Canada
e-mail: corey.johnson@uwaterloo.ca

D. C. Parry et al. (eds.), *Digital Dilemmas*,
https://doi.org/10.1007/978-3-319-95300-7_11

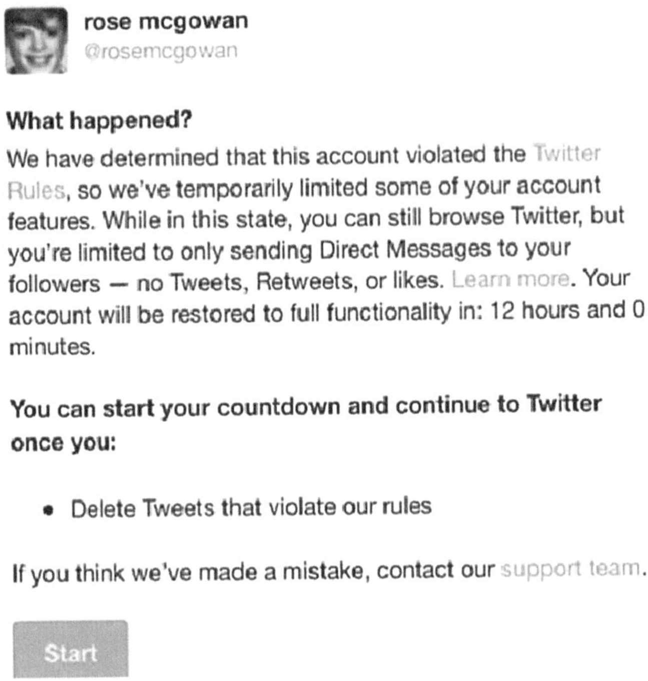

Fig. 1 @rosemcgowan Twitter suspension notice. (McGowan, 2017)

tensions raised as the digital landscape is used to and for the shaping of society (Fig. 1).

As we articulated in our introduction, the purpose of this book was to take up the challenge of understanding how gender is performed, resisted, re-enacted, regulated, and transformed through rapidly changing digital contexts. To do so, wc have explored a diversity of feminist dilemmas shaping everyday life in advanced liberalism—popular culture, dating practices, sport and active lifestyles, mental health, along with a focus on marginalized bodies, stories, and practices and how to study these new landscapes. Writing through different feminisms including their various perspectives and methodological approaches, each chapter has contributed to the collective project of reshaping the contours of digital practices that frame ways of re-presenting, knowing, and doing gender. In this concluding chapter, we focus specifically on gender as a *material-discursive phenomena* through which identities and social relations are enacted as everyday forms of digital culture and leisure-related practices. The tangible and intangible aspects of our gendered lives are also embedded within the less visible ways digital spaces are designed, mined, collated, and navigated (Bivens, 2017). Through this new materialist informed approach, we consider how gender norms, patterns, and power relations are bound in and among the increasingly indistinguishable sociotechnical relations that entangle our online and offline lives.

With rapidly proliferating digital platforms, sites, and complex mediated power relations (affective, surveillant, intersectional, global publics), heteronormative, homonormative, and other binary formulations of masculinity and femininity are being contested, reinvented, and abandoned. For example, the entangled social media landscapes of sport and celebrity culture have foregrounded debates about different enactments of gendered personhood and injustices (Caitlin Jenner as a former Olympian; Caster Semenya's sex testing treatment; Serena Williams speaking out on racism, the gender pay gap, and rebuffing sexism as a mother; and Billie Jean-King's cisgender, queer narrative retold through the popular film *Battle of the Sexes*[1]). As Morrison has argued in this book (chapter "Theory in Digital and Leisure Contexts"), the prosumer practices afforded by social media possibilities (# or hashtags) are assembling new digital publics and politics with capacities to collectively articulate issues in diverse ways, often with subversive humour. Exploring the *gendering* of our digital lives involves thinking 'across' multiple sites of visibility/invisibility and intersections with normative categories of race, gender, sexuality, class, (dis)ability, religion, age, and so on, that, as Butler says, constitute identities in ways that are "purported to be" acceptably feminine or masculine (1990, p. 25).

Following Butler's recasting of gender as performative, feminist scholars have argued that the 'empowering' possibilities of social media (greater visibility, being heard, and exercising agency through speaking back to/at sexism) are bound up with complex gender relations entwined in neoliberalmarket logics (post-feminist hetero/homo sexy bodies, accommodating

[1] https://www.youtube.com/watch?v=WMdzBwsZRX8

femininity, geek masculinity, self-branding) (Banet-Weiser, 2015; Harris & Dobson, 2015; Toffoletti & Thorpe, 2018). For instance, Banet-Weiser's (2015) argument for a shift from thinking about the politics of visibility to the gendered economics of visibility is taken up by Toffeletti and Thorpe (2018) in their analysis of how popular sportswomen position themselves through social media as 'becoming' empowered subjects (where self-love, self-esteem, and sharing one's authentic self are the primary vehicles of change). Questions arise about which gendered bodies become visible commodities within the intersection of identity politics. Rather than offer closure in this chapter, we use the opportunity to think critically and creatively about the shifting gender relations of visibility and invisibility in the digital dilemmas explored in this collection. Both theoretical and methodological questions arise about how to explore (and intervene in) the *gendering* of digital cultures in diverse leisure-related contexts, along with feminist disruptions of ways of knowing and interventions on the doing and re-presenting gender (Green & Singleton, 2013).

Digital Cultures: Materializing Gender

The incredibly diverse global and local sites through which the 'gender order' is digitally mediated creates particular challenge for feminist researchers to examine the specificity of data flows, power relations, and visualization that is assembled through the practices of corporations, governments, activists, citizens, and so on (Gill, in press). The theoretical and methodological inventiveness of feminist work in digital culture is part of wider debates (new materialist feminism, third- and fourth-wave feminism, feminist science and technology studies, digital humanities) that are reshaping the ontological, ethical, and epistemological boundaries of 'doing' knowledge to effect change (Luka, Millette, & Wallace, 2018). This material discursive approach situates "digital cultures as material practices of appropriation, and new media objects as material assemblages of hardware, software, and wetware" (Boomen, Lammes, Lehmann, Raessens, & Schäfer, 2009, p. 9).

New materialist feminist scholars are 're-turning' to and extending feminist theorizations of 'patriarchal' power beyond overly determinist and dualistic formulations of structure/agency, oppression/liberation, virtual/real to reinvent gender relations and feminist ways of knowing through lively, material practices (Bivens & Hasinoff, 2017; Hughes & Lury, 2013; Ringrose & Coleman, 2013). Barad (2014) has argued that this process of analysis involves "re-turning – not by returning as in reflecting on or going back to a past that was, but re-turning as in turning it over and over again...We might imagine re-turning as a multiplicity of processes" (p. 169). In this way, materialist thought breathes 'new life' into the concept of patriarchy to move beyond static representations or constructivist notions of meaning, assumed to exist apart from use in feminist knowledge (Hook & Wolfe, 2017). Alongside academic reworking, there has been a cultural revitalization of feminist terms, such as misogyny, that we have seen through social media that has amplified a politics of the personal (e.g. Australian Prime Minster, Julia Gillard's 'misogyny speech'[2] in parliament) (Mclean & Maalsen, 2013).

Feminist media studies (Colman, 2014; Keller, 2012; Weare, 2016) has opened up key questions about our embodied relationship with technology through understanding data as a lively materiality entangled with *affective* intensities (Keller, Mendes, & Ringrose, 2018; Sumartojo, Pink, Lupton, & LaBond, 2016). Such intensities are understood to be not merely examples of personalized feeling, but rather emphasize how intimate, visceral responses (anger, rage, shame, joy, despair, etc.) are implicated in affective economies and micropolitical assemblages that reiterate and destabilize patriarchal meanings and identities (Ringrose & Coleman, 2013). The seemingly endless eruptions of sexism and homophobia through social media and mainstream reporting across the spheres of politics, sport, work, leisure, and culture have fuelled powerful affects and amplified feminist desires to be heard, to contest, and to collectively mobilize rage (#metoo, #everydaysexism, #Blacklivesmatter, #genderpaygap, #TraditionallySubmissive, #TimesUp). Such forms of hashtag activism produce new, loosely affiliated collectives that voice people's diverse views in ways that clearly contest norms of niceness, pleasantness, accommodating traditional normative gender and sexual expectations. Ahmed's (2017) figure of the 'feminist killjoy' also captures this subversive

[2] Please see https://www.youtube.com/watch?v=ihd7ofrwQX0

humour that enacts different thinking-feeling subjectivities not premised upon highly individualized, decontextualized, and self-sacrificing notions of personal happiness. Drawing upon these material-discursive insights, we return to the question of how the gendering of leisure-related practices is made thinkable through the affective, cultural, economic, political, and sociotechnical contours of patriarchal relations. As Hemmings (2012) has suggested, "to know differently, we have to feel differently … (feminist) politics can be characterized as that which moves us, rather than that which confirms us in what we already know" (pp. 150–151).

Digital Labour and Leisure

Luka, Millette, and Wallace's (2018) observation that research is increasingly focused on how (often feminized) digital labour shapes the global knowledge economy also highlights the entanglement with leisure practices and questions of wellbeing, "networked technologies have engendered an 'always on' work culture (Luka, Millette, & Wallace, 2018) that is changing the very nature of work and its relationship to social and leisure time" (p. 26). Digital cultures reconfigure work-leisure relations in more permeable ways—neoliberal subjects are urged to work at our leisure through digital labour that remains largely immaterial while also investing in successful (paid) work identities—both which maintain to ensure data flows for global capitalism. Leisure practices can no longer be thought of in dualistic terms or through spatial metaphors that divide everyday life into 'containers' of human action that are online or offline. Rose and Spencer (2015) emphasize this interrelation, when they said:

> The largest online leisure environment and social media site in history, Facebook, has 1.39 billion users and growing (more than one in every seven people on the planet). Facebook is arguably the largest shared leisure space on earth… where leisure and labour become intertwined, where users' lives are the object, subject and site of commodification, commerce and consumption. (p. 810)

As everyday life is increasingly mediated by digital practices, our leisure worlds and subjectivities are produced through entangled, gendered 'intra-actions' of humans, data objects, screens, mobile technologies, algorithms, and so on (Barad, 2007). This materialist understanding moves away from considering how leisure is experienced as a humanist form of engagement with new digital objects and online contexts, and towards a conceptualization of leisure practices as produced through the cultural, political, and embodied processes of digital mediation (Kember & Zylinska, 2012). We emphasize the feminist perspective on mediation as "a key trope for understanding and articulating our being in, and becoming with, the technological world, our emergence and ways of intra-acting with it, as well as the acts and processes of temporarily stabilizing the world into media, agents, relations, and networks" (italics in original, Kember & Zylinska, 2012, p. xv).

In many ways, the early feminist critique of leisure as a dualistic concept and premised upon a universalized masculine agentic subject (exercising free will) is radically extended by feminist analysis of digital culture that starts with different ontological assumptions about how power and privilege materialize—the datification and surveilling of everyday life through the gendered fragmentation of agentic capacities (as personal information and identity data is gathered, stored, and re-presented across a myriad of sites and institutions). Our focus on the gendering of power relations in this book extends earlier work that has called for critical analysis of digital leisure practices that question "traditional binaries between work/leisure, production/consumption, material/digital and human/non-human" (Silk, Millington, Rich, & Bush, 2016, p. 713). In addition, there has been little exploration of methodological questions about how digital dilemmas can be researched with respect to the workings of nuanced gender-power relations. The chapters by Cousineau, Oakes, and Johnson (chapter "Appnography: Modifying Ethnography for App-based Culture"), as well as Trussell, Apgar, and Kovac (chapter. "Online Qualitative Methods: Confronting New Possibilities and Challenges within a Social Justice Perspective"), offer different examples of empirical research involving digital sites and methods (ethnographies of digital apps and digitally curated groups) that has identified opportunities and potential difficulties for future scholarship.

Networked Gender Assemblages

Exploring how digital leisure practices are gendered requires an analysis of platforms within the wider sociocultural context and micropolitical forces shaping how gender is negotiated in localized ways. Platforms and software are authored by programmers, and, purposefully or not, these programmers imbricate their own social experiences and biases into that software (Lessig, 2006; Sandvig, Hamilton, Karahalios, & Langbort, 2016). Where the coders, developers, and decision-makers in a company (e.g. YouTube or Facebook) are mostly men, then they can, and likely do, privilege male perspective and male voices over all other voices (Nakamura, 2012). In terms of broad cultural reach, the identification of gender bias in image collections demonstrates how digital repositories work to reiterate normative gender identities, bodies, and practices as desirable and acceptable. Simonite (2017) reports on research that makes visible how gender bias materializes through the normative practices of software development, organizational culture, and the production of images for consumption, "Two prominent research-image collections—including one supported by Microsoft and Facebook—display a predictable gender bias in their depiction of activities such as cooking and sports. Images of shopping and washing are linked to women, for example, while coaching and shooting are tied to men. Machine-learning software trained on the datasets didn't just mirror those biases, it amplified them" (p. 1).

The significance of these gender-biased depictions extends beyond their representational nature and into the very core of the way that the computational systems and sorting algorithms which power them are designed. As computers moved into homes, the significant work of gendering these technologies male was already at work. Because of their novelty, complexity, and antisocial nature (working with the hardware of computers is often a solitary task), computer work was often relegated to 'computer rooms', basements, and garages—solitary spaces not built for socialization and, therefore, off limits to many girls (Cheryan, Plaut, Davies, & Steele, 2009). The result is a hardware, and subsequently the software to run it, which increasingly becomes the purview of men and boys, and we see a near-steady decline in women's participation in computer science and technology studies from the early 1980s, with percentages of women students in these areas significantly lower than in 1980 (Accenture, 2016).

The significance of such modes of 'seeing' gender is not simply a question of abstract representation but rather, as Pedwell (2017b) argues, "visual digital media become folded into our embodied habits and modes of perception" (p. 19) The production, collation, and circulation of stereotyped gendered images raises questions about how to continue iteration of such meanings through the networked assemblages of digital cultures that entangle users, producers, bodies, and spaces through leisure and labour. As Pedwell (2017b) and other feminists have argued, we need to understand not just "the potential effects of one image, one GIF or one video in isolation, but rather, the affective relations among multiple, changing digital files and configurations" (p. 19) Such assemblages bring into relation the multiple directions of gendered power (top-down, bottom-up, horizontal) through the structural dimensions governing our digital lives and the micropractices that shape cultural life (as our opening Twitter example demonstrates).

Gill (2019) has argued for the importance of feminist thinking in the emergent field of surveillance studies as a means of mapping out the gendered practices through which women are judged, and in turn judge themselves and their peers, within digitized markets of neoliberalism. These concerns about gendered surveillance of active feminine bodies is explored in the chapters by Rich (chapter. "Making Gender and Motherhood through Pedagogies of Digital Health and Fitness Consumption: 'Soon it Made us More Active as a Family'"), as well as Depper, Fullagar and Francombe-Webb (chapter "This Girl Can?: The Limitations of Digital Do-it-Yourself Empowerment in Women's Active Embodiment Campaigns"), through examples of how mothers and daughters are positioned within the 'healthy family' advertisements of commercial self-tracking fitness devices, as well as how sport policy promotion urges 'fun' self and peer surveillance through social media in the UK *This Girl Can* campaign. With a focus on understanding personal information (data, images) that is collected and managed (knowingly and unknowingly) by state and corporate organizations that seek to influence those individuals, feminist surveillance studies have focused on how gendered bodies and vulnerable subjects are produced in differential ways (offering intersectional, interventionist, and activist approaches) (Dubrofsky & Magnet, 2015).

One example that connects with the focus of two chapters on mental health and wellbeing, by Fullagar and Small (chapter "Writing Recovery from Depression Through a Creative Research Assemblage: Mindshackles, Digital Mental Health and a Feminist Politics of Self-Care"), and Swist and Collin (chapter "Playing with Zombie Problems: Exploring the Gender-Digital-Play Assemblage in Online Mental Health Campaigns"), is the case of a Canadian woman with depression who lost her disability insurance benefits after holiday photos of her looking 'too happy' were taken from her Facebook page (Dubrofsky & Magnet, 2015). The circulation of gendered norms about how mental ill health should be enacted and 'look like' for women and men can be understood as part of a broader diagnostic assemblage that governs health and wellbeing through all kinds of digital technologies used in medicine, by insurance companies, and employers (Fullagar, Rich, Francombe-Webb, & Maturo, 2017). Against this context of medicalized surveillance and the production of digitally disordered lives, Fullagar and Small write through a creative-academic assemblage to explore the way micro-publics (such as Small's Mindshackles website) enable the visualization of diverse meanings and affects that contest pathologization. In their chapter, Swist and Collin also articulate alternative ways of thinking beyond the limitations of gendered stereotyping of masculinity in mental health promotion campaigns through a participatory approach involving young people in designing creative help-seeking options. They demonstrate how digital practices, architectures, and networks of participation have materialized as platformed 'playgrounds' through which gender, wellbeing, and problematized subjectivities (mental ill health) are enacted in conventional and transformative ways.

Questioning the gender neutrality of networked assemblages and alternative digital possibilities, feminist work offers a challenge to the gendered obligation to monitor and manage wellbeing through "'psycho-technology apps' (for example around developing mindfulness, positive thinking, happiness and confidence/self-esteem); dieting apps which inform, evaluate, and track food intake; the enormous range of applications marketed to women around menstruation, conception, pregnancy, and parenting; and proliferating 'beauty apps'"(Gill, 2019, n.p.). Alongside this work, on the more visible aspects of digital surveillance, is feminist analysis of the normative logics "under the hood" that inform the design, coding, and operation of software (Bivens, 2015). As Bivens (2015) argues, "if we work only on the surface—dealing with users, content, representation, discourse—we chip away at the problems feminism seeks to transform within and through social media, while the deeper manifestations continue to flourish" (p. 715). Her research into Facebook has been particularly revealing with respect to the unanticipated effects of gender blindness that have implications for women's safety. For example, the algorithm that automatically identifies people in a user's broader network that can generate unwanted connections between survivors of sexual assault and perpetrators (and pinpointing one's exact geographical location for those who most of know women in some way).

In another key paper, Bivens (2017) has identified how Facebook *produces* digital subjects through design practices that embed and materialize gender identities within an entanglement of corporation-user-software that both *reveals* and *conceals*. She states that, in 2014, Facebook introduced changes where, "Instead of two options for users to choose from when identifying their gender ('male' and 'female'), users were given a third option ('custom') that, if selected, offered 56 additional options" (Bivens, 2017, pp. 880–881). Queer organizations praised the move to recognize gender diversity, while more reactionary individuals and organizations protested the move away from a 'natural' gender binary. However, Bivens' (2017) analysis of the coding practices "revealed how underneath the surface, these conditions are severed in favour of the binary. The design strategy that generates these conditions simultaneously reconfigures gender into data that conforms to the hegemonic regime embraced by marketing and advertising institutions" (p. 886). Despite the self-identification of preferred gender, Facebook reassigns gender in terms of male, female, or custom to, paradoxically, capture user preferences for targeted marketing. This finding adds to a long list of gender (along with racial and other forms of discrimination) issues identified with social media platforms like Facebook that deceptively enact public inclusiveness while pursuing concealed agendas with little accountability.

Understanding what known and unknown digital mediations 'do' to shape our mobile leisure lives requires a shift towards thinking about leisure-related practices as performative and transformative of gendered bodies and relations as we "become part of a specific configuration, or ecology, of persons and things" (Pink, 2011, p. 344). With the growing popularity of wearable technologies for self-tracking and sharing personal sport performance data (along with calorie intake and a host of other body measures), feminists have begun to explore how mobile data-bodies are produced with gendered effects (Depper & Howe, 2017; Rich, 2018). The following account by a woman runner provides an everyday example of how gendered surveillance materializes through wearable technologies where unexpected data sharing is enabled by Strava's default settings:

> After I'd completed my usual 5-kilometer loop near my London flat, a stranger I didn't know "liked" my workout—even though I had enabled stricter privacy settings, which I thought would shield my workouts from public view. This happened several more times while I jogged the same route.... Alarmed at the idea that strangers could see the routes I run on two or three times a week, I embarked on an investigation into the privacy settings of Strava. What I learned wasn't reassuring for an urban woman—or anyone concerned about location-based privacy. (Spinks, 2017, p. 1)

Software coding does not consider how gendered risks can be amplified through data sharing as women negotiate mobility through public spaces. Nor are users often aware of settings, data sharing, and basic privacy concerns. While the statistical risk of being attacked by a stranger in public is lower for women than being subjected to sexual assault, rape, and child abuse by (largely) men who are familiar in some way, these apps give men they know the details of their lives. Women's risk perceptions are bound up with a gendered economy of affect that amplifies and individualizes fear. Objectification of women's bodies, norms of feminine weakness, and racialized-sexualized-classed discourses about sexual availability for men all circulate through everyday cultural sites. Anxieties about being alone, moving through public spaces in the night-time leisure economy, and being attacked have become the objects of digital interventions (rape prevention apps) that evoke feelings of safety. Yet, feminist research into the features and content of such apps has identified how "anti-rape app design generally reinforces and reflects pervasive rape myths, both by targeting potential victims and by reinforcing stranger-danger" (Bivens & Hasinoff, 2017, p. 2). Feminist scholars continue to highlight, in particular ways, how greater visibility through social media also generates complex reactions and affects—hatred and shaming bound up with misogyny, racism, homo/transphobia, and so on—in the contested visual terrain of digital corporeal culture (Renold & Ringrose, 2017). In their chapter, Lebel, Pegoraro, and Harman outlined how sportswomen and journalists developed self-preservation strategies to deal with sexist trolls as part of the new normal on Instagram. The failure of social media platforms to address repeated cyberviolence is an ongoing intersectional feminist issue and one that Matamoros-Fernández conceptualized as 'platformed racism'. Matamoros-Fernández (2017) analysed how the assemblage of social media practices contributed to the amplification of racist reactions when a high-profile Australian Aboriginal footballer challenged racist slurs. She observed that "By liking and watching racist content directed to Adam Goodes on Facebook and YouTube, the platforms' recommendation algorithms generated similar content about controversial humour and the opinions of Australian public figures known for their racist remarks towards Aboriginal people" (Matamoros-Fernández, 2017, p. 939). In this way, technical design, affordances, commercial models, and policies can be seen as fundamentally entangled with the relations that govern social media platforms, sport and media organizations, and the cultural specificity of user practices (see also, Mohrman & Fischer, 2016 for an example of the complexities of countering racism via Facebook livestreaming as a form of resistant sousveillance).

Feminist research critically questions the gendered complexities that shape the relationship between technical design and social norms rather than positioning technology as an individual solution to pervasive forms of gender injustice. Alongside important critical insights into the gendering of digital culture is the growing body of feminist work that emphasizes the inventive possibilities of digital activism and disruption. As fourth-wave feminists have claimed and scholars such as Baer (2016) have argued, "digital activism constitutes a paradigm shift within feminist protest culture" as feminist politics moves away from "conventional legal and legislative channels" (p. 18). Next, we consider the possibilities of engaging critically and creatively with the gendering of digital cultures through what Durham, Cooper, and Morris (2013) articulate as a kind of 'percussive feminism'.

Percussive Feminisms: Digital Inventiveness

> The Crunk Feminist Collective argues that the tension between competing and often contradictory political and cultural projects like hip-hop and feminism is percussive in that it is both disruptive and generative. Percussive feminism allows for the creativity that ensues from placing modes or objects of inquiry together that might not traditionally fit, hiphop and feminism being only the most obvious example (Durham, Cooper, & Morris, 2013, pp. 723–24).

As a group of hip-hop generation Black Feminist scholars and activists, The Crunk Feminist Collective (CFC)[3] mobilize a 'percussive' feminism in their desire to foreground tensions (within cultural practices and also feminisms) as producing disruptive and generative effects. Hip-hop feminism and pedagogy are an example of flourishing digital activism that draws from, and enacts change through, the cultural conditions shaping black women's lives. In her chapter on Digital Black Feminism, Love also explores the historical context and present possibilities of percussive movements such as #blackgirlmagic. In their feminist work, Durham, Cooper, and Morris (2013) elaborate upon how diverse hip-hop feminisms in the US work upon and through social media to contest and make visible racialized and heterosexist practices. The launch of a successful Facebook and Twitter campaign by the We Are the 44% Coalition pressured a

> major hip-hop magazine to fire the editor and demand a public apology for publishing a video interview by popular pimp rapper Too $hort, who advised adolescent boys on how to sexually assault girls. The swift response to misogynoir not only resulted in a retraction by the rapper but also provided an opportunity for serious dialogue about sexual violence in communities across the country. (Durham, Cooper & Morris, 2013, p. 731)

[3] http://www.crunkfeministcollective.com/

The inventiveness of diverse digital feminist activism has mobilized new collectivities to challenge rape culture (#BeenRapedNeverReported hashtag, anti-street harassment website Hollaback!) and hence generate different ways of enacting feminism through affective relations that connect and challenge silence (Keller et al., 2018). Activists and writers of the Fembot Collective[4] have produced the Fembot toolbox through which "strategies for coping and resistance" are shared. Other feminist-academic collaborations have produced collections documenting feminist hacktivism and cultural making, such as *Disobedient Electronics* (Hertz, 2018), which includes examples of performative practices that disrupt and enact gender imaginatively. One example is the performance-creation of an app–Periodshare—that enables the self-tracking of women's bodies to counter taboo and invites participants to share their personal data as a means of disobeying market logics that commodify data by using uncanny humour. The second example relevant to our exploration of leisure is the "gender pay gap clock" that alerts women to stop work after they have completed the proportion of hours they are paid in relation to men. This clock could be reimagined to include different rates of pay for women of colour and across different occupations, while also marking the time women often do during the 'second shift' with unpaid household and childcare labour.

Feminist strategies that mobilize digital interventions and the collective force of social media work to challenge the individualization of sexism (by increasing confidence, assertiveness, or even 'leaning in'). Importantly, they make visible and intervene in the networked assemblages that produce the shifting gender order (sociotechnical, historical, economic, political, and cultural contours) (Pedwell, 2017a). In this way, material discursive ways of theorizing, performing, and enacting feminist knowing-doing also advance our understanding of leisure practices as always mediated rather than being conventionally thought of as individualized human-centred activity that exists apart from digital realms. Pursuing an understanding of the entanglement of leisure with digital cultures requires methods and theories that enable us to think through the mediating forces that shape how gender is made visible and invisible within the context of "white supremacist capitalist heteropatriarchal surveillance" (Dubrofsky & Magnet, 2015, p. 7).

[4] http://fembot.adanewmedia.org/

References

Accenture. (2016). *Cracking the gender code: Get 3X more women in computing*. Dublin, Ireland: Accenture.

Ahmed, S. (2017). *Living a feminist life*. Durham, NC: Duke University Press.

Baer, H. (2016). Redoing feminism: Digital activism, body politics, and neoliberalism. *Feminist Media Studies, 16*(1), 17–34. https://doi.org/10.1080/14680777.2015.1093070.

Banet-Weiser, S. (2015). Keynote address: media, markets, gender: Economies of visibility in a neoliberal moment. *Communication Review, 18*(1), 53–70. https://doi.org/10.1080/10714421.2015.996398.

Barad, K. (2007). *Meeting the universe halfway: Quantum physics and the entanglement of matter and meaning*. Durham, NC: Duke University.

Barad, K. (2014). Diffracting diffraction: Cutting together-apart. *Parallax, 20*(3), 37–41. https://doi.org/10.1080/13534645.2014.927623.

Bivens, R. (2015). Under the hood: The software in your feminist approach. *Feminist Media Studies, 15*(4), 714–717. https://doi.org/10.1080/14680777.2015.1053717.

Bivens, R. (2017). The gender binary will not be deprogrammed: Ten years of coding gender on Facebook. *New Media and Society, 19*(6), 880–898. https://doi.org/10.1177/1461444815621527.

Bivens, R., & Hasinoff, A. A. (2017). Rape: Is there an app for that? An empirical analysis of the features of anti-rape apps. *Information Communication and Society, 4462*, 1–18. https://doi.org/10.1080/1369118X.2017.1309444.

van den Boomen, M., Lammes, S., Lehmann, A.-S., Raessens, J., & Schäfer, M. T. (2009). *Digital material: Tracing new media in everyday life and technology*. Amsterdam: Amsterdam University Press.

Bowles, N., & Buckley, C. (2017, October 12). Rose McGowan's twitter account locked after posts about Weinstein. *The New York Times*, Retrieved from https://www.nytimes.com/2017/10/12/arts/rose-mcgowan-twitter-weinstein.html

Butler, J. (1990). *Gender trouble: Feminism and the subversion of identity*. New York: Routledge.

Cheryan, S., Plaut, V. C., Davies, P. G., & Steele, C. M. (2009). Ambient belonging: How stereotypical cues impact gender participation in computer science. *Journal of Personality and Social Psychology, 97*(6), 1045–1060. https://doi.org/10.1037/a0016239.

Colman, F. (2014). Feminicidad digital: Predicación y medida, informática materialista e imágenes. *Artnodes, 14*(14), 7–17. https://doi.org/10.7238/a.v0i14.2408.

Depper, A., & Howe, P. D. (2017). Are we fit yet? English adolescent girls' experiences of health and fitness apps. *Health Sociology Review, 26*(1), 98–112. https://doi.org/10.1080/14461242.2016.1196599.

Dubrofsky, R. E., & Magnet, S. A. (2015). *Feminist surveillance studies*. Durham, NC: Duke University Press.

Durham, A., Cooper, B. C., & Morris, S. M. (2013). The stage hip-hop feminism built: A new directions essay. *Signs, 38*(3), 721–737. https://doi.org/10.1086/668843.

Fullagar, S., Rich, E., Francombe-Webb, J., & Maturo, A. (2017). Digital ecologies of youth mental health: Apps, therapeutic publics and pedagogy as affective arrangements. *Social Sciences, 6*(4), 135. https://doi.org/10.3390/socsci6040135.

Gill, R. (2019). Surveillance is a feminist issue. In T. Ouren & A. Press (Eds.), *Handbook of contemporary feminism*. New York: Routledge.

Green, E., & Singleton, C. (2013). "Gendering the Digital": The impact of gender and technology perspectives on the sociological imagination. In K. Orton-Johnson & N. Prior (Eds.), *Digital sociology* (pp. 34–50). London: Palgrave Macmillan.

Harris, A., & Dobson, A. S. (2015). Theorizing agency in post-girlpower times. *Continuum, 29*(2), 145–156. https://doi.org/10.1080/10304312.2015.1022955.

Hemmings, C. (2012). Affective solidarity: Feminist reflexivity and political transformation. *Feminist Theory, 13*(2), 147–161.

Hertz, G. (2018). *Disobedient electronics. The studio for critical making*. Retrieved from http://www.disobedientelectronics.com

Hook, G. A., & Wolfe, M. J. (2017). Affective violence: Re/negotiating gendered-feminism within new materialism. *Journal of Gender Studies*. https://doi.org/10.1080/09589236.2017.1340151.

Hughes, C., & Lury, C. (2013). Re-turning feminist methodologies: From a social to an ecological epistemology. *Gender and Education, 25*(6), 786–799. https://doi.org/10.1080/09540253.2013.829910.

Keller, J. (2012). Virtual feminisms: Girls' blogging communities, feminist activism, and participatory politics. Information. *Communication and Society, 15*(3), 419–429. https://doi.org/10.1080/1369118X.2011.642890.

Keller, J., Mendes, K., & Ringrose, J. (2018). Speaking "unspeakable things": Documenting digital feminist responses to rape culture. *Journal of Gender Studies, 27*(1), 22–36. https://doi.org/10.1080/09589236.2016.1211511.

Kember, S., & Zylinska, J. (2012). *Life after new media: Mediation as a vital process*. Cambridge, MA: The MIT Press https://doi.org/cb-pdf.

Lessig, L. (2006). *Code* (Version 2.0 ed.). New York: Basic Books.

Luka, M. E., Millette, M., & Wallace, J. (2018). A feminist perspective on ethical digital methods. In M. Zimmer & K. Kinder-Kurlanda (Eds.), *Internet research ethics for the social age* (pp. 21–36). New York: Peter Lang.

Matamoros-Fernández, A. (2017). Platformed racism: the mediation and circulation of an Australian race-based controversy on Twitter, Facebook and YouTube. *Information Communication and Society, 20*(6), 930–946. https://doi.org/10.1080/1369118X.2017.1293130.

McGowan, R., [@rosemcgowan]. (2017, October 12). [@rosemcgowan Twitter suspension notification screenshot]. Retrieved from https://www.instagram.com/p/BaImG1Mle7b/

Mclean, J., & Maalsen, S. (2013). Destroying the joint and dying of shame? A geography of revitalised feminism in social media and beyond. *Geographical Research, 51*(3), 243–256. https://doi.org/10.1111/1745-5871.12023.

Mohrman, K., & Fischer, M. (2016). Black deaths matter? Sousveillance and the invisibility of black life. *Ada: A Journal of Gender, New Media, and Technology*, (10), 1–13. https://doi.org/10.7264/N3F47MDV.

Nakamura, L. (2012). Queer female of color: The highest difficulty setting there is? Gaming rhetoric as gender capital. *Ada: A Journal of Gender, New Media, and Technology*, (1). https://doi.org/10.7264/N37P8W9V.

Pedwell, C. (2017a). Habit and the Politics of Social Change. *Body and Society, 23*(4), 1357034X1773461. https://doi.org/10.1177/1357034X17734619.

Pedwell, C. (2017b). Mediated habits : Images, networked affect and social change. *Subjectivity, 10*(2), 147–169. https://doi.org/10.1057/s41286-017-0025-y

Pink, S. (2011). From embodiment to emplacement: Re-thinking competing bodies, senses and spatialities. *Sport, Education and Society, 16*(3), 343–355. https://doi.org/10.1080/13573322.2011.565965.

Renold, E., & Ringrose, J. (2017). Selfies, relfies and phallic tagging: Posthuman participations in teen digital sexuality assemblages. *Educational Philosophy and Theory, 49*(11), 1066–1079. https://doi.org/10.1080/00131857.2016.1185686.

Rich, E. (2018). Healthism, girls' embodiment, and contemporary health and physical education: From weight management to digital practices of optimization. In *The palgrave handbook of feminism and sport, leisure and physical education* (pp. 523–536). London: Springer.

Ringrose, J., & Coleman, R. (2013). Looking and desiring machines: A feminist Deleuzian mapping of bodies and affects. In *Deleuze and research methodologies* (pp. 125–144). Edinburgh, UK: Edinburgh University Press Edinburgh.

Rose, J., & Spencer, C. (2015). Immaterial labour in spaces of leisure: Producing biopolitical subjectivities through Facebook. *Leisure Studies, 4367*(March), 1–18. https://doi.org/10.1080/02614367.2015.1031271.

Sandvig, C., Hamilton, K., Karahalios, K., & Langbort, C. (2016). Automation, algorithms, and politics| when the algorithm itself is a racist: Diagnosing ethical harm in the basic components of software. *International Journal of Communication, 10*, 19.

Silk, M., Millington, B., Rich, E., & Bush, A. (2016). (Re-)thinking digital leisure. *Leisure Studies, 35*(6), 712–723. https://doi.org/10.1080/02614367.2016.1240223.

Simonite, T. (2017). *Machines taught by photos learn a sexist view of women.* Retrieved January 24, 2018, from https://www.wired.com/story/machines-taught-by-photos-learn-a-sexist-view-of-women/amp?__twitter_impression=true

Spinks, R. (2017). *Using a fitness app taught me the scary truth about why privacy settings are a feminist issue.* Retrieved February 3, 2018, from https://qz.com/1042852/using-a-fitness-app-taught-me-the-scary-truth-about-why-privacy-settings-are-a-feminist-issue/

Sumartojo, S., Pink, S., Lupton, D., & LaBond, C. H. (2016). The affective intensities of datafied space. *Emotion, Space and Society, 21*, 33–40. https://doi.org/10.1016/j.emospa.2016.10.004.

Toffoletti, K., & Thorpe, H. (2018). Female athletes' self-representation on social media: A feminist analysis of neoliberal marketing strategies in "'economies of visibility'". *Feminism and Psychology, 28*(1), 11–31. https://doi.org/10.1177/0959353517726705.

Weare, A. M. (2016). Special issue on digital feminist media studies. *Journal of Communication Inquiry, 40*(4), 311–312. https://doi.org/10.1177/0196859916667660.

Index[1]

[1] Note: Page numbers followed by 'n' refer to notes.

D. C. Parry et al. (eds.), *Digital Dilemmas*,
https://doi.org/10.1007/978-3-319-95300-7

The manufacturer's authorised representative in the EU is Springer Nature Customer Service Centre GmbH, Europaplatz 3, 69115 Heidelberg, Germany. If you have any concerns regarding our products, please contact ProductSafety@springernature.com

Printed and bound by CPI Group (UK) Ltd, Croydon, CR0 4YY
22/09/2026
02221070-0003